RICH MKHONDO
REPORTING
SOUTH AFRICA

JAMES CURREY
LONDON

HEINEMANN
PORTSMOUTH (N.H.)

James Currey Ltd
54b Thornhill Square, Islington
London N1 1BE

Heinemann
A division of Reed Publishing (USA) Inc.
361 Hanover Street
Portsmouth, New Hampshire 03801-3912

Agents in Southern Africa
David Philip Publishers
PO Box 23408
Claremont 7735, Cape

First published 1993

1 2 3 4 5   97 96 95 94 93

ISBN 0-85255-369-2 (James Currey Cloth)
ISBN 0-85255-364-1 (James Currey Paper)

ISBN 0-435-08089-X (Heinemann Cloth)
ISBN 0-435-08096-2 (Heinemann Paper)

British Library Cataloguing in Publication Data
Mkhondo, Rich
  Reporting South Africa
  I. Title
  320.968

Library of Congress Cataloging-in-Publication Data
Mkhondo, Rich.
  Reporting South Africa / Rich Mkhondo.
       p.   cm.
  Includes bibliographical references and index.
  ISBN 0-435-08089-X (Heinemann cloth)
  ISBN 0-435-08096-2 (Heinemann paper)
  1. South Africa -- Politics and government--1989- 2. South Africa-
  -Race relations. 3. African National Congress.   I. Title.
  DT1970.M57 1993
  305.8'00968--dc20   93-32149
                                                        CIP

Typeset in Monotype Bembo, with Helvetica Narrow Display
by Opus 43, Cumbria, UK
and printed in Britain
by Villiers Publications Ltd, London N3

CONTENTS

ABOUT THE AUTHOR

Rich Mkhondo is a correspondent/journalist in South Africa for Reuters, the world's biggest news and information service. Mkhondo has also worked for South Africa's biggest daily newspaper, *The Star,* and the sadly missed liberal *Rand Daily Mail.*

Since 1984, Mkhondo has covered the anti-apartheid activities that have led the government of President F.W. de Klerk to unban all opposition groups and begin negotiating a non-racial constitution with opposition leader Nelson Mandela.

He has interviewed most of South Africa's leaders, black and white.

His job has taken him to many parts of South Africa. He has also covered Namibia's transition to democracy.

He has travelled extensively in the United States on speaking engagements. In 1986 he spent eight months as a press fellow with *The Philadelphia Inquirer.*

He is a graduate of Rhodes University, Grahamstown, South Africa, where he was one of the first blacks to be admitted to a white South African college in 1981. He holds a degree in Journalism.

Comment in *The Citizen*, Johannesburg:

Read this description by Rich Mkhondo, who has lived in Katlehong all his 36 years and is a correspondent for Reuters.

Read it and weep:

The smell of roasting human flesh hung in the air. A crowd of 20 with spears, axes and stones gathered round three burning bodies lying behind refuse bins.

'Sizitholile Izinja, Siyazitshisa,' they chanted – 'We found the dogs and we are burning them.'

'Viva, ANC, viva' – Long live the African National Congress.

The victims – two men and a woman – were supporters of Mangosuthu Buthelezi's Zulu-based Inkatha Freedom Party.

From a SAPA-Reuters story widely used in international newspapers:

A white right-winger hit me in the face, kicked me, insulted me and called me an ape threatening the survival of the Afrikaner nation.

I am a black correspondent for Reuters.

My assailant was a khaki-clad member of the Afrikaner Weerstandsbeweging.

I was at the World Trade Centre on Friday when AWB supporters carrying Nazi-style banners smashed their way into the country's democracy negotiations.

White colleagues intervened to prevent a second AWB man from attacking me as the invaders finally withdrew from the conference site on the outskirts of Johannesburg.

PREFACE

Apartheid convinced my parents whites were God-like creatures, and urged me to believe the same. As a young boy, I did not know what apartheid meant. I knew vaguely there was something wrong with our country when I wanted to play in a park reserved for white children and my mother smacked me for insisting.

When I was 19 the government sent bulldozers to flatten my ancestral village of Doornkop. Until then my aunts, uncles, cousins and grandparents had all lived in one place. Since that day my family has been scattered all over the country. In the name of white authority, the demolishers deliberately broke the oneness in my community. I will remember forever the tears and anguish on the faces of my mother and aunt, and the bitterness across the entire village, as they were forced to abandon their homes.

As a young and angry man in the 1970s, I was detained for belonging to an anti-apartheid poetry writing group. When I was arrested in 1975 for being in Johannesburg illegally, and for not carrying the pass compulsory for blacks, apartheid and its ravages began to dawn on me fully. The pass book or, as whites called it, the *dompas* (or pass for stupid people), literally controlled every aspect of our lives: where we were born, where we lived, where we worked, and where we were buried.

I was growing up in South Africa, where anything white people did was right because, they said, God was on their side. I was a student at Rhodes University, one of the first blacks to attend, when the authorities had to intervene to stop whites defacing our rooms with graffiti demanding 'coons' move out. The apostles of apartheid applied racial separation to everything. Nature permitting, they would have separated the very air that blacks and whites breathed.

In 1984, after years of schooling, I got my first job as a journalist, and since then I have covered historical events in South Africa on a day-to-day basis. As a black South African living in the often battle-ridden townships, I have witnessed at first hand the reluctant unfolding of political change. I have lived through the terror of 'necklacing' – people killed by petrol-soaked tyres hung around their necks and set ablaze. I have seen raging and rampaging Zulu *impis* (regiments) from migrant workers' hostels kill township residents. I have seen township residents kill Zulus living in hostels for single men. I have interviewed white right-wing militants who regard blacks as less than human.

Because of the sorry mess created by apartheid, I have always been convinced that it would take a terrible bloodbath to free South Africa from the shackles of racial domination. My country was not only a closed society, it was also morally destructive and physically violent. It destroyed the social cohesion in black communities, sundered families, ruined marriages, and deprived black children of their youth and the chance to grow up in an environment free from terror.

But that is all supposed to be ancient history now.

On 2 February 1990, Frederick Willem de Klerk turned the tide of history. He unbanned liberation movements, released political prisoners from jail, allowed exiles to return from abroad, and began the process of normalizing politics inside the country so that whites and blacks could live at peace. Two years later, on 20 and 21 December 1991, South Africa had its first multi-party, interracial, constitutional convention, otherwise known as the Convention for a Democratic South Africa (CODESA). On that day, old political enemies came together as friends to deliberate over the future of South Africa. I listened as black and white politicians, like Germans attacking the Berlin Wall from both sides, set about plotting the downfall of apartheid with destructive glee. It was clear we had entered a new political era.

All of us who have spent our lives on the receiving end of apartheid were optimistic that CODESA would be a vehicle to take us to a better future. But in the years between 1990 and the present, the mood in the country has soared with hope one month and plummeted in despair the next. There has been so much suspicion, fear, and expectation.

Given South Africa's peculiar legacy of apartheid, ethnic diversity, poverty and isolation, nation-building was never going to be easy. The transition to multiracial rule proved difficult and bloody. Whites battled to preserve some power and privilege, sharing with blacks a crisis of confidence about their future. It seemed that the birth of our new nation might be aborted by the pressures and dynamics of political transition. Violence was pervasive, a dread which hung over all races and lingered in every household as crime, political killings, police brutality and suicides filled morgues and hospitals. The economy slumped, entering its worst recession for 80 years, and the government reeled under a series of dirty tricks scandals, financial and military. Whites suffered unusual hardship with almost a quarter of the five million population floundering below the poverty line. White right-wingers fiercely opposed the changes our leaders intended to implement. Black communities were tortured by rampant violence. Fierce fighting between ANC and Inkatha supporters claimed hundreds of lives. Police and soldiers, some conducting an unofficial rearguard defence of apartheid, added to the carnage. The transition to democracy was seriously threatened.

Wherever the fault lies, violence is a fact of South African political life and will remain so for several years to come. Apartheid was a violent system, violently imposed; and more violence is the legacy apartheid is leaving us. I will never forget seeing the charred and hacked bodies of close friends, caught in the horror of township massacres. Each day I still picture in my mind a tall, extremely neat, courteous friend named Johannes, who greeted everyone with his irrepressibly sunny smile. Johannes was shot, then hacked to death; they set his car alight after placing his body in the boot. Even today his family cannot come to grips with the manner in which he died. That my friend, a teacher, who never uttered a word of politics, could have met his death in such a manner at the hands of the community he served was tragic, to put it mildly. To put it crudely, it was barbaric. The fate of Johannes, and countless others who will never see the new South Africa, highlights the nightmare existence of thousands of decent black people who yearn for peace and security, yet have become victims of endless violence, crime and intimidation in the townships. In the townships death and violence are a heartbeat away from home. There have been times when we who survive woke up surprised our families had not been butchered.

What do the perpetrators of this appalling violence hope to achieve? Innocent people like Johannes, who have long suffered the injustices of apartheid, are now being subjected to a worse form of oppression and brutality by members of their own race. Denied the basic human right of living without fear, they deserve all our sympathy. Sadly, our white South African fellows are unaware of the full extent of the horror and suffering in our squalid townships, and of its causes. Most remain indifferent, as long as the violence does not intrude upon their own lives.

But the problem cannot be dismissed as one that concerns only blacks. A culture of violence, in which killings created vendettas that created more killings, has taken hold in a society which, largely as a result of apartheid, has no democratic traditions to fall back on. The apartheid era legitimized violence, both on the part of the government in securing power, and on the part of blacks in resisting apartheid. In the wake of the unbanning of black liberation groups, this conflict has moved to centre stage, with open warfare between different political factions, the police, the South African Defence Force (SADF) and right-wing organizations. This violence has interrupted progress in the negotiations for a future democratic South Africa, eroding hope of a peaceful solution to our country's problems.

A fact overlooked by many people, and especially by whites in their heavily fortified homes, is that reports of the death of apartheid have been greatly exaggerated. Terrible deprivation continues to exist outside the comfortable white suburbs. Although so many apartheid laws have been repealed, the lot of most black South Africans will remain unchanged for many years to come.

Most blacks will judge the progress of reform by what material benefits it brings them, and how speedily. As long as blacks are kept poor by an economy built for and maintained by whites, and as long as they are degraded by white attitudes fostered by decades of official racialism, apartheid will live on. It will remain a mind-set and an inheritance of legalized inequality for decades to come.

This book is about South Africa's reluctant but inevitable transition to democracy, the perils and the pitfalls caused by competing forces, the agony of enduring violence, the re-emergence of the ANC and its preparedness to govern, and the new wave of Afrikaner pragmatism. From the perspective of a black South African journalist, it chronicles South Africa's road to democracy by reporting the personalities and issues that shaped it.

The reader joins me on this journey when I attend the first plenary session of CODESA, at which our leaders earnestly begin to chart a new path. On those two days before Christmas of 1991, we entered the tortuous road to a new political order. The book also looks at the first groundbreaking 'talks about talks' between the government and the ANC as a prelude to CODESA. Other important topics are the role of the police and security establishment in fomenting political fighting, and the position of the Zulu nation and Chief Mangosuthu Buthelezi in the process of building a new nation.

The book's main focus is the leadership of the two men most responsible for South Africa's profound political changes: F. W. de Klerk and the man who may well succeed him, Nelson Mandela. Because South Africa's new political order plainly lies in their hands, these two men influence and shape each of the book's three sections and 12 chapters. De Klerk and Mandela astounded the world by announcing constitutional negotiations; nevertheless, their failure to prevent anarchy and the slide to economic ruin remains deeply disturbing.

The involvement of other actors in the process of creating a new political dispensation – men, women, and children whose lives have been transformed by this enduring struggle – also features in some chapters of this book. The violence – both from the white right, stoking the embers of apartheid, and from left-wing groups whose supporters have fought for turf in South Africa's sprawling townships – is analysed in terms of its effects on community life and the transition to democracy.

I have reported the story of South Africa's transition to a non-racial democracy as a personal journey that is also an indispensable passage in South Africa's history: the birth pangs of our new nation.

Katlehong, South Africa
August 1993

ACKNOWLEDGEMENTS

For their initial encouragement to write the book and later for their thoughtful comments, I should like to thank my New York-based friends Michael Clough and Nomsa Daniels. Daniels gave long hours to a careful scrutiny of the manuscript. Her sharp eye and understanding of the complexities of the subject helped turn the manuscript into what I hope will be a valuable contribution to the birth of our new nation.

Thanks are also due to those who granted me interviews during difficult and exciting times in the history of my country. I am grateful to my wife Lindiwe, my daughters Noluvuyo and Nothemba, and my friends for the long and lonely hours they had to endure without me when I was writing this book.

Special thanks are owed to my colleagues at Reuters – Rodney Pinder for his invaluable editorial advice, Andrew Steele for the thoughts we shared about this project at the beginning, William Maclean, Anton Ferreira and Judith Matloff, whose reports influenced follow-up interviews, Rory Channing and Brendan Boyle. Boyle spent many hours each week in the parliamentary press gallery of the outgoing white parliament and often shared his thoughts with me. Lastly, my appreciation goes to my two photographic division colleagues Ulli Michel and Juda Ngwenya, who allowed me to use some of the photographs in this book.

FACTS

1 South Africa: Population Profile

	Numbers	%
Black	29 108 434	74.8
Coloured	3 307 776	8.5
Asian	1 011 790	2.6
White	5 487 018	14.1
TOTAL	38 915 018	100

Source: Development Bank of Southern Africa (DBSA)

2 Predictions for the Year 2000

Black	78.3%
Coloured	8.0%
Asian	2.3%
White	11.4%
TOTAL	47.5 million

Source: DBSA

3 Home Languages (%)

Blacks

Xhosa	12.7	Sotho	1.2
Zulu	38.8	Tswana	6.8
Swazi	3.5	Shangaan/Tsonga	6.1
South Ndebele	0.9	Venda	0.5
North Ndebele	0.5	English	0.2
Ndebele	0.6	Afrikaans	0.4
North Sotho	15.1	Other	1.3
South Sotho	11.4		

Whites

Afrikaans	57.6
English	38.7
Afrikaans and English	
(to the same extent)	0.8
Dutch	0.2
French	0.1
German	0.7
Greek	0.2
Italian	0.4
Portuguese	0.8
Other	0.7

Asians

English	95.1
Afrikaans	1.3
Afrikaans and English	
(to the same extent)	0.1
Tamil	0.4
Hindi	0.5
Telegu	0.1
Gujerati	0.9
Urdu	0.4
Chinese	0.2
Zulu	0.2
Other	0.8

Coloureds

Afrikaans	83.0
English	15.1
Afrikaans and English	
(to the same extent)	0.7
Other	1.2

Source: Central Statistical Service and South Africa Foundation.

4 Political Parties and Groups

African Democratic Movement	A party based in the nominally independent homeland of Ciskei.
African National Congress (ANC)	South Africa's largest political organization. Formed in 1912, banned in 1960 and unbanned on 2 February 1990.
Afrikaner Broederbond (AB)	A secret Afrikaner political movement, membership by invitation, dominated by the Afrikaner élite. For years the group has influenced government policy from behind closed doors.
Afrikaner Volksunie (AVU)	A party founded by former members of the Conservative Party protesting against the party's hard-line apartheid stand.
Afrikaner Volkswag (AV)	A right-wing movement that broke away from the Afrikaner Broederbond.
Afrikaner Vryheidstigting	An Afrikaner party which believes in the self-determination of whites in their own homeland.
Afrikaner Weerstandsbeweging (AWB)	A neo-Nazi white supremacist movement.
Azanian People's Organization (AZAPO)	A black consciousness movement with strong socialist leanings.
Black Consciousness Movement of Azania (BCMA)	The ideological cousin of AZAPO, established in exile.
Boerestaat Party (BSP)	A white party that believes in a return to the white republics of Transvaal, Natal and the Orange Free State.
Congress of Traditional Leaders (Contralesa)	A movement formed by traditional leaders.
Conservative Party (CP)	A pro-apartheid right-wing party founded by former National Party members protesting against apartheid reforms in 1982.

Democratic Party (DP)	A liberal pro-federalist party which fought for the enfranchisement of the black majority during the dark days of white minority rule. Official opposition until the 1987 elections, when it was still known as the Progressive Federal Party (PFP). The DP came about through the merger of the National Democratic Movement, Independent Party and PFP in 1989.
Dikwankwetla Party	A party based in the QwaQwa homeland
Herstigte Nasionale Party (HNP)	A white party which still believe in Verwoerdian hard-line apartheid.
Inkatha Freedom Party (IFP)	Federalist party with a strong base in Natal. Ruling party in the KwaZulu homeland.
Intando Yesizwe Party	A party based in the homeland of KwaNdebele.
Inyandza National Movement	A party based in the KaNgwane homeland.
Labour Party	A party with strong support among coloured people.
Natal Indian Congress/Transvaal Indian Congress	Anti-apartheid groups allied to the ANC.
National Party (NP)	The party which entrenched statutory racial discrimination and began a process of abandoning it in February 1990.
National People's Party	An Indian party that served in the white-dominated Tricameral Parliament.
Pan-Africanist Congress (PAC)	A socialist movement stressing black self-reliance and the return of the land to its indigenous people.
Sindawonye Progressive Party	A KwaNdebele-based party.
Solidarity Party	An Indian party that served in the white-dominated Tricameral Parliament.
South African Communist Party	A strong ally of the ANC which believes lack of democracy led to the collapse of communism in Eastern Europe. It says its own brand of participatory communism can still work in South Africa.
United Federal Party	A new federalist party.
United People's Front	A party based in the Lebowa homeland, mainly for Northern Sotho speakers.
Ximoko Progressive Party	A party based in the Tsonga/Shangaan-speaking Gazankulu homeland.

5 Military Wings

Umkhonto we Sizwe (MK)	Military wing of the ANC.
Azanian People's Liberation Army (APLA)	Military wing of the PAC.
Azanian National Liberation Army	Military wing of BCMA and its ideological cousin, AZAPO.

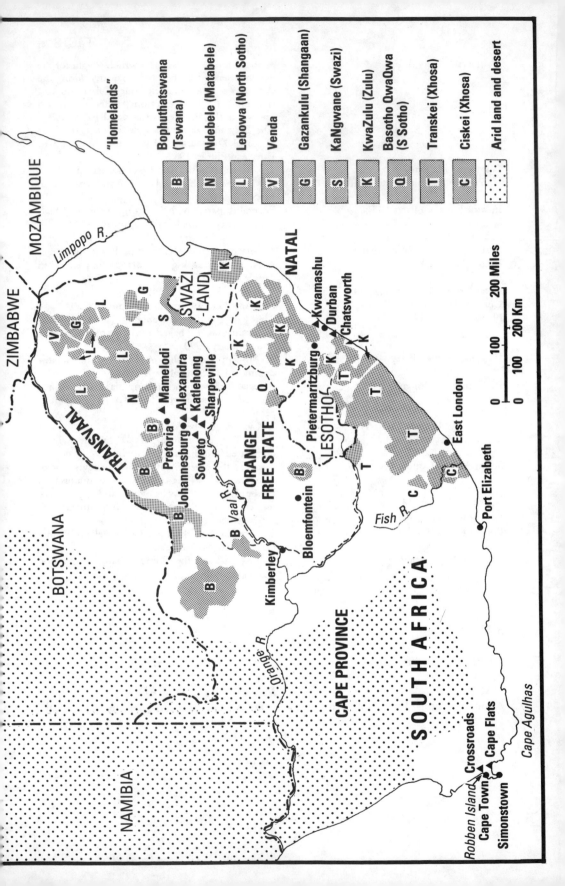

1

TO THE
FUTURE

1 *Nelson Mandela's first picture, taken by a government photographer and distributed to the media to avoid public clamour for the image of a man silenced and hidden for 27 years. After his last meeting as a prisoner with F.W de Klerk, Mandela agreed to pose for a picture with the president he called 'a man of integrity'.*

▲2   ▼3

4

4 *A buoyant Mandela during a membership drive in Soweto. The ANC failed to reach its target of two million paid-up members within 18 months of its unbanning. But the organisation commands a large following among blacks.*

2 *Nelson Mandela, F.W de Klerk and their delegates at the end of the first 'talks about talks' at Groote Schuur which ushered in a full-scale negotiation process on the transition to democracy, including other South African political parties and groupings.*

3 *Mandela, Joe Slovo and other ANC leaders doing a lap of honour around First National Bank stadium outside Soweto before addressing supporters to report back on the first 'talks about talks', held on 2–4 May 1990.*

5 *Mandela often found time to address branch meetings to boost his organisation's membership. But because of the heavy load of work and international travels, such duties were later delegated to younger officials.*

6 *Mandela welcomes his predecessor Oliver Tambo on his return to South Africa on 13 December 1990, after 30 years in exile. Tambo died after suffering a stroke on 26 April 1993. He had been credited with building the ANC into a powerful organisation after it had been banned and forced to operate from exile.*

1
THE FINAL MILE

We, the duly authorized representatives of political parties, political organizations, administrations and the South African government, coming together at this first meeting of the Convention for a Democratic South Africa, declare our solemn commitment: To bring about an undivided South Africa with one nation sharing a common citizenship, patriotism and loyalty, pursuing amidst our diversity, freedom, equality, and security for all irrespective of race, colour, sex or creed: a country free from apartheid or any other form of discrimination and domination. . . .

Declaration of Intent, CODESA, 21 December 1991.

The hall of the World Trade Centre, with its chandeliers, red upholstered silver chairs and white cloth-draped tables, resembled the United Nations. But it was not the UN Plaza in New York. This building stood along the Jan Smuts airport motorway near the eastern Johannesburg suburb of Kempton Park in South Africa. Inside the World Trade Centre, a large conference room decorated with a huge banner (the sun against a bright yellow and red background, incorporating black and white silhouettes and posters of three black and two white faces) provided the setting for the historic multi-party Convention for a Democratic South Africa, or CODESA for short. The two-day meeting held on 20 and 21 December 1991 marked the formal beginning of a process that would lead to a new constitution and a new democratic South Africa.

I was one of the first to arrive at the convention. In the first place I was anxious to catch a glimpse of all the men and women who would be shaping my future. Secondly, if I was going to record history in the making, I wanted to be there for the kick-off.

In a setting replete with ironies, black and white security men escorted delegates amid the bright lights of photographers and television cameras. Plain-clothed African National Congress (ANC) and South African Communist Party (SACP) guerrillas worked with white policemen under a special agreement on security. 'In the past week here I have spotted 12 policemen who were guarding me in jail . . . now they see me chatting amicably with the Minister of Defence and Chief of Police,' said smiling convention manager Murphy Morobe, who spent a total of eight years in prison for his anti-apartheid activities. For most of us, black and white, CODESA had become more than a vehicle of our search for coexistence; it had become the instrument of our survival.

3

When Nelson Mandela and F. W. de Klerk arrived, they loomed large, demonstrating that the hopes and fears, doubts and expectations of a democratic South Africa rested on their shoulders. For a little under 20 months, the two had conducted a political high-wire act that transformed South Africa, bringing hope to millions who had despaired. From this day the political futures of Mandela and de Klerk would be two sides of the same coin. Charged with keeping the negotiation process going, they would try to unite the country's fragmented groups, end township political killings and bring leftists and right-wingers to the negotiating table. Between them they would determine whether there was a peaceful transition to a new South Africa or whether we would be plunged into ever-worsening violence.

Preparing for CODESA: Participants and Absentees

The ANC first raised the issue of an 'all party congress' in its annual state-of-the-nation address on 8 January 1991. At that time the government was also toying with the idea of a 'multi-party conference'. The ANC wanted such a conference to include all political parties to discuss the mechanisms of transition to democracy, such as constitutional principles, an interim government and an elected constituent assembly. After the 8 January policy speech, the ANC entered into behind-the-scenes talks with the government. A steering committee was set up to organize the preliminary talks.

Although incessant political violence clouded the talks, the ANC decided to begin preparations for the constitutional conference. It held discussions with various political organizations, trade unions and religious bodies. A number of meetings on the structure of the conference – its possible agenda, functions, venue, participants and principles – were held. It was during this time that intense wrangling occurred over the shape and size of the all-party congress, its venue, and who should be its convener.

Eventually, the parties and groups that were involved in CODESA ranged from the white government, which wanted power sharing, to radical left-wing groups calling for an immediate transfer of power. The National Party (NP), led by President F. W. de Klerk, wanted a non-racial country with a free-market economy, an entrenched Bill of Rights, a guarantee of regular, multi-party elections for a government with a limited lifespan, and an independent judiciary. The ruling party representation at CODESA was boosted by a separate delegation from the all-white executive arm of government which comprised senior cabinet ministers led by de Klerk. The ANC, led by its president Nelson Mandela, was the main anti-apartheid movement that embodied the aspirations of millions of blacks and some whites. It was committed to redressing inequalities of wealth and the creation of a unitary, non-racial, non-sexist democratic state. ANC allies included the SACP and NP allies included the Inkatha Freedom Party (IFP), led by its chairman Frank Mdlalose.

There were two Indian parties: Solidarity, the majority party in the Indians-only chamber, and its opposition, the National People's Party. Coloureds (those of mixed race) were represented by the Labour Party, formerly the majority party in the coloured chamber of the Tricameral (coloureds, Indians, whites) Parliament. The remaining participants were from the 10 homelands, four of them nominally independent and six others self-governing. The quasi-independent homelands included two Xhosa 'states', Transkei along the Indian ocean west of the province of Natal and Ciskei, in the Cape Province. Both were run by military strongmen who snatched power through coups. The other two were Venda, for Venda-speaking South Africans and situated in the northern Transvaal, and Bophuthatswana, with seven patches of territory for the Tswana people scattered across three South African provinces. The leaders of Transkei and Venda broadly aligned themselves with the ANC, while those of Ciskei and Bophuthatswana were virulently anti-ANC.

The remaining six self-governing black territories were represented by parties: the Inyandza National Movement from the Swazi homeland of KaNgwane in the south-eastern Transvaal; the Ximoko Progressive Party from the Shangaan homeland of Gazankulu in the eastern Transvaal; the Dikwankwetla Party from the South Sotho homeland of QwaQwa in the Orange Free State province; Intando Yesizwe from the Ndebele homeland in the north-eastern Transvaal; and the United People Party, representing the North Sotho homeland of Lebowa. Four of the six – Dikwankwetla and Ximoko were the exceptions – had healthy relationships with the ANC.

Impressive as the roster of parties present was, suspicions were voiced from the right and the left that CODESA was a gigantic fraud. Some said it was designed to preserve minority power and privilege. Others feared de Klerk and his party were giving up power to the black majority controlled by communists. Notably absent were the Pan-Africanist Congress (PAC), and the Conservative Party (CP) which championed right-wing interests.

The absence of the PAC was all the more noticeable since, in Durban only two months before the convention, the PAC and the ANC formed a patriotic front to give de Klerk and his regime the 'knock-out punch'. In the words of their joint statement, 'The purpose of the front was to strengthen the hand of extra-parliamentary forces in future constitutional negotiations.' The front, which had also enjoyed the support of the Azanian People's Organization (AZAPO) in its pre-conference stage, agreed to push for an elected constituent assembly and an interim government. During discussions leading to CODESA, it was suggested that a preparatory multi-party meeting be scheduled for the end of November to discuss CODESA's formalities.

A few days before the meeting on 29 November 1991, things rapidly fell apart between the ANC and the PAC. The PAC, a socialist party demanding the complete restoration to blacks of land taken by white settlers over 350 years, announced it had received what it was certain were transcripts of a confidential address by ANC Director for International Affairs Thabo Mbeki to African ambassadors to the United Nations. In the briefing, Mbeki was reported to have broken all the aims and objectives of the patriotic front by telling the diplomats the ANC had entered into agreements with the government on a host of issues such as the interim government and a constituent assembly without the knowledge of patriotic front members. 'We believe the ANC, in cahoots with the regime, is aborting our common resolve,' PAC general secretary Benny Alexander said. The ANC denied any wrongdoing. 'The ANC utterly repudiates the unfounded assertions,' ANC secretary general Cyril Ramaphosa said. 'It is certainly not a record of the meeting I attended,' Mbeki added.

After denials by the government and the ANC that they were conniving with each other, CODESA's preparatory meeting was eventually held at the end of November with the PAC still fuming. Former PAC deputy president, Dikgang Moseneke, said it became clear to him and his colleagues at the preparatory meeting that the front was dead. The government and the ANC were initiating all decisions at the meeting and everyone else was 'rubber stamping' them, he said. 'Throughout the proceedings parties, except the PAC, did no more than endorse positions which were the result of prior consultation and agreement principally between the ANC and the regime,' Moseneke added. 'Without exception proposals made by the PAC were opposed by the ANC or the regime and would not be supported by the homeland or tricameral leaders. It became very clear that this pattern would persist throughout the rest of the meeting,' he said, adding the PAC had no alternative but to walk out to seek fresh consultations and a new mandate. A week later the PAC's extraordinary congress resolved to stay out of the talks, saying they were a charade.

Speaking to journalists at his home on 1 December 1991, Mandela dismissed the PAC's radical stance as a 'storm in a tea-cup'. 'The forward move towards a democratic South Africa does not depend on the attitude of the PAC nor can they do anything to slow down the process,' he said. He attempted to minimize the damage the accusations could have on the front. 'We do not think the patriotic front is going to be weakened. The patriotic front does not consist of the PAC and ANC alone. The PAC alleges collusion between the government and the ANC in order to create the perception that they are the true revolutionaries of our country,' Mandela said.

Also absent from the talks was AZAPO, a black consciousness, socialist party stressing black self-reliance. It had not taken part in preliminary talks in November because it had vowed never to talk to an 'illegitimate regime and its puppets'. AZAPO predicted that more people would join de Klerk's 'gravy train' as a result of the negotiations. Blacks, AZAPO said, had become depoliticized and had been hood-winked into the politics of negotiation with nothing to show for it.

The pro-apartheid CP, the official white opposition party in parliament, also refused to attend any talks until the autonomy of the white nation was guaranteed. The Afrikaner Weerstandsbeweging (AWB), a neo-Nazi group which is calling for a whites-only homeland, said it would never sit at the same table 'with ANC–Communist murderers' and accused de Klerk of selling the white nation out to the ANC. The Herstigte Nasionale Party (HNP), which has similar views to the AWB and demands a whites-only homeland in the Transvaal, Orange Free State, and Northern Natal, also refused to participate in CODESA.

Some of right-wing groups even tried to sabotage the talks by planting bombs in government buildings. 'The Boer *volk* [nation] is growing increasingly angry and frustrated at seeing their own land stolen away from them, something which will surely happen by the decisions taken at CODESA,' said Robert van Tonder, leader of the Boerestaat Party, in December 1991. White right-wingers said they would campaign against the convention on the grounds that its agenda 'does not make any sincere effort to pre-acknowledge the Afrikaner-Boer nation's right to autonomy.' A joint statement issued by five right-wing parties on 8 December said: 'It is not enough merely to place the right of nations to self-determination on the agenda at a meeting where it could merely be wiped off the table by a majority.' The CP, in spite of heavy lobbying by a pro-negotiations faction within its ranks, also refused to participate.

Despite the absence of the PAC, AZAPO, the CP and others, parties at the first preparatory meeting had won much more than they had lost. More than ever before, I was convinced that we were walking the final mile to political freedom. The possibility of achieving a democratic South Africa through negotiations had become real. The successful conclusion of the preparatory meeting marked the opening of genuine negotiations. After overcoming a series of obstacles in the long process of talks about talks, we had now come to where the real talks commenced. CODESA participants were going to be faced with the challenge of laying the foundations of a new South Africa.

The main purpose of the talks was for party leaders to commit themselves publicly to the negotiation process, setting out goals and principles; then working groups or committees could set to work on main areas such as constitutional principles, an interim government, the future of the homelands and suitable time frames for implementing a non-racial democracy. Delegates elected five of these working groups.

Working Group 1 was charged with easing the climate of negotiations by levelling the political playing field and identifying all obstacles to non-racial elections. This group was to make recommendations on how to oil the wheels of the constitutional process.

The main bones of contention included the release of remaining political prisoners, the return of political exiles, the repeal of contentious laws, political intimidation, arranging a ceasefire in township warfare, the use of the security forces and the funding of political parties. This group was also given the task of working with international organizations such as the United Nations to find ways in which the international community could assist the process.

The second working group was charged with the task of making suggestions on how South Africa might be governed during the transfer of power from the white government to a post-apartheid governing authority. The committee was to come up with transitional arrangements acceptable to all parties.

Working Group 3 was to consider options for a new constitution under the guidelines laid down by the convention. Its job was to analyse different types of electoral systems, a non-racial voters' roll, the power of the law over the constitution, a bill of human rights, the role of the president, financial control and economic principles. Its most thorny task was to recommend ways of implementing a new consti- tution – through a referendum, a constituent assembly, or an all-party conference.

The fourth group was to recommend ways of federalizing or reincorporating the 10 tribal homelands, four of which were considered independent states by South Africa's unique definition. Matters of citizenship and the method for reincorporating homeland residents would be on the agenda. The fifth and last working group was to set an agenda for the constitutional process, and set target dates or time limits for the transfer of power to a non-racial government.

Beyond Disagreements to 'Sufficient Consensus'

Before the convention, there were several main areas of disagreement between the government, the ANC and other groups involved in negotiations for a non-racial constitution. The ANC and its allies wanted a constituent assembly. De Klerk and his ruling party did not. The ANC said the new constitution should be drawn up by a body elected by universal suffrage within 12 months. The government and its ruling party wanted the constitution to emerge from the talks.

The ANC and its allies said an interim government comprising all parties was essential to oversee the transitional period because it believed de Klerk could not be trusted with the task. Such a government would control the security forces, the budget, state media and the electoral process. The ANC wanted as quick a transition as possible, with an interim government within 18 months of December 1991 and elections for a constituent assembly six months later. The government had spoken of transitional arrangements being in place for up to 10 years. The government said it was ready to accept other parties joining it in a form of 'transitional authority' but parliament must retain sovereignty.

The ANC insisted on a unitary state with no special protection for minorities, but the NP and the IFP wanted devolution of power to regions. While the ANC wanted centralized government, de Klerk's ruling group wanted decentralization, giving more responsibility to the regions. Linked to this was the future of the homelands – the ANC wanted them reincorporated into South Africa, the government and Inkatha believed any homelands wanting autonomy should be allowed to claim it under some form of federation. The ANC supported participation by groups such as the Commonwealth, the United Nations, the Organization of African Unity and the Non-Aligned Movement in the transition. The government would accept observers, but resisted any repetition of the facilitating role the United Nations had played in Namibian independence.

CODESA introduced new words into South Africa's political lexicon, the most important being the term 'sufficient consensus'. The new phrase was a product of pre-negotiation talks between the main actors. They decided that the negotiation process should proceed on the basis of consensus or, failing that, sufficient consensus. When I interviewed him on 12 December 1991, it took almost an hour for the ANC's constitutional negotiation expert, Mahomed Valli Moosa, to explain that phrase to me. 'The way I understood it, sufficient consensus implied more than a mere majority, 51 per cent of the votes. A greater preponderance of support than that, a decisive majority emerging after a sustained bid to reach consensus. More than a simple majority but less than unanimity, but without pinpointing a definite cut-off point.' If this is still tricky, maybe NP leader Dawie de Villiers had been more precise in trying to unscramble the doctrine to me a fortnight earlier. 'At all times the chairmen of a meeting or a committee must seek unanimity, but we must accept the principle that the convention cannot be held up by a small minority.'

Political organizations committed to CODESA constituted a sufficient consensus to conclude a political settlement. De Klerk's ruling National Party and the liberal Democratic Party represented the majority of whites, while the ANC and Inkatha reflected a clear majority in the black community. At the preparatory meeting, CODESA chairmen Justice Piet Schabort and Justice Ismael Mahomed applied the notion of sufficient consensus in overruling party dissent and mud-slinging, which caused the PAC's walk-out. This could be bad news for organizations such as the PAC and CP, who stayed out of CODESA and its future conventions. The white pro-apartheid parties and black radical groups needed to realize that, with or without them, a settlement would be reached. By staying out they marginalized themselves, yet could not prevent decisions being taken without them.

Playing the Man: Mandela Tackles de Klerk

Chief Justice Michael Corbett opened the convention and called on delegates to bow for prayers offered in several languages by clergymen from several denominations. After the prayers and preliminary remarks, Corbett handed over to co-chairmen Schabort and Mahomed. Opening remarks by delegation leaders followed, with each speaker limited to 15 minutes. The order was alphabetical, which meant that the ANC, led by Nelson Mandela, spoke first and a National Party spokesman in the middle. Down to speak third last, for the RSA government, F. W. de Klerk then asked to slip two places down the order, past Transkei and the Ximoko Progressive Party, and speak last of all.

Talking in a calm, measured tone, Mandela called on the government to make way for an interim government of national unity to supervise the transition to a non-racial democratic South Africa. 'The invalidation of the prevailing constitution is the most persuasive argument in support of the view that the incumbent government is unsuited to the task of overseeing the transition to democracy. Its often-stated commitment to democracy must now compel it to make way for an interim government of national unity to supervise the transition . . . . There is a compelling urgency about this task,' he said. Switching to Afrikaans (the language of white Afrikaners), Mandela continued: 'The message of the ANC . . . is plain and simple, and for all South Africans, the time for one South Africa, one nation, one vote, one future, is here,' he said.

De Klerk was the last to speak. For the first time he said his government was committed as a matter of urgency to admitting blacks to the country's white-dominated parliament in a bid to help the transfer of power to a post-apartheid authority. 'We are convinced it is in the best interests of South Africa and all its people for us to institute expeditiously a government that is broadly representative of the whole population. We are convinced that the composition of parliament should be changed during this initial phase already to include the total population in an equitable manner.' But the delegates' excitement was soured when the reformist white president said he was not prepared to suspend the constitution until South Africans of all races could have a say in a referendum to decide the fate of a post-apartheid state.

Despite moving closer to conceding ANC demands for an interim government and a constituent assembly, de Klerk prompted a major clash on an otherwise trouble-free day when he attacked the refusal of the ANC to end the armed struggle which it had suspended indefinitely 15 months earlier. 'An organization which remains committed to an armed struggle cannot be trusted completely when it also commits itself to peacefully negotiated solutions.' De Klerk lashed out at the ANC for failing to live up to the spirit of the peace accord signed on 14 September with regard to its military wing. De Klerk reminded the ANC that a stipulation in the peace accord that no political party should have a private army placed a question mark over the ANC's participation in a convention which, essentially, was taking place among political parties. 'The choices are between peace through negotiation or a power struggle through violence. The ANC and other organizations still sitting on two stools, such as the PAC, now have to make this choice,' de Klerk said.

The mood of the conference changed dramatically. Mandela took the stage at the end of the day to denounce de Klerk furiously as an illegitimate ruler seen by blacks as a killer. It was the prelude to a verbal brawl, captured live on prime-time television, that burst like a thunderstorm at the end of the sedate first day of South Africa's reform talks. Their unscripted spat about the ANC's guerrilla army capped a day of firsts for black assertiveness on a political stage long dominated by the ruling minority. Never before had South African state television viewers been allowed to see a black man giving a white president an uninterrupted, angry lecture on his alleged political failings.

I am gravely concerned about the behaviour of Mr de Klerk today. He has launched an attack on the ANC and in doing so he has been less than friendly. Even the head of an illegitimate, discredited minority regime as he has certain moral standards to uphold. If a man can come to a conference of this nature and play the type of politics in his paper . . . very few people would like to deal with such a man. Mr de Klerk has been less than frank. Just because he is the representative of a discredited, illegitimate minority regime, he has no excuse not to uphold moral standards. We must make allowances for the fact that he is a product of apartheid.

And he pointed to a glum-looking de Klerk, ten metres away.

De Klerk sat impassively, his hand clamped angrily over his mouth while Mandela made his unscripted attack. Stunned delegates, dignitaries and journalists, who only minutes earlier had heard speaker after speaker applaud de Klerk as the co-architect of this historic convention, sat motionless, paralysis written on their faces. The exchange made them forget earlier speeches larded with references to peace, democracy, cooperation and new dawns. De Klerk's colleagues in government and his party stared stonily downwards, some covering their eyes with their hands through anger, hatred or shame at what was happening to their president. In South African politics, it was unprecedented. De Klerk flushed, started taking notes, dropped his pen and angrily clasped his chin. His colleagues, Foreign Minister Pik Botha and chief negotiator Gerrit Viljoen, whispered into his left and right ears.

A calm but icy Mandela continued the tirade. He said de Klerk had not indicated to him right up to late the previous night that he was just about to launch an attack on the *bona fides* of the ANC. 'The members of the government persuaded us to allow them to speak last. It is now clear why they did so. He has abused his position because he hoped

I would not reply. He was mistaken because I am doing so now.' Despite de Klerk's attack, the ANC was still prepared to continue discussions with the government and the NP. But he warned: 'He must forget [it] if he thinks he can impose conditions on the ANC and, I dare say, [on] the [other] political organizations here. He continues to undermine the ANC . . . [but] we are going to stop him. He is not fit to be a head of government. He has little idea of what democracy means.' Mandela reminded the convention that he, and not the government, had initiated the negotiating process in 1986 when he was still in jail.

Mandela lambasted the government for using taxpayers' money to fund certain political organizations and contemptuously dismissed de Klerk's earlier statement that he had not known about state funding for an Inkatha rally held in January. He said de Klerk had been less than frank not to tell the convention that the ANC had agreed to hand over its weapons to joint ANC–government control once the political process had reached the stage where the liberation organization had a form of political say. 'When the process reaches such a stage when we have an effective say in government, we would relinquish everything. I say you are asking us to commit suicide because when your government is not prepared to intervene and stop the violence . . . when our people are asking to be armed . . . what political organization can hand over the weapons to the very person that kills him?'

Mandela said the two of them had discussed the issue the previous week, but de Klerk had decided to use CODESA for 'petty political gain. If he plays this double game, we will not disband MK [Umkhonto we Sizwe, the ANC's armed wing] – he can do as he wants. I ask him to place his cards on the table face upwards. Let there be no secret agendas. I hope this is the last time he will [have to] do so.'

De Klerk, who heard the protracted attack out in silence, was granted right of reply. Visibly charged, he struggled for control of his voice. 'I did not intend to attack Mr Mandela,' he began. 'I prefer to play the ball and not the man.' At times searching for breath, searching for words, de Klerk launched into a rebuttal of Mandela's accusations, saying it was a vital matter of principle that no party should have a private army. He said he had reluctantly raised the issue at CODESA because no progress had been made in extended meetings with the ANC on the subject. The president said he had no intention of apologizing for his words. 'Yes sir, I said we cannot have a party with a pen in one hand and claiming the right to hold arms in the other.' He said the question of the ANC's armed struggle, which was suspended in August 1990, but has never been officially ended, remained one of the greatest stumbling blocks to peace in South Africa. 'Only one group in this room admits to possessing illegal arm caches. We will constantly raise [with the ANC] this . . . issue of deep concern.' He said the disagreement was an example of how 'democracy should really work', adding that he hoped that, having cleared the air in the best interests of South Africa, they would find a way to resolve the problem. He then made an impassioned plea for goodwill at CODESA.

When the confrontation ended, we all sat in silence, unable to believe what we had just witnessed. An American television journalist turned to me and asked what I thought. I was speechless. I could not recall any head of state, anywhere, however illegitimate, being subjected to such verbal abuse as Mandela levelled at de Klerk. I had known for a long time that there were tensions beneath the surface between the two rival parties, but I had not expected such an outburst. The unprecedented gloves-off exchange was the opening salvo in the battle for control of the country. Mandela's angry rejoinder proved that old-style politics, where white leaders lectured black ones, was a thing of the past.

My friends in the townships applauded Mandela's fiery attack, saying de Klerk's demand that the ANC disband its military wing was tantamount to asking the ANC to commit suicide at a time when there was a common perception among blacks that government-led police and soldiers were somehow responsible for the township political fighting. We were all reminded that, even if 19 parties and organizations had agreed to negotiate, old enemies had not buried their ideological differences; when practical issues were tackled, some blood would stain the negotiation table.

The Mandela–de Klerk fracas showed that in the months ahead the government was going to fight dirty as well as hard, while the ANC would also reply viciously. To some of us, who for many years had wanted all leaders irrespective of colour and creed to build a post-apartheid future together, it was a warm welcome to real negotiations. CODESA's first session had started out predictably, with 17 speakers giving their views about how South Africa should arrive at a democratic settlement. It ended in spectacular fireworks with South Africa's men of destiny at each other's throats in front of hundreds of delegates, observers and journalists, and millions of television viewers across the world. No one who witnessed the event would forget the sight of a black leader lecturing a white head of state about his failings.

The drama overshadowed what was perhaps the most important aspect of CODESA – the Declaration of Intent. The document, signed by 17 of the 19 participants, was a noble inscription for the foundation stone of a new South Africa. It said:

We, the duly authorised representatives of political parties, political organisations, administrations and the South African government, coming together at the first meeting of the Convention for a Democratic South Africa, declare our solemn commitment:

To bring about an undivided South Africa with one nation sharing a common citizenship, patriotism and loyalty, pursuing amidst our diversity, freedom, equality, and security for all irrespective of race, colour, sex or creed: a country free from apartheid or any other form of discrimination and domination. To work to heal the divisions of the past, to secure the advancement of all, and to establish a free and open society based on democratic values where the dignity, worth and rights of every South African are protected by law.

To strive to improve the quality of life of our people through the policies that will promote economic growth and human development and ensure equal opportunities and social justice for all South Africans. To create a climate conducive to peaceful constitutional change by eliminating violence, intimidation and destabilisation and by promoting free political participation, discussion and debate.

To set in motion the process of drawing up and establishing a constitution that will ensure, inter alia: That South Africa will be a united democratic, non-racial and non-sexist state in which sovereign authority is exercised over the whole of its territory: That the constitution will be the supreme law and that it will be guarded over by an independent, non-racial and impartial judiciary: That there will be a multi-party democracy with the right to form and join political parties and with regular elections on the basis of universal adult suffrage on a common voters' roll; in general the basic electoral system shall be that of proportional representation: That there shall be a separation of powers between the legislature, executive and judiciary with appropriate checks and balances: That the diversity of languages, cultures and religions of the other people of South Africa shall be acknowledged: That all shall enjoy universally accepted human rights, freedoms, and civil liberties including freedom of religion, speech and assembly protected by an entrenched and justiciable bill of rights and a legal system that guarantees equality of all before the law.

We agree: That the present and future participants shall be entitled to put forward freely to the convention any proposal consistent with democracy: That CODESA will establish a mechanism whose task it will be, in cooperation with the administration of the South African government, to draft the text of all legislation required to give effect to the agreements reached at CODESA. We, the representatives of the political parties, political organisations and administrations, further solemnly commit ourselves to be bound by the agreement of CODESA and in good faith to take all such steps as are within our power and authority to realise their implementation.

The declaration was the unifying centrepiece of CODESA, a sign of progress for South Africa which had never known such unity. It bound parties with the basic tenets of multi-party democracy, regular elections, an independent judiciary, the supremacy of the constitution, and a division of executive, legislative and judicial power. Two participants, the IFP and the government of Bophuthatswana, did not sign the declaration. The IFP disagreed with the formulation of the declaration because it appeared to favour a unitary state to the exclusion of federal principles. Bophuthatswana said it would make its own decision on reincorporation into South Africa because the people of the homeland must have the final say in the future. Mandela said fellow ANC leaders also had reservations about the declaration, but he had persuaded them that the movement should sign in the interests of reconciliation. He said some of his aides wanted the convention resolutions to become law. As the declaration stands, the government committed itself to converting resolutions into legislation through parliament.

Delegates came to the second day of talks having digested what their rivals or allies had said the previous day. 'Our very presence presumes that there is agreement among ourselves to act in a constructive manner. None of us should act in a manner designed to weaken any of the parts of CODESA,' Mandela said. To dissenting murmurs from the audience, Foreign Minister Pik Botha said, 'I do not think we will achieve much by further acrimonious exchanges. We are like the Zebra – it does not matter if you put the bullet through the white stripe or the black stripe. If you hit the animal, it will die.' Despite these words, it was clear on Saturday that tempers had cooled and harsh words had been tempered. The day's agenda concerned the nitty-gritty of committee work rather than the sweeping policy statements of the first day.

By the end of the second day, my anxieties had disappeared. I was convinced there could be no turning back now. With CODESA we entered an entirely new phase of politics. It was a phase which involved chipping away at the white nation's exclusive hold on power. In this new era parties outside parliament got the recognition that they had been denied for decades. For that reason, delegates from the 19 parties had made history. Under the scrutiny of the white electorate, they showed that blacks had no horns and could work together with whites as equals.

CODESA: First Parliament of the New South Africa?

What then did CODESA achieve? It did not settle any of the tremendous problems facing the country such as violence, the economic downswing, unemployment, the housing backlog and other socio-economic ills. But then, it was never meant to; its purpose was only to prepare the ground. The first and most important test for the members of CODESA was likely to occur when the convention met again to grapple with the challenges of how to set up an interim government, how a new constitution would be written, and how to appoint the body that would write it. That would determine the course of negotiations, when the political battle over the new society would begin in earnest. For some time, anxieties among South Africans would centre around whether a non-racial South Africa would be the one suggested by de Klerk and his party or Mandela and his ANC; whether power would be shared, as de Klerk wanted, or simply transferred from a minority government to a majority government.

In effect, CODESA meant that the march towards a democratic non-racial state had entered its climactic and, perhaps, most volatile phase. Apart from running the country, the new government would have the task of making arrangements for a constituent assembly which would, in turn, draw up a final constitution. After the final constitution had been drawn, elections for South Africa's first democratic government would be held. CODESA had indeed set the country irrevocably on the road to a new South Africa. Despite the hiccups, it was a great success.

No one argued that CODESA represented final liberation. Those attending represented many millions of people, and though the political views of some of them may have been poles apart, their presence signified a willingness to compromise in the interests of the country. There was no other way to reach these goals. The signs were all around us: parties to the negotiation process had finally rolled up their sleeves, quit their sloganeering and grandstanding, and got down to the real business of fashioning a new political system. Although no magic solutions and quick fixes emerged from the first two days of CODESA, the excitement and tension, compounded by the blaze of international publicity, made it more than a ceremonial occasion. The day belonged to blacks and whites mapping their future together. It was the most important gathering since the founding of the Union of South Africa in 1910. It was, in a sense, the first parliament of the new South Africa.

2

THE LAST WHITE PRESIDENT

De Klerk, a man bred into privilege, educated for leadership, and trained for power, is a different breed of cat. Where President Botha is rough, he is smooth; where President Botha smashes, he bends; where President Botha confronts and rages, he yields and mollifies. His career is a tale of compromises, of making the best out of bad situations, of smoothing over difficulties.

Ken Owen, Editor, Sunday Times, *August 1989*

When de Klerk was sworn in as State President on 20 September 1989, he found the National Party in political turmoil. Battered by years of fighting to maintain apartheid, it was ideologically incoherent and divided. Some of its key leaders wanted to move rightwards to reunify Afrikanerdom, others wanted to talk to black opposition groups such as the ANC. Twenty ministers announced that they would not stand for re-election in the 6 September 1989 elections. Most who chose to resign were loyal supporters of de Klerk's predecessor, P. W. Botha.

At the same time as the National Party was facing internal problems, South Africa was at the height of increasing isolation and pressure from the international community to abolish apartheid. The country's economy was being slowly wrecked by sanctions and trade embargoes. I did not share the euphoria over de Klerk's election as president. I was not in the least convinced that his presidency would be any different from those of his predecessors. I remembered very well how in the 1970s euphoria greeted John Vorster's plea to the world to be given six months to dismantle apartheid. After Vorster, P. W. Botha called on whites 'to adapt or die', saying apartheid was an outdated concept. These two leaders failed even to tinker with the grand pillars of apartheid.

For me as for millions of other blacks, de Klerk was one more white National Party leader to give apartheid one more lease of life. I was one of two blacks among a group of journalists invited to de Klerk's party congress soon after he became president. Through discussions over coffee, and later at several media conferences, he struck me as an open man with more than just a touch of pragmatism. I could not be moved to call him 'a man of integrity', as Nelson Mandela later would, though he was impressive. In his conversation, there was both a sense of urgency and a sparkle of confidence. He spoke about his commitment to reform while at the same time suggesting and implying that white domination would remain long after the grim demise of apartheid. To millions of blacks like me, it appeared that there were two de Klerks: the smiling Dr Jekyll of apartheid reform, and the grim-faced Mr Hyde of apartheid proper.

The Ascent of 'F.W.'

Frederick Willem de Klerk, or F. W. as almost everyone calls him, often speaks about how he, his father (a cabinet minister in three National Party governments), and his grandfather have striven over three generations to realize the apartheid dream of partitioning South Africa into racial states. A fourth-generation Afrikaner nationalist born into a prominent conservative political family and trained as a lawyer, de Klerk was elected to parliament from the blue-collar Transvaal town of Vereeniging where he first set up his law firm. De Klerk's father had played a key role in bringing the National Party to power in 1948. His late uncle, J. G. Strijdom, was once prime minister. He was twelve years old in 1948 when his father became a member of parliament and the National Party rose to power on the platform of grand apartheid. His own rise in the party was rapid. He became a cabinet minister in 1977, Transvaal provincial leader in 1982, and home affairs minister and national education minister in 1984. When P. W. Botha unexpectedly resigned as party leader in February 1989 following a stroke, de Klerk was chosen as his successor.

Unlike his predecessors, de Klerk came to power without a major institutional power base in government. Hendrik Verwoerd was the architect of the apartheid empire. John Vorster was the strongman of the police establishment who helped drive black dissent underground and into exile. P. W. Botha was a military man who wanted to reform apartheid on his own terms, initiating cosmetic changes while launching cross-border raids against anti-apartheid guerrillas. One of Botha's legacies was the creation of a huge military bureaucracy which controlled government from behind the scenes.

De Klerk brought nothing into the power game. I first heard of him when, as Minister of Home Affairs, he signed a deportation order for a woman who hit P. W. Botha with a tomato during the height of apartheid repression in 1987. A surprising statesman, he was never part of the National Party's so-called *verligte* or 'enlightened' wing. Considered a dyed-in-the-wool conservative, he had the background of looking after white sectional interests as chairman of the white Minister's Council and Minister of National (white) Education, Minister of the Interior and, later, of Home Affairs. By the stiff-backed standards of his party he was considered a cautious centrist. I saw him as essentially pragmatic rather than visionary – a South African Mikhail Gorbachev trying to check the tide of change before it overwhelmed him and his Afrikaner *volk*.

De Klerk's advantage was that he was more outward-looking than any of his predecessors. He has often spoken of his first trip to the United States in 1976, where he witnessed more racial incidents in a month than he had previously witnessed in South Africa. He related an incident where a bus driver called a black American 'boy' and an ugly fight erupted. His American experience convinced him that racial discrimination was not limited to his own country – that in a country with great conflict potential like his own, it was only necessary to manage the conflict. This conviction is still inherent in de Klerk's philosophy as one who has tried to manage the transition to democracy.

His closest brush with the tragedies and sufferings of blacks under apartheid came soon after he returned from the United States in 1976, when as Minister of Education (a white minister of education was the overall director of all 14 racially segregated departments) he witnessed the black student riots which killed more than 600 people in protests against the use of Afrikaans as a compulsory medium of instruction in black schools. He stood resolutely behind the principle of Bantu education, which prescribed a separate and inferior education for blacks.

When de Klerk became president, he had two choices: either he could continue the old strategy of repression while coopting compliant blacks into white political structures that would enable whites to maintain control, or he could accept that majority rule was inevitable and start negotiating the terms for a new dispensation with credible black liberation movements such as the ANC.

He chose the latter, though in reality he had no other choice. Mass dissent had not been crushed after the uprising of the mid-1980s, the way it was after Sharpeville in 1960 and Soweto in 1976. Mass mobilization had become a permanent, structurally ingrained feature of South Africa's political life, and no amount of repression short of a total civil war could contain it. Anti-apartheid protests were tearing the country apart, confirming a long-held view that apartheid was simply unworkable. Extra-parliamentary politics dominated the local and international political scene. White South African leaders were regarded as outcasts worldwide, while their anti-apartheid opponents were accorded the status of heads of government.

Moreover, the South African economy had become chronically sick as sanctions, disinvestment, and a whole host of other ills had taken their toll, causing the South African rand to plunge in value, while prices soared and inflation hit its highest peak in years. In this tense climate, voteless blacks were speaking out from the factory floors, streets, schools and other places, despite the most draconian security legislation the country had ever seen. School boycotts spread nationally, trade unions flexed their muscles, popular structures such as civic organizations replaced government-created community councils, and political militancy persisted in spite of the crippling State of Emergency. Alternative structures in the townships, from those dealing with justice to those dealing with education, gave blacks an experience of having a say in their own affairs. Anti-apartheid organizations developed a myriad tactics and strategies, mounting the most sustained, resilient and widespread resistance ever offered to white rule.

The Balancing Act: Between Black Hopes and White Fears

As President, de Klerk knew he had to act quickly in the deteriorating political and socio-economic climate. But first he had to move on a number of fronts to consolidate his position and establish his credibility as a leader in government. He needed to consolidate his position and win the hearts of those of his colleagues who had voted for former Finance Minister Barend du Plessis during the race for the party leadership. In a short time he had gained a reputation for decency and devotion to duty, a legacy of his father's stern admonition that politics was a 'calling' rather than a profession.

On the international front, one of his first goals was to convince the international community of his bona fides. He visited Britain's Margaret Thatcher, Germany's Chancellor Helmut Kohl, and government leaders in Italy and Portugal. In Africa he met Mozambique's Joachim Chissano, and the leaders of Zaire and Lesotho as well as moderate black leaders inside South Africa. At home, he promised to negotiate with disenfranchised blacks about political rights at the national level. He pledged a new South Africa that would be acceptable to all, but also stressed that the country's future lay in the recognition and protection of separate groups.

His political position had six basic elements: constitutional negotiations with black moderates, maintenance of group rights on a non-discriminatory basis, political incorporation of all groups with no domination of one by another, security, the normalization of foreign relations, and maximum devolution of state functions at a regional and local level. This meant switching from the institutionalized formalities of white politics to the volatile uncertainties of black politics. It meant looking into demands by the black majority to unban all political groups, allow all exiles to return, release political prisoners, lift the State of Emergency, remove troops from the black townships, and begin to dismantle apartheid.

De Klerk knew he had to maintain a delicate balancing act. While promising blacks a vote, he assured whites again and again that their segregated residential areas, schools and hospitals would be protected under what he termed segregation without discrimination. 'To the white electorate,' he told a party congress in November 1989, 'I want to give this assurance. The National Party will carefully guard against your security and your interest. The National Party will never leave you in the lurch.'

Immediately upon becoming president, de Klerk tried to win friends in the black community with his promise of substantial reforms. But clashes between police and anti-apartheid demonstrators, most of whom were members of the United Democratic Front (UDF), soured his reformist image. Twenty-three people were killed by police during township clashes on polling night in the white general election to test his new policies. 'I do not understand how people could become vaguely excited about these elections, when, on the same night, the man who calls for reform and a new South Africa allowed this kind of massacre of innocent unarmed demonstrators to happen,' anti-apartheid clergyman Allan Boesak told journalists on 14 September 1989. The results of the elections hardly impressed the black leaders, who expected de Klerk to continue governing South Africa through a mixture of reform and repression, like his predecessor. I still regarded de Klerk's plans for a negotiated power-sharing settlement as new labels for old dogmas.

The government tried to refute such charges by publishing a draft bill setting out vague proposals for a black franchise at a higher level than their existing voting right, which limited them to municipal polls. The bill showed that Pretoria accepted the notion of black political voting rights, but only after negotiations leading to constitutional reform. A week before taking oath as President, de Klerk took the unusual step of allowing a march through the centre of Cape Town to protest against the election night killings. The march was the first to be allowed to go ahead without violent incident since Botha imposed emergency rule in 1986 to stop political unrest. It was also the largest in 30 years. De Klerk's aides said the move showed that his administration might tolerate protest provided it was peaceful, in contrast to the draconian security policies of Botha.

De Klerk also raised hopes of accelerated reform by taking the unusual step of allowing dissidents to stage mass marches throughout the country. He extended his hands-off policy by allowing mass political funerals for victims of unrest despite the illegality of open-air protest under the State of Emergency imposed by P. W. Botha. 'It is not necessary in South Africa for any person to give vent to his political aspirations through disorderly protest,' de Klerk told journalists on the eve of the march. The demonstrators responded by warning de Klerk that his expected confirmation as President signalled the end of white rule. 'We say to Mr de Klerk. We have already won. If you know what is good for you, join us in the struggle for a new South Africa,' Archbishop Desmond Tutu told the marchers.

The white leader's tolerance of opposing political views was the first indication that he was committed to his decision to normalize the political process. By giving the go-ahead to the protest marches, he took a calculated gamble, defying his security establishment and some of his cabinet colleagues and thereby breaking every precedent set by a government that has always stifled dissent. His handling of marches provided a whole new perspective on the man. 'I have no illusions about the great responsibility attached to this position [the presidency],' he said on 20 September. 'Our country is going through one of the most decisive phases in history. What happens in the next five years, will be decisive for many decades to come. We must accept the risk that goes with new initiatives. The risk of staying in a dead end street is far higher. Everything we do, we do it to avoid revolution.'

A month after taking the reins of presidency, de Klerk released Mandela's closest comrade, Walter Sisulu, and seven other prominent political prisoners. The announcement was the strongest signal yet that the government might be ready to negotiate with the banned ANC and that de Klerk would live up to his reformist promises for a new non-discriminatory constitution, breaking the deadlock between the country's white-led government and its voteless black majority. Soon after releasing the ANC leaders, de Klerk threw open South African's beaches to all races and vowed to scrap another segregationist law, the Group Areas Act. Reserved under one of the key apartheid laws, the Separate Amenities Act, the beaches were among the areas targeted for defiance by anti-apartheid movements and church groups led by Archbishop Tutu. The beaches were opened two weeks before the country's summer holidays began, just three months after police had used dogs, whips and teargas to drive Archbishop Tutu and hundreds of anti-apartheid protestors from beaches near Cape Town.

Continuing his steady series of reforms, de Klerk cut the power of South Africa's security chiefs and returned government authority to the cabinet. The security chiefs, known in political circles as 'securocrats', had set themselves up as the power behind the cabinet. The cabal brought together the cabinet ministers in charge of police and defence and the heads of the defence force, police and secret service. Parliament was accountable; the chiefs of the defence force, the police and national intelligence were not. These moves to restore parliament as the decision-making and law-making authority were welcomed by white lawmakers.

De Klerk downgraded the shadowy State Security Council and the National Security Management System, widely regarded as an 'inner cabinet' or cabal of selected government ministers and appointed security chiefs, to the rank of a parliamentary committee, a step towards government accountability. For more than a decade, the National Security Management System had combined the civilian administration, the police and the military into a nationwide chain of command that ran from the lowest municipal authority to the State Security Council at the top. Civil rights campaigners called the system a 'government within a government' and said it was an instrument of repression. The two councils were extremely powerful, with horizontal and vertical tentacles that embraced almost every aspect of public policy making. De Klerk's action reduced the power of heads of the military, police and intelligence, who challenged the cabinet.

Along with the securocrats, de Klerk also scrapped a controversial system of administration by police, military and civilian officials known as the Joint Management Committees (JMCs). The JMCs were introduced in 1986 by P. W. Botha as the local instruments of the National Security Management System and the State Security Council to contain political tension in black townships. They were presented as a more effective means of coordinating government efforts to 'win hearts and minds' in the black townships by responding to complaints that required special attention. But the government also used its network, which was headed at every level by military or police officers, to keep track of dissent and identify and often detain those trying to mobilize opposition to apartheid. Blacks generally saw the system as a network for domestic espionage and suppression. Critics of the system also complained at the time that it gave the security forces too much influence in civilian matters. Helen Suzman, a retired liberal anti-apartheid parliamentarian, derided it as 'a creeping *coup d'état* by consent'.

South African white males received a Christmas bonus when de Klerk cut military conscription from two years to one in 1990. Whites were liable for military service from the ages of 18 to 55. The cut in military service, which had been expected because of the decreasing military threat on South African borders, was welcomed by the white community. Conscription was seen as a drain on South Africa's limited pool of skilled labour and many conscripts disliked being deployed at the borders to defend apartheid or into black townships to quell political unrest. The past years had seen a steep rise in the number of conscientious objectors. Scores had publicly denounced the military and refused to obey call-up papers. Several objectors accepted stiff jail terms rather than serve in the armed forces.

Ultimately, de Klerk had been compelled to acknowledge the futility of apartheid for pragmatic reasons. In the words of his Foreign Minister, Pik Botha, 'The government began to shift away from apartheid when it realized that it was impossible to stem the tide of blacks moving to the urban areas in search of employment, signalling that the homeland system did not work. As the economic realities overwhelmed the dream, so did we come to realize that there were consequences of those policies that were indeed oppressive and humiliating.'

Justice Minister Kobie Coetzee revealed another secret behind his government's reforms: 'By the end of 1989, the National Party leadership, with de Klerk at the helm, found its options for the future, as a government and a party, to be extremely limited.' Coetzee explained to a party congress in November 1990 how he visited a friend's farm and found that all his friend's fruit was marketed using the stamp of another country. 'Nobody accepted us in the outside world. The National Party therefore decided that this was enough – we decided to create a new South Africa.'

De Klerk himself said there had been no Damascus conversion, just a realization that 'if we continued as we were, we were in a cul-de sac.' As he put it in a speech at a by-election rally in February 1992, 'If responsible leaders do not act with determination, our country will remain locked in this situation and will sink further into a morass of distrust, poverty, growing isolation and power struggle.' As if resigned to the programme of change he and his government faced, he remarked, 'Of course we would all like to live in our own state. We would like a nice, near homogeneous existence without all the problems and tensions of having to live together with other people. But it is meaningless to vote for what you would like to see. You must vote for what you think can work.'

Leading the *Volk* across the Rubicon: De Klerk's Reforms and the Afrikaner Context

Despite the dizzying pace of his reforms, de Klerk initially remained committed to the notion of separate development for black and white South Africans. Months before he became president, his speeches showed him to be firmly committed to apartheid, albeit a more benign version. Like Botha, he tried to discourage contact between white South Africans and black liberation leaders. De Klerk reproved his elder brother, Willem, a former newspaper editor and influential analyst, for talking to the ANC, the largest and most influential black liberation movement. 'Participants in such talks are playing into the hands of forces that are set on destabilizing South Africa and destroying law and order,' he warned his brother in November 1988.

Secondly, he told parliament that he wanted even more 'own affairs', or separate development in line with self-determination, for South Africa's different ethnic groups. He gave a clear indication that the government would negotiate with the blacks on the basis of 'own affairs' rights in which each race group would run separate adminis-trations. 'Our strong emphasis on group rights alongside individual rights is based on the reality of South Africa and not on ideological obsession or racial prejudice,' he said in the August 1989 election campaign. He claimed that the variety of groups in South Africa made it essential to recognize 'own interests' in addition to general interests. In a speech given in September 1989 he said that 'We will promote this standpoint in the negotiation process in the road ahead, because we believe that there is a place for the broadening of own affairs.' A year before he was elected National Party leader, he had explained that 'In itself, own affairs as a developing concept, and as concept in the making, is the key to the granting of security of every group.'

In de Klerk's view, the complexity of the South African society required that two realities, power-sharing and self-determination, be accommodated. Although the reality was that blacks and whites needed to stand together, to work together and to take decisions together in all matters affecting their interests, he was not prepared to allow whites to lose their power in the process. In effect, de Klerk reaffirmed that the NP stood for 'own community life, own residential areas, schools, institutions and systems'.

De Klerk's pragmatism reflected a tendency within the famous Afrikaner Broederbond or Brotherhood – a secret society of élite Afrikaners to which he was admitted at the youthful age of 27. The Broederbond was created in June 1918 as a private organization to defend Afrikaner interests against British colonialism. After their defeat in the Anglo–Boer War, which ended in 1902, Afrikaners found themselves second-class citizens, politically, economically and socially. Facing intimidation by British authorities, the Broederbond went underground. It recruited a network of members who helped each other rise in virtually every aspect of South African society and was a driving force behind the Afrikaner nationalism that swept the National Party into power in 1948, giving rise to apartheid. Membership in the organization is extended by invitation only to those who are white, male, Protestant, Afrikaans-speaking, and well-connected. Even today, the Broederbond remains influential in white politics, education, broadcasting and the Dutch Reformed Church. Its rituals and membership remain secret.

Since 1980, the Broederbond has moved steadily to the left, preparing the ground for de Klerk to dismantle apartheid. Pieter de Lange, chairman of the movement since 1984 once told me:'Some of us became convinced that Afrikaner interests had become so entwined with everyone's interests in South Africa and internationally that you could not promote Afrikaner interests in isolation. You had to promote everyone's interests.' Indeed, a change in Afrikaner thinking was confirmed by a working document of new guidelines circulated among its 20,000 members earlier in 1990. The guidelines, leaked to journalists, contained three cardinal propositions. The first was that a new constitution had to be drawn up in consultation with all groups including, by implication, the then outlawed ANC. Secondly, that Afrikaner survival was compatible with a black president and a cabinet in which most members were black. And thirdly, that white control could be built into or entrenched in a future constitution which would provide for power sharing.

The document argued that 'The abolition of statutory discriminatory measures must not be seen as concessions but a prerequisite for survival.' The guidelines suggested that 'The majority of the government members will indeed be black, but the system and procedure [will operate] in such a way that all groups can participate effectively and not be dominated by one group.' The document further argued that the 'exclusion of effective black power sharing in political processes at the highest level is a threat to the white man which cannot be countered by maintaining the *status quo* or by a further consolidation of power in white hands.' And, in a shift away from the government's long preoccupation with racial groups, it said: 'It must be borne in mind that group interests may cross over colour barriers.'

Broeders, including de Klerk's brother Willem and de Lange, set the scene in the late 1980s by travelling abroad to hold secret discussions with the ANC. According to the ANC a score of such meetings were held in the early 1980s, but were never publicized. De Klerk was linked fraternally to the talks in more ways than one. He was linked firstly through the participation of his brother and secondly as a member himself. With de Klerk at the helm as leader of the National Party and president, the Broederbond's new policies became National Party policies. His first chief negotiator, and former Minister of Constitutional Affairs, Gerrit Viljoen, was both former chairman of the Brotherhood and a close friend of present chairman de Lange.

There are striking similarities between de Klerk's 1989 Five Year Plan and Broederbond guidelines, for example. In 1988 the movement raised the idea of rotating the presidency and of government by consensus or 'concurrent majorities', in which each group would have to approve any law separately before it could be passed. This has become a major platform of the National Party which de Klerk has put forth in the negotiations for a new constitution.

By declaring his readiness to negotiate with black leaders, and draft a new constitution which would guarantee the vote to South Africa's disenfranchised blacks, de Klerk had crossed the Rubicon of apartheid that had deterred the defeated P. W. Botha. When he gave an interview on national television in November 1990, de Klerk avoided any similarities between his government and white-dominated Rhodesia (now black-ruled Zimbabwe): 'In Rhodesia the mistake was that the opportunity for constructive negotiation was not exploited. They waited too long. We are determined not to repeat that mistake.'

'Comrade F. W.': 'I Feel Very Near to the People'

On 1 February 1990 the sun set on the old South Africa. On the first anniversary of his election as leader of the ruling white National Party, and after six months as president, F. W. de Klerk stunned the world. He lifted a 30-year ban on the ANC and other organizations, and allowed political exiles to return. He eased restrictions on the 38 other opposition groups including the ANC's close ally, the UDF. He ended restrictions on the movements and political activities of 500 anti-government activists. In announcing that the government would release Nelson Mandela, de Klerk declared, 'The season of violence is over. The time for reconstruction and reconciliation has arrived.'

Black leaders were cautious with their reactions. Mrs Winnie Mandela told a street rally that de Klerk had not gone far enough: apartheid should be scrapped immediately. 'We are not prepared to accept a bone with no meat, unbanning the ANC and leaving apartheid as it is is no deal,' Mrs Mandela said. ANC official Pallo Jordan, then still exiled, could not believe the news when I telephoned him in Lusaka. He said that de Klerk had made some 'substantive changes', but had failed to meet the movement's demands in full. 'It's like a buffet dinner. He took the parts he liked and left the parts he did not like,' Jordan said. 'Victory is in sight,' Mandela's friend and comrade-in-arms Walter Sisulu said when the news was broken to him in Stockholm. 'This has taken my breath away. I want to give him considerable credit. He has not given us everything, but he has gone a very long way along the road,' Archbishop Tutu said. Inkatha Freedom Party leader Mangosuthu Buthelezi said: 'If blacks now fail to bring about the radical change they have struggled for so long through non-violent means, they will only have themselves to blame.'

De Klerk also meant to take white right-wing parties by surprise. The CP, the official opposition in parliament, said de Klerk had no mandate from whites for his reforms. Eugene Terre'Blanche, leader of the AWB, said de Klerk had capitulated to left-wing radicals by unbanning the ANC. He threatened to fight for a whites-only state, saying: 'We will restore law and order with force and create a state for the *volk* [Afrikaner people].' CP leader Andries Treurnicht said: 'The CP challenges Mr de Klerk to hold a general election immediately to give white voters the opportunity to decide on the National Party's drastic announcements.' Robert van Tonder, whose Boerestaat Party advocates the creation of a Boer republic for whites, warned that the policies outlined in de Klerk's speech could lead to the re-emergence of the extreme right-wing Ossewa Brandwag guerrilla movement of the 1940s, and to possible civil war. Other smaller right-wing factions echoed these sentiments. 'Fools rush in where angels fear to tread,' said Marie van Zyl, head of the Kappiekommando, of the de Klerk initiative. The Kommando, a grouping of Afrikaner women, holds silent protests wearing nineteenth-century bonnets and clothes to uphold the views on race held by early settlers.

Despite such detractors, euphoria swept the country like wildfire. Blacks poured into the streets in a spontaneous celebration not seen even when de Klerk released several top ANC officials the previous October. Tens of thousands of blacks thronged city streets to celebrate the above-ground re-emergence of their long-exiled organizations and the possible return of their exiled leaders. De Klerk had shown more skill than all his predecessors. In unbanning the ANC, he opened the way to negotiations. After 2 February, he was hailed as 'Comrade F. W.' by hundreds of cheering blacks during a whistle-stop tour of Soweto township.

Only a few months before, many white South Africans had been warned that talking to the ANC was tantamount to treason. Now de Klerk had invited the same organization that the National Party had demonized for years to 'walk through the open door, and take [its] place at the negotiating table.' However, in unbanning black opposition groups so unexpectedly, de Klerk clearly meant to throw them off balance. He meant to exploit the differences in age, personality and ideology within the ANC leadership. His problem was how to move fast enough to thwart international pressure for tougher sanctions against his government, fast enough to entice the ANC, and yet carefully enough to keep the whites from turning against him.

By inviting the black opposition groups to the negotiating table, de Klerk offered something for everyone. Those who were at the forefront of international sanctions claimed victory. The ANC and its allies also claimed the 'people's victory' brought about by 'people's power' and the 'people's struggle'. Chief Buthelezi claimed that his commitment to negotiations with the white government had been vindicated. They were all right. De Klerk was not offering 'one person, one vote', but his reforms still granted everyone significant gains. All formerly banned groups would have the same standing as any other political party. They could open offices, hold rallies, raise funds and recruit members.

Some believed it was the collapse of communism in 1989 that persuaded de Klerk to send his country hurtling down the road to reform. But while the world applauded his boldness, others, especially white South Africans, were aghast at the possibility that de Klerk, like Gorbachev, would lose control of the beast he had unleashed, plunging South Africa into further chaos. But in answering a question I put to him at a press conference on 26 September 1992, de Klerk denied he would suffer the same fate as Gorbachev.

There are some comparisons, but Gorbachev had to deal with an economy which was totally destroyed by communism. I do not have that. Gorbachev had a problem with states which never really wanted to be part of the Soviet Union. We do not have that. My problems are different, and easier. So I don't think a Gorbachev case study applies. I feel very near to the people. I know their worries. I realize that to say we are going to change the system through negotiation makes for uncertainty.

That's why I believe it is in the best interests of all that we move fast. Yes, you run a risk of increasing uncertainty, but that way you get to the point where you can remove it that much sooner. When you go slowly you play into the hands of the radicals to the left and the right – and they are minorities – who do not want us to succeed.

Whether yielding to the inevitable like Gorbachev or pursuing a personal vision of a new South Africa, de Klerk showed a willingness to take the kind of risks that ultimately determine a leader's greatness or his folly. 'The old order, in which a white minority exercised all the meaningful power and dominated others, is untenable,' he said in February 1992. 'Each and every South African must realize this. There is but one way to avoid devastating conflict and that is fundamental and orderly reform towards full sharing of power and opportunity.' A year later, de Klerk had this to say about Mandela and the ANC: 'I think Mr Mandela has the typical qualifications, personal qualifications and qualities, expected of people who will fill high office. But the ANC lacks the experience necessary to rule the country. To me they are unacceptable because of their adherence to communism. I think they need direction.'

3

THE MYTH
THE LEGEND
& THE MAN

White South Africans must accept that there will never be
peace and stability in this country until the·principle of
majority rule is accepted....We are not in favour of black
majority rule. We are in favour of majority rule.

Nelson Mandela, August 1991

Between 1986 and 1989, Nelson Mandela was periodically spirited away from prison
late in the afternoon for long secret meetings with government officials. From 1986,
Mandela held at least 22 meetings with a team of government officials; from November
1989, he held regular sessions with cabinet ministers. He later explained that these
preliminary meetings with the government were not negotiations, but that he was only
playing the role of a 'facilitator'. Mandela said he took the initiative to meet with the
government without consulting the ANC because of what he called 'the deepening
political crisis in South Africa'. In an extraordinary, prescient memorandum written
from his prison cell to former President P. W. Botha in 1989 (and published in *South*
newspaper on 1 August), he said: 'I am concerned about the spectre of South Africa
split into two hostile camps ... the key to the whole situation is a negotiated settlement.
An accord with the ANC, and the introduction of a non-racial society, is the only way
in which our rich and beautiful country will be saved....' He added: 'Most South
Africans, black and white, hope to see the ANC and the government working closely
together for a new era in our country in which racial discrimination and prejudice,
coercion and confrontation, death and destruction will be forgotten.'

In the following months Mandela submitted another more formal document to the
government regarding steps it should take to create a climate for negotiations and his
release. These included the release of all political prisoners and the lifting of the State of
Emergency, as well as the unbanning of all opposition groups including his ANC, the
PAC and the SACP. Following de Klerk's election as president, government talks with
Mandela took on real meaning. In October 1989, they worked out the release of
Walter Sisulu and seven other prisoners. Over the next three months, Mandela pressed
de Klerk's government to meet the ANC's terms of negotiations, the unbanning of
political organizations, the release of political prisoners, the lifting of the State of
Emergency and the beginning of a process to dismantle apartheid.

On 13 December 1989, Mandela and de Klerk met at Tuynhuis, the presidential
offices in Cape Town, in what was to be the beginning of a series of meetings on ways
to convene preliminary negotiations to address future demands of the unbanned ANC.

The meeting signalled that, unlike his predecessors, de Klerk was prepared to negotiate with the ANC. People who saw Mandela during that period gained the impression that the two men had come to respect each other greatly. The government, which had for years demonized him as a terrorist, now regarded Mandela as 'a man you can negotiate with', while de Klerk confided that Mandela 'is a man of integrity, a man you can trust.'

In the Shadow of Mount Nelson: The Mandela Legend

Like millions of youngsters in South Africa, I grew up in the shadow of Nelson Mandela. His 27-year imprisonment represented our daily oppression. His degree of self-sacrifice was what we as youngsters strove for to prove our commitment to 'the struggle'. Yet few of us matched his nobility. On Robben Island, in Cape Town's modern Pollsmoor prison and later alone in a luxury bungalow among the vineyards of Paarl, his influence remained undiminished through what he called 'these long, lonely, wasted years'. Township revolutionaries and moderate black leaders invoked his name in heroic terms. Moderate whites saw him as the only person who could prevent a bloody civil war. He was perceived as a Moses waiting to be released from Canaan to lead his people to the Promised Land.

On my first trip to the United States and London in 1986, I spent all of my stipend on books by him or about him. Because such books were banned at home, and as it was a treasonable offence to be found in possession of many anti-apartheid books, especially those on Mandela, I quickly devoured whatever information about the man I could lay my hands on. I was to find out why an unseen and scarcely heard man had for more than a quarter of a century dominated the fight for black rights in South Africa, and why he had become an enduring worldwide symbol of opposition to racial domination. After my reading, I concluded that only Mandela could lead anti-apartheid South Africans into talks with the government. The white government had also reached a similar conclusion. Any negotiations or talks without him would be useless.

The first suggestion of Mandela's release occurred in 1985 when Botha made the offer provided that Mandela 'unconditionally reject violence as a political instrument.' Mandela's response, read out by his daughter Zinzi at a rally, was that 'prisoners cannot enter into contracts.' Meanwhile, his stature grew to near-mythic proportions.

Everyone who visited him in prison spoke of his commanding presence – a lean, gentle, white-haired man who spoke softly and deliberately. Friends from earlier days remarked on his charisma, eloquence and powerful voice. A close friend said that as an orator he had 'an animal magnetism that attracts the masses like pollen attracts bees.' Even government ministers talked about Mandela's unflinching dignity, his great style, charm, humility, his respect for education, his generosity and compassion, his sense of humour, his respect for others and his desire to listen to other people's views before giving his own.

His fellow prisoner, Ahmed Kathrada, spoke in an interview of a lesser-known side which was revealed to Mandela's prison mates. 'We had problems with him at Pollsmoor Prison, for instance, when we were living in a communal cell and there were crickets making terrible noise. We would want to kill them. He wouldn't. He'd go carefully and pick up a cricket. If the window was open, he'd let it out. But he would never kill not even an ant, a cricket or a bee,' said Kathrada.

Retired veteran anti-apartheid politician Helen Suzman was amazed by Mandela's frankness and straightforward talk. 'I first met Nelson Mandela in 1967. He just told me about all their grievances quite openly in front of a commanding officer. His manner was very self-assured,' she said. On Robben Island, Mandela and the other top ANC officials slept in one-man stone cells, two metres by two metres, lit by a 40-watt bulb and furnished with a bed, mat and bookshelves.

In 1975, all but three political prisoners on Robben Island fell ill for five days with influenza and were too weak to get up. In the mornings, Mandela, who remained in good health, went from cell to cell, emptying and washing each cell's toilet bucket. He also helped feed the prisoners.

Most remarkable of all was the recognition Mandela commanded from his own white jailers. Reports of the special respect they showed him were legion. Fikile Bam, who was with him on Robben Island for ten years, said the warders addressed him as 'Mr Mandela', 'an unusual courtesy for a prisoner, and ... he addressed them by rank and name, never showing any animosity.' 'He has had an experience of tremendous power. He has had a tremendous amount of contact with other people. A lot of it adulatory, and it is not going to stop,' said Azar Cachalia.

Three months after negotiating for the release of his friend Walter Sisulu, Mandela was himself freed, after almost 10,000 days in jail, at a quarter to four in the afternoon of 11 February 1990, much to the amazement of South Africans and the world at large. Mandela's release from jail ensured that, after only six months in office, de Klerk had done more to resolve the political crisis in South Africa than P. W. Botha had in more than a decade.

Freedom marked a great personal triumph for Mandela, who had repeatedly refused offers for his conditional release and never wavered from his demand for a multiracial South Africa based on a system of one person, one vote. Some people questioned whether Mandela, then 71, would be able to cope with life on the outside and adjust to the hectic pace likely to be demanded of the country's pre-eminent black leader. 'His present home is so quiet and peaceful. I do not know how well prepared he is for Soweto,' said Amina Cachalia, who visited him while he was still being held at Victor Verster prison. 'He has lived in a cloistered environment for so long. He may quickly get tired from all the movement,' said Audrey Coleman, who ran an organization helping detainees. But all agreed that Mandela was a formidable personality who survived prison with little psychological damage. 'Mandela is in a class of his own as a survivor,' said Ahmed Kathrada.

Like many journalists, I had the opportunity to observe Mandela closely after his release and was astonished at his lack of bitterness and his ability to step into the high-profile role of political leadership. During an interview shortly after his release, Mandela told me: 'We never felt a sense of hopelessness because we went to jail under a cloud of praise and support and demands for our release by heads of government and state.' Asked if his jailers warmed to the man revered by the black majority as the hero of their liberation struggle, he said: 'Oh yes. If a man fights back, he is likely to get more respect than if he merely capitulates.... There were bad men, there were good men, and the good men tried to make things easy for us. We met remarkable people in prison who enriched our lives. We also had the opportunity of reflecting on the past mistakes and planning how we would handle problems when we were released from prison. It was a rewarding experience.'

In jail, Mandela said, he and other political prisoners tried to improve their education, organizing seminars among themselves and seeking ways of getting news into prison. This kind of positive thinking, of planning ahead, kept them in high morale and helped keep bitterness at bay. 'It is not easy to remain bitter if one is busy with constructive things,' Mandela said. He said he had never felt 'against whites as such' – not even against the police force as a whole, a symbol of enmity to many black South Africans.

Mayibuye Mandela

In his first public addresses, Mandela signalled a tough stance towards the government by reaffirming the ANC's commitment to armed resistance which had earned him a life sentence in jail in 1964 for plotting against apartheid rule. His very first rally in Cape Town turned into bedlam as youths began smashing windows and looting stores. The police retaliated with teargas and gunfire that left at least one person dead and 69 injured. Mandela began his first public address from the mayor's balcony of the Cape Town city hall with the traditional ANC rallying cries *Mayibuye iAfrika!* (Come back Africa!) and *Amandla!* (Power!). It was a carefully crafted speech which balanced the demands of the ANC hardliners against the requirements of the man who freed him. Unmistakably a statesman, Mandela showed he was a man of compromise, compassion and hope who aimed to lead his people into a brighter tomorrow. The main task of negotiations would be to reconcile black demands for one person, one vote with white fears about black domination, but he cautioned blacks that they 'must not be too impatient.'

To whites he gave this assurance: 'Whites are fellow South Africans and we want them to feel safe.... We appreciate the contribution they have made towards the development of this country.' At another point he said the ANC sincerely wanted to address the question of the concern of whites over one person, one vote. 'They insist on structural guarantees to ensure that the realization of this demand does not result in the domination of whites by blacks. We understand those feelings, and the ANC is concerned to address that problem and to find a solution which will suit both the blacks and the whites of this country.'

The next day, roaring crowds gave Mandela a hero's welcome when he returned to Soweto to a rally attended by over 120,000 people. He called on all South Africans to join him in ending the 'dark hell of apartheid'. 'During the past 27 years,' he said, 'I have looked forward to the day when I would come back to an area which I regard as my home.' His speech included a powerful appeal for discipline and a condemnation of mindless violence, a message welcomed by President de Klerk. 'This bodes well for the possibility of reasonable discussions in the negotiating process,' said Gerrit Viljoen, then Minister of Constitutional Development.

While the world and millions of South African blacks shouted Hallelujah, Mandela's release and his message horrified conservative and far-right whites. While ecstatic residents of South African townships danced for joy, neo-Nazis yelled 'Hang Mandela!'. White supremacist leader Eugene Terre'Blanche said de Klerk had betrayed minority whites and threatened to ignite a civil war to defend white supremacy. There was a mood of outrage among Terre'Blanche's khaki-shirted AWB, which delivered a coffin symbolizing the fate of five million whites to government headquarters in Pretoria. On top of the coffin, 30 coins symbolized the 30 pieces of silver paid for the betrayal of Jesus Christ.

Conservative Party leader Andries Treurnicht called Mandela a proven communist who had refused to renounce the ANC's armed struggle and had threatened to destabilize the country if blacks were not granted majority rule. 'It is amazing that such a man could be treated like a hero. In view of the offences which Mandela committed – the same as high treason – his refusal to renounce the armed struggle, the fact that he is a proven communist and that he demands majority rule or no internal stability, we find most disturbing and alarming,' he said. 'It is an injustice against the nation. The Afrikaner is a friendly tiger, but don't mess with him,' he added, responding to Mandela's first public address in 27 years.

Despite these signs of animosity from right-wingers, Mandela demonstrated his abilities as a reconciler by his praise for de Klerk's reforms. About de Klerk he said

(11 February): 'It must be added that Mr de Klerk himself is a man of integrity, who is acutely aware of the dangers of a public figure not honouring his undertakings. Mr de Klerk has gone further than any other nationalist president in taking real steps to normalize the situation.' He said he was sure de Klerk wanted to complete the normalization of political life that had already begun.

At times he questioned whether all government officials were committed to de Klerk's initiatives, suggesting that some civil servants might sabotage the envisaged changes. But a greater worry was the security forces, whose position was not clearly defined. Mandela's supporters argued that a majority of security force personnel were opposed to change and might engage in dangerous acts of sabotage to derail negotiations. They also believed that right-wing parties drew their support from these organs of state. Mandela was predicting the difficulties and dangers facing him and de Klerk as they tried to chart the route to democracy.

In a strange way, the two men found themselves locked in a mutual dependence. The success or failure of one rested on the success or failure of the other. For Mandela, the challenge was to unite the fractious and sometimes violent elements of the black community beneath a common banner. Mandela and the ANC needed to transform the raw emotions of their supporters into a disciplined political force ready to back any deal which could be struck with the de Klerk government. For de Klerk, the no less daunting task was to face down assaults from the white right wing and the security forces. If Mandela promised to be a leader of great emotional presence, de Klerk was also showing more skill than any of his predecessors.

The Messiah and the Organization Man

Following Mandela's release, the ANC tried to make the most of his martyrdom to consolidate their support base. The movement wasted no time in capitalizing on its advantage by organizing high-profile rallies around the country to galvanize their supporters in large urban communities. Mandela travelled across the country wooing homeland leaders and other people who served in government-created structures, urging them to 'to join the winning side.'

Plunging himself into the international arena, he kept up a punishing schedule as he criss-crossed the world, addressing mass rallies which attracted thousands. South Africans and the international community hung on his every word, followed him in his travels and debated his opinions. In the first few weeks of his freedom, Mandela's most notable success was his ability to maintain the cohesion of the ANC's leadership, which was scattered all over the world, while pursuing his attempts to enter into preliminary talks with the government. To this end he had to persuade the ANC to accept his reading of de Klerk and to pursue negotiations as their primary strategy.

At the same time, he never wanted to abandon his dual role as both militant and moderate leader. He often reminded blacks and whites that the factors which necessitated the armed struggle still existed, that his movement had no option but to continue its campaigns. 'We have no vote. The only way in which we can focus attention on our grievances, when we fail to convince through persuasion and argument, is to exercise our power, to go into the streets and demonstrate. We are going to do that,' he declared in the speech that celebrated his return to the public arena. To him defiance and other campaigns could only culminate in the establishment of democracy, a fact many whites disagreed with, charging that never-ending protests hurt the already sanctions-battered economy. In a moderate tone, he often expressed the hope that de Klerk would create a climate conducive to begin talks so that there would no longer be the need for an armed struggle.

As a committed anti-apartheid activist, Mandela called on his followers to strengthen their pro-democracy protests to build peace and security. Some regarded him as a Messiah, but Mandela himself often cautioned against unrealistic expectations. First and foremost, as an organization man, he never wanted to deviate from ANC policies – something he made plain in his 11 February speech: 'As a disciplined member of the ANC, I am therefore in full agreement with all of its objectives, strategies and tactics.' He often stressed this point, even though he knew that some ANC strategies, policies and objectives were outdated and strongly criticized at home and abroad.

But he was soon to realize that he had to accommodate the realities of the new world order that had swept away the ideologies of the 1960s. When he began his life sentence, newly independent African nations were looking forward to prosperity under African socialism, while the world was locked in the opening phase of a cold war battle. When he walked to freedom almost three decades later, African socialism and world communism were on their death beds. Mandela soon discovered that any leader who displayed socialist leanings was treated with disdain.

Shifts in Our Thinking: Mandela and the Nationalization Issue

One of his first controversial positions, which touched off a heated debate in South Africa and abroad, was his embrace of nationalizing the so-called commanding heights of the economy as a way of redistributing wealth in a post-apartheid South Africa. Initially Mandela stood by his position, arguing that 'Much debate has been sparked off by the ANC policies on the economy relating to nationalization and redistribution of wealth. South Africa is a wealthy country. It is the labour of black workers that has made the cities, roads and factories. They cannot be excluded from sharing this wealth.'

South African economic growth had declined steadily while Mandela was in jail, largely because of foreign financial and trade sanctions and the cost of administering wasteful apartheid bureaucracies. Inflation-adjusted growth in gross domestic product fell to an average of less than 2 per cent in the 1970s compared with nearly 6 per cent in the 1960s. While many businesses felt that the lifting of sanctions and, especially, a resumption of foreign loans could give a major boost to the economy, they also feared the threat of nationalization under a future ANC government. They feared that the ANC, with little or no proven economic experience, would mismanage state-owned businesses and wreck the country's already fragile economy.

But Mandela dismissed concern among the white business community and foreign investors about his support for nationalization. He said whites had lost interest in state ownership of industry only because there was now a prospect of blacks winning a share of political power. 'The question of nationalization is being looked at from the white point of view alone, and not from the point of view of the whole country,' he told the media conference on 12 February 1990. 'The whites are now changing their minds, saying let us privatize, because they want to keep the wealth to themselves.'

This was partially true. Months before Mandela's release, the National Party government had begun privatizing some of its huge state-owned corporations, many of which had provided safe jobs for whites. The first major sale was the Iron and Steel Corporation (ISCOR) in 1989. State transport, telecommunications, forestry and other concerns were also earmarked for privatization. Mandela fuelled this debate by openly espousing nationalization, which epitomized the hopes of blacks and the fears of whites.

Months later, though, Mandela appeared to be backing down in the face of stiff criticism. Some people described him as just an old, muddled, out-of-date politician with some goodwill but also with a lot of impractical and dangerous ideas. His response this time was more flexible and compromising: 'Nationalization is our policy, but there is a shift in our thinking,' he said. 'We have observed the hostility and concern of businessmen towards nationalization, and we cannot ignore their perceptions.' Again, these were the qualities of a flexible leader. As a result of internal and external pressure, the nationalization and redistribution hysteria has subsided because of the ANC promise that it would keep them as options, but not as policies.

Although Mandela recognized that he had to be flexible on nationalization, he refused to do so with regard to sanctions. He kept on hammering countries which insisted that sanctions against South Africa should be eased. 'There is no question of sanctions ending, because the conditions for which sanctions were applied still exist. I still do not have a vote. Until every South African has a vote, our call for sanctions remains unchanged' (media conference, 12 February 1990). Much to the chagrin of ANC leaders, this call had been largely ignored, and instead foreign governments had rushed to lift sanctions to reward de Klerk for dismantling statutory apartheid. Despite cries from some disaffected blacks who had borne the costs of sanctions over the years much more than whites, the ANC chose to continue its campaign for the economic isolation of South Africa. This was clearly a political rather than an economic decision: the longer sanctions stayed, the more chance that blacks were going to inherit a country in ruins.

Mandela's freedom, the debate over sanctions, and the debate over what line to pursue in the negotiations – these developments confronted the ANC with a host of thorny questions about how to adapt their strategies to the new political terrain. Almost all black organizations were caught off balance and disorganized. After years of bannings, detentions, restrictions, jailings and mass protests, they suddenly found themselves having to accept de Klerk's challenge of reconstructing South Africa. De Klerk believed he was turning Mandela the myth into Mandela the man. By legalizing the ANC, he removed its cloak of underground heroism and turned it into an ordinary political party which would have to make hard choices and unpopular compromises. These compromises were expected to anger and disillusion segments of the black majority, giving the government an additional opportunity to divide the opposition.

Along with external challenges, Mandela also faced challenges inside his own organization. His first and most daunting task was to unify his party and to persuade the various factions of the black community to move forward together. As well as turning emotional support into disciplined political action, the ANC needed to heal the wounds caused by factional violence. If a deal was to be struck with the government, it had to be acceptable to a broad black constituency. The biggest challenge came from a new generation of militant youth within the ANC who resented his automatic resumption of leadership. They considered him too willing to compromise and were angered by his initiating a personal dialogue with de Klerk. This prompted people like powerful trade union leader Cyril Ramaphosa to declare that Mandela's status was no different from the status of any other ANC member.

Mandela's role as a peace broker went beyond his dealings with the government. He was drawn into a range of domestic conflicts, which showed no signs of abating. For example, the perilous state of education in the black community demanded his urgent attention. Since a nationwide uprising against the introduction of Afrikaans in schools as a medium of instruction in 1976, students and pupils – with the support of community organizations, unions and other groups – have been at the forefront of political protest. Young protesters shouting Mandela's name took to township streets, determined to change a policy that has doomed them to second-rate schools. This made students part and parcel of the nationwide anti-apartheid struggle, prompting slogans such as

'Liberation now, education later'. But because of frequent disruptions to their education, black students paid the price at examination time. Results of the all-important school-leaving examinations revealed high failure rates among black students each year: black education seemed to be getting steadily worse. In some years, youths chanting 'Pass one, pass all' demanded to be promoted to the next class despite the fact that they had failed to sit for examination at the end of the previous year. In this volatile atmosphere, Mandela's call for peace, and for pupils to return to school, went largely unheeded, causing speculation that he was unable to control the youth.

A major problem for Mandela and the ANC was growing political violence. Mandela came out of prison at the height of fighting between his supporters and those of Inkatha. Divisions across the political spectrum quickly grew into major rifts that threatened the image of the ANC and hampered its recruitment efforts. Township political violence took up a large part of Mandela's time and energy. To some, his inability to curb the violence diminished his near mythical image and seriously damaged his credibility. When Mandela travelled to the hardest-hit province, Natal, and asked people to 'throw your pangas [machetes] into the sea', his followers made it clear that they could not disarm themselves without risking the safety of their communities.

Ongoing intimidation of rival organizations by self-proclaimed ANC supporters constantly undermined Mandela's claims that his organization abided by democratic principles of freedom of choice and association. Addressing the question of violence and political intolerance, Mandela said: 'The right of people to differ from us must be preserved.' And he warned his followers that 'we are attacking the government for the fact that they are showing this political intolerance. We must not be accused of the same' (speech in Natal, March 1990).

To the world at large (media conference, 12 February 1990) Mandela offered this lengthier explanation:

Our organization has been banned for the last 30 years. Experienced leaders of the organization have been forced into exile. Other well-trained and experienced leaders of the movement have been thrown into jail, and those members who have remained inside the country have been detained, harassed and some killed. Therefore there was nobody to explain the policy of the organization, to instil discipline. You must remember that many of the youths who are active today were born during the last 30 years, when the organization was illegal and when there was nobody to explain the policy of the organization.

If therefore any of our members were guilty of intimidation, you must judge their action against this background. Now that the organization has been legalized, we have considered it to be our duty to stress the question of discipline, the question of tolerance, and I think we are getting support from our membership.

Another problem Mandela faced was the constraint of operating under consensus. A few months after his release, Mandela had shown himself to be a man with a strong sense of mission; but he was also seriously constrained in his individual freedom of action by the ANC's tendency to seek broad, grassroots input before taking any firm decisions. This style of operating restricted Mandela's room to manoeuvre and to make bold, unilateral decisions. At times Mandela seemed torn between a sense that he had a personal and historic mission and his duty to his organization. For example, when he sought, on his own, to make peace with Chief Buthelezi, he ran into serious resistance from hardliners at both the organizational and grassroots levels. Their distrust of the white minority government, and of Chief Buthelezi, ran so deep that the idea of Mandela meeting, and possibly compromising with, either of them was anathema. After talking to families of Inkatha victims, Mandela bowed to local pressure and cancelled his meeting with Chief Buthelezi. A meeting did take place a year later, but never helped to end the carnage.

While he trusted de Klerk as a man who was serious about change, Mandela had continually to question the degree to which de Klerk exercised control over the state to end political violence, and the degree to which the various elements which constitute the state shared his vision. Against such a background, and given the often conflicting demands and concerns of the various sections of his constituency, Mandela could not avoid making statements that were contradictory. The most obvious example came at the peak of the township wars, when Mandela called on de Klerk to use the coercive power of the state to end the violence, and then turned round to denounce de Klerk when he did just that.

People feared cataclysm during the first months of Mandela's freedom, but it did not materialize. Violence and economic decay worsened, however, ruining thousands of lives and terminating thousands more. The scale and savagery of the apparently mindless violence left most South Africans stunned and grasping for reason. People said Mandela had invested too much in the authority of his own personality, while the enmity between his followers and their rivals intensified. Five weeks after his release, up to 300 people had been killed.

Soon enough, Mandela suffered the setbacks of a mortal politician caught in the harsh realities of South Africa's divided society. His opponents in other black organizations presented him as a sell-out. 'When a man has his foot on my neck, should I call him a man of integrity?' asked PAC leader, the late Zeph Mothopeng, after Mandela's description of de Klerk as a man of integrity. Chief Buthelezi lamented Mandela's blunder in hesitating to meet him to try and find ways of ending township violence. The government-supporting media depicted him as old and ineffective. Meanwhile, his personal life was also taking its toll.

Winnie

As he juggled the dual roles of head of the Mandela family and leader of black South Africa's struggle for political rights, one of his major concerns was his wife Winnie, who was only 27 when he went to jail. She herself had been detained, frequently harassed, and once spent over a year in solitary confinement. 'I have wondered whether any kind of commitment can ever be sufficient excuse for abandoning a young and inexperienced woman,' he wrote in 1985. He added that sometimes, because of her, 'conscience and guilt have ravaged every part of my being.'

A few months after his release, Mandela's personal problems concerning his wife's conduct became a public scandal. Her remarks were often in sharp contrast to those of her husband, earning her the reputation of a militant and a firebrand. Unlike her husband, who often emphasized his lack of bitterness, his belief in the integrity of de Klerk and his government, and the flexibility of the ANC on the question of armed struggle, Mrs Mandela expressed total commitment to the armed struggle, harboured a great deal more bitterness toward the 'Afrikaner ruling class' and declared she had no reason to trust the integrity of de Klerk. Some ANC leaders viewed Mrs Mandela as an embarrassment. Time and time again, she mounted public platforms to propound what she claimed to be ANC policy, only to find ANC officials contradicting her.

Often dressed in designer battle fatigues, in contrast to her husband's choice of designer suits with matching ties and shirts, she used emotive language which most ANC officials eschewed, promising to 'return to the bush' to take up arms against the white man. She toured battle-scarred townships encouraging ANC supporters to use force in self-defence when other leaders were working for peace. Her comments regularly unsettled a white community already fearful for its future. Despite their disagreements, Mandela promoted his wife within the ANC, overriding objections by some of his colleagues.

But even as Winnie sought to solidify her status on the ANC executive, the ghosts of the Mandela football club came back to haunt her. Mr Mandela supported his wife as she faced four charges of assault and four of kidnapping in connection with the severe beatings of four young blacks at her home in Soweto in 1988. One of them, a 14-year-old activist named Stompie Seipei, was later found dead. Some blacks believed the government was bent on destroying the ANC by framing her. Many others felt she had shamed the black nation. Mrs Mandela was found guilty and sentenced to six years' imprisonment. On appeal, her conviction was upheld but the prison sentence was commuted to a fine. Chief Justice Corbett said in his 192-page judgement that Mrs Mandela was on occasion evasive, untruthful, contradictory and capable of dishonest improvisation. She was ordered to pay a R15,000 fine, with an additional two years' imprisonment conditionally suspended, in place of the six-year jail term. She was also ordered to pay R5,000 compensation to each of the three surviving victims of the kidnappings and assaults.

Slowly, the long-admired marriage began to disintegrate a year and half after Mr Mandela's release from prison. Family members say Winnie refused to listen to her husband. When she faced a spate of new allegations about her possible involvement in the deaths and disappearances of more activists, coupled with allegations that she was having an affair with a lawyer 29 years younger than her, Mr and Mrs Mandela mutually agreed to separate, making a tough and brave decision to save the ANC from humiliation and embarrassment. A few days later she also resigned from her position as head of the ANC's social welfare department. 'Those who have rejoiced in reading about our problems and those who for selfish political and personal reasons waged a vicious and malicious campaign against me, and through me the leadership of my husband and our organization, have unfortunately partly succeeded in their aims,' she wrote in her resignation letter.

Despite a life of immeasurable suffering under apartheid, and his own personal tragedies, Mandela has been willing to put the past behind him to fulfil a dream for which he spent 27 years in jail. The name Mandela still draws huge crowds. Though he is not the martyr he once was, his stature remains undiminished. He remains calm and composed, dispassionately assessing situations and weighing up options in the creation of a new South Africa. He has emerged as a powerful force for reason and reconciliation amid the violence and chaos of change.

4
TALKS
ABOUT TALKS

We of Umkhonto we Sizwe have always sought – as the liberation movement has sought – to achieve liberation without bloodshed and civil clash. We do so still. We hope – even at this late hour – that our first actions will awaken everyone to a realization of the disastrous situation to which the Nationalist policy is heading.

MK Leaflet, 16 December 1961

The ANC has taken the initiative in regard to getting the government and the ANC to sit down together and hammer out a peaceful solution and these discussions, we look at them with satisfaction, because it is the realization of a dream for which we have worked patiently and consistently over the last three years. We say so not in a spirit of either boasting or claiming credit for the success of the discussions. We went into these discussions in the spirit that there should neither be victors nor losers and, at the end of these discussions, not only are we closer to one another, the ANC and the government, but we are all victors. South Africa is a victor.

Nelson Mandela, 4 May 1990

In May 1961, Nelson Mandela wrote to South African Prime Minister Hendrik Verwoerd deploring apartheid's savage attacks on the rights and living conditions of the black people under a government 'notorious the world over for its obnoxious policies'. In his letter he warned the government that a dangerous outcome could be averted through a national convention of all South Africans to hammer out a non-racial constitution. 'Such a convention', he said, 'would discuss our national problems in a sane and sober manner, and would work out solutions which sought to preserve and safeguard the interests of all sections of the population.'

Writing as secretary of the All-in African National Action Council, a body representing hundreds of religious, social, cultural, sporting and political bodies, Mandela said: 'Conference noted that your government, after receiving a mandate from a section of the European population, decided to proclaim a republic on 31 May 1961. It was the firm view of delegates that your government, which represents only a minority of the population in this country, is not entitled to take such a decision without first seeking the views and obtaining the express consent of the African people.'

The government's response was to ban, arrest and harass leaders of all races, including Mandela. The police and army were deployed in the townships to raid houses and arrest anti-apartheid protesters. On the morning of 17 December 1961, 18 months after the ANC and others had been banned, ANC leaders met in an underground hideout, in fear of a police raid, to draft an historic statement which was in effect a declaration of war against the apartheid regime. On that day acts of sabotage marked the emergence of Umkhonto we Sizwe (MK), the military wing of the ANC. Mandela was its first commander-in-chief. For the next 29 years, South Africa was to experience a simmering guerrilla war.

Speaking from court during his trial in 1964, Mandela explained the decision to form Umkhonto we Sizwe: 'After a long and anxious assessment of the South African situation, I and some of my colleagues came to the conclusion that as violence in this country was inevitable, it would be unrealistic and wrong for African leaders to continue preaching peace and non-violence at a time when the government met our peaceful demands with force.' He went on to add that 'The government policy of force, repression and violence will no longer be met with non-violent resistance only. The choice is not ours, it has been made by the Nationalist government, which has rejected every peaceful demand by the people for rights and freedom and answered every such demand with force and yet more force.'

During the period of the armed struggle, hundreds of South Africans – white and black – have been killed in bombings, gun battles and rocket attacks launched by Umkhonto we Sizwe. The group's first attacks in December 1961 occurred within 18 months of the worst mass shooting of blacks in modern history – the killing of 69 people by police in the township of Sharpeville. 'With the launch of "MK" suddenly there was hope again. Things were happening. People in the townships became eager for political news,' Mandela told the court.

But for the next 15 years, MK could field only a few hundred poorly trained guerrillas who used home-made bombs to attack army, police and government targets. MK was transformed from June 1976 when harsh police action to quell the Soweto uprising drove thousands of radicalized youths out of South Africa and into the ranks of the ANC in exile. It is estimated that, in 1976 alone, the exodus of youths from troubled townships swelled the ranks of MK by at least 8,000 guerrillas. The Soviet Union and East Germany provided advance training and modern rifles, rocket launchers and mines. Guerrillas based in neighbouring black states infiltrated back into South Africa and trained military cells in the townships in preparation for a mass uprising.

The government pursued MK relentlessly, launching air raids against alleged ANC bases in Zimbabwe, Mozambique, Botswana, Swaziland and Lesotho. The destabilization campaign sowed confusion and demoralization and was calculated to confirm the racist stereotype that black rule does not work. The governments of these neighbouring states denied they harboured ANC guerrillas, accusing Pretoria of launching raids to please restive white voters. South Africa deployed an army of informers inside the ANC and patrolled the borders against infiltration. While the apartheid regime has never had to use more than a fraction of its military arsenal against ANC guerrillas, armed action directed from ANC bases in exile has exerted considerable psychological pressure on whites to grant political rights to the black majority.

Nevertheless, many whites have scoffed at the ANC's armed struggle as an amateurish guerrilla operation which did virtually no harm to the mighty South African state. Such critics point out that the ineffectiveness of the armed struggle made it a weak bargaining point. A car bomb that killed up to 19 people and wounded 200 in the capital city of Pretoria in May 1983 was the bloodiest single attack. Without the armed struggle, however, the ANC would never have attracted to its ranks the thousands of black students who fled the country after the Soweto rebellion of 1976. Nor, without it, could the ANC have capitalized so successfully on the township revolts of 1984–6. The ANC's bombing campaign in 1986–8 struck fear into whites by treating as open targets the shopping centres, restaurants and bars frequented by residents of wealthy suburbs previously untouched by the country's political turmoil.

No One in the Room Had Horns: African and Afrikaner Nationalists, May 1990

Since the ANC was founded in 1912, black South Africans have done everything possible to get successive white governments to the negotiating table. The ANC did not discover its belief in political solutions in the 1990s. The entire history of the organization is strewn with attempts to seek peace through negotiations. This has been symbolized by fifty years of non-violent mass protests, civil disobedience campaigns, the general strikes now known as 'stay-aways', and written appeals to the authorities. Even when it formed Umkhonto we Sizwe to launch the armed struggle, the ANC merely wanted to pressure the government to talk to the majority as a step towards democratic government. It was not pressing for a military victory.

Three decades later, on 2 May 1990, this impasse was finally broken in the first series of talks between the National Party government and the ANC about a new political dispensation. The meeting was held in Cape Town at Groote Schuur, a residence used by successive white prime ministers and presidents. For the first time since the inception of apartheid, a serious meeting was taking place between anti-apartheid leaders and the white government officials who have ruled our country down the years. 'It indicates the deadly weight of the terrible tradition of a dialogue between master and servant which we have to overcome,' Mandela said at the beginning of the talks.

Soon after taking their seats, delegates from both the government and the ANC realized 'how foolish we'd all been,' ANC diplomatic head Thabo Mbeki said. 'We were all of us a bit surprised . . . within a matter of minutes, everyone understood there was no one in the room who had horns – and that, in fact, discussions ought to have taken place years ago. And when we closed after the first few hours of talks, the general feeling was that not only is forward movement necessary, but that it is also possible.'

Bizarre elements of the meeting were driven home by his account of their preparations for the talks and their first trip home in 30 years.

> When the pilot of the aircraft announced that we were crossing the Limpopo river, we all stood up and stared out of the window. There was a lot of excitement building up as we were moving further south. There was a lot of happiness that people were coming back. But there was also some sadness that it was ever necessary that we should have been outside this country for so long. When we landed at D. F. Malan airport [in Cape Town] there was no earthquake, no white children died, no bombs went off. Why didn't we do that 28 years ago? Why didn't the government realize the futility of the apartheid system? But then, life in exile has in a way been rewarding. Out there are people who will make a very important contribution to change in this country.

Talking about the difficulties of life in exile, Mbeki added:

> Admittedly, it has not been very easy for many of our people. We have got kids at our school in Tanzania who even when the schools were closed for the holidays had nowhere else to go. What has sustained everybody is that nobody spent a life of

idleness. People learned something. The other thing that sustained them is that they never lost confidence that one day the apartheid system will go and that one day they will return home and everybody would have played a role in the process. There is really no bitterness against the people who caused all the suffering. The bitterness is really against the system and not against the people.

Communist leader Joe Slovo, formerly white South Africa's enemy number one, had this to say:

We have come in a spirit of conciliation, but we have not come as petitioners, we have come as claimants for a people who have been kept down for too long. We are here with our hearts filled with hope. We left by the back door and we have entered through the very front door. For those of us who have suffered the curse of exile for almost 30 years, this is a moment of great joy, although we continue to live in a country that is chained by apartheid. The vote, the land remain a virtual monopoly of the white minority. We have come to talk to the government in a spirit of conciliation. If there is a real way forward without bloodshed, the whole world knows we will grab it. We have come to the table in search of a future of peace and equality.

De Klerk's government had tried to bar Slovo from taking part in the pioneering talks because of his affiliation to the South African Communist Party (SACP). But Mandela stuck to his guns, insisting that he would be a member of the ANC's team. 'I suggested to them that they should regard the matter as closed. I pointed out that I had risked my own reputation and told my organization that Mr de Klerk is an honest man. I said to them they should risk their political reputation and explain to their own people that Mr Slovo is a true son of South Africa.'

At the moment that the Zambia Airways jet conveying Slovo and five other ANC delegates touched down at Cape Town's D. F. Malan airport on 27 April 1990, one of South Africa's most enduring psychological barriers crumbled: the unthinkable and unusual began to happen. South African Police handed out ANC press cards with the 'ANC lives' logo showing the spear, shield and flag of the organization. Controlling access to the international arrivals lounge was a tall, burly white policeman. Helping was ANC activist Willie Hofmeyr, who only a month earlier had begun legal pro-ceedings against the government demanding R100,000 rands ($45,000 dollars) for keeping him under solitary confinement in detention. A few months earlier, he had gone on a devastating and much publicized hunger strike to demand his release. In the welcoming lounge Govan Mbeki (Thabo Mbeki's father) said: 'From Africa, always something new comes. Strange things happen. In the days before the delegates left the country, we could never have gathered like this. The gentlemen on the other side [the security police] would have been trailing us. It is a very different story today.'

Indeed, unusual things happened. Police and members of the white-led security forces helped guard ANC leaders. Only four months before, the security forces might have shot them on sight. But in those hopeful days in May, it was the police, soldiers and government who rolled out a red carpet for the people they had denounced for so long as 'terrorists and murderers'. The government also picked up the tab for the ANC delegation at a five-star hotel. The hotel was named after Lord Charles Somerset, one of South Africa's nineteenth-century colonial rulers.

Walking Past van Riebeeck: 2 May 1990 and its Aftermath

Groote Schuur, for seven decades the official residence of South African prime ministers and presidents, was the richly ironic venue for the historic 'talk about talks'.

Groote Schuur was brought to its splendour, replete with art collections and antiques, by South Africa's apostle of imperialism, Cecil John Rhodes, notorious colonizer of Zambia and Zimbabwe. Groote Schuur became the Prime Minister's residence in 1910. Within its walls, white ministers had concocted a long list of apartheid measures to deny the black majority a say in governing their country. Now, here were Mandela, Mbeki and several other ANC leaders entering the building which for years was one of those used to plot their downfall, this time to begin talks which promised to lead South Africa to a non-racial democracy.

The rectangular dining room was converted into a conference chamber. The ANC was given the lounge as its caucus room; the government chose the Rhodes study. The rooms were fully equipped with modern technology, special lights, microphones and control boxes, sophisticated recording equipment. A huge tent festooned with flowers was erected outside to provide the delegates with meals and refreshments.

De Klerk and his entourage arrived in a fleet of German limousines. The ANC delegates arrived in similar cars, together with a mini-bus taxi. After brief preliminary remarks, the parties disappeared into the building through the main entrance, past the bronze frieze that shows Jan van Riebeeck at his first meeting with the indigenous people of South Africa, the Khoi and San. Van Riebeeck's arrival in 1652 marked the beginning of 350 years of dispossession and domination of South Africa's indigenous people, as Mandela noted when he addressed the media.

Standing beside de Klerk in the lush garden of Groote Schuur, Mandela declared: 'The sacrifices that our people have made to end the system of apartheid demand that all of us act with the necessary sense of responsibility so that the dreams of millions of people, in South Africa, southern Africa, Africa and the rest of the world, for an end to the system of white minority domination are transformed into reality. The time to reach this end has come.'

In his opening remarks, de Klerk said he was irreversibly committed to change and wanted obstacles to substantive constitutional negotiations removed as soon as possible. 'There are bound to be difficulties, but there is cautious optimism, as well as faith and conviction that our problems will be solved by negotiation. The government has accepted the challenge of doing everything possible to achieve this.' Turning to him, Mandela responded in Afrikaans: 'Dit was 'n lekker gespraak.' (That was a nice speech.) The black and white delegations lined up behind their leaders broke into smiles.

Day One was spent getting acquainted and reviewing issues. Mandela delivered a moving chronology of the events that led to the ANC resorting to armed action against the government. Both delegations were astounded to find that they were so much in agreement, that they had so much in common as inhabitants of the same country. At no stage was there any tension or threat of a breakdown. Even Communist Party leader Joe Slovo said he never encountered any hostility but only 'bemused curiosity' from some government delegates who would have locked him up and thrown away the key a few months before. The smooth completion of the meeting reflected a breakthrough in personal relations and attitudes among the country's major political players.

Day Two saw the two parties getting into more serious discussions about several obstacles in the way of formal talks on a new constitution for a non-racial democratic South Africa. They were: security laws, the return of exiles, the presence of white-led troops in black townships, the release of political prisoners, the State of Emergency, the ANC's commitment to armed struggle and the need to end violence in black communities.

On Day Three, the parties deliberated on the agreement which had to be reached to clear obstacles to negotiations, such as the release of all political prisoners, the safe return of all exiles, the lifting of the State of Emergency, the suspension of political trials, the withdrawal of troops from the townships and the steps to be taken to curb political unrest in the townships.

Working groups were set up to look at ways of improving the political climate and speeding the process towards real constitutional talks. Another committee would look at time scales and mechanisms for dealing with the release of political prisoners and the granting of immunity in respect of political offences to those inside and outside South Africa. Delegates agreed there was a need for temporary immunity from prosecution for political offences committed before the agreement. This would enable members of the ANC's National Executive Committee and selected members of the ANC outside the country to return and help with the establishment and management of political activities and negotiations. The government committed itself to review existing security legislation in order to ensure normal and free political activity and the lifting of the State of Emergency. The ANC committed itself to review its position on the armed struggle, although this did not form part of the agreement.

The outcome of the historic three-day talks went beyond the wildest dreams of the parties and most of us who have watched our country degenerate into chaos. The Groote Schuur Minute showed that the government and the ANC had agreed on a common commitment towards the resolution of apartheid's problems through a peaceful process of negotiation. Prominent in the joint communique released at the first joint press conference was the acceptance by both parties of their need to work together to end the violence which was ravaging the country's towns, cities and townships.

About the agreement, de Klerk said: 'I regard what is contained in this document as an important breakthrough in the peaceful process which we want to take place in South Africa. It has been this government's goal to normalize the political process. Today we can say a great step forward has been taken in the process. It has been our goal to improve the climate for negotiation.'

Mandela added: 'The important thing is going to be the implementation of the agreement and there is a realization on the part of both delegates that it is important that these obstacles, which we have identified in the document, should be removed at the earliest possible convenience. We in the ANC are convinced that both our organization and the government mean just to do just that and we hope we will get the support of all South Africans and the international community in this important objective.' Mandela also stressed that 'the ANC and the government are the main players in this country in the search for peace.' 'However,' he said, 'we recognize the fact, which we have stated over and over again, that there are other interested parties in this regard and it would only be proper at some stage to seek their views on the important questions which we have been discussing over the last few days.'

The agreement, while lauded in South Africa and abroad, caused a stir in several quarters inside South Africa. The ANC's arch-rival, the PAC, criticized the ANC for selling out by agreeing to talks. 'As far as we are concerned, we will not be going within spitting distance of that negotiation table,' PAC spokesman Barney Desai said. 'We would like to see the government meeting some of our preconditions, such as the scrapping of the Land Acts, Group Areas Act, Population Registration Act and security laws that are all inconsistent with human rights.'

AZAPO said future talks would fail because de Klerk had stressed his rejection of one person, one vote in a unitary state, and the redistribution of land and wealth. The organization predicted that de Klerk would also refuse to budge on the crucial issue of minority rights and the maintenance of a free enterprise system.

CP leader Andries Treurnicht staged a walk-out from parliament's chambers. Flanked by his party members, he said the government had turned its back on the mandate from the white electorate. He said de Klerk had no legal right to give 'ANC terrorists indemnity against prosecution or to prevent the police from acting against them.'

After decades of apartheid repression, critics of negotiations such as the PAC, AZAPO and others refused to place their trust in a government with such a record. This section of the black South African community firmly believed that de Klerk was not serious about genuine negotiations. His aim, they said, was to liquidate internal resistance, and put an end to the international isolation of South Africa and sanctions. They supported their claim by emphasizing de Klerk's insistence that one person, one vote, or simple majority rule, was not the answer to South Africa's problems. They also recalled de Klerk's staunch belief in the protection of minority rights.

For de Klerk and his government, the announcement of their commitment to negotiations ended their isolation by the rest of the world. The Poles and Hungarians wanted trade links. Madagascar wanted air links and, for the first time in four decades, an Afrikaner leader received red-carpet treatment in the United States at a meeting with an American president.

Whether the ANC believed the government to be sincere was not the issue. The issue was that, for the first time in the history of apartheid rule, the government had expressed its willingness to negotiate a future democracy. If the government was not sincere, the people of South Africa and the international community would pass judgement. For that reason, the outcome of the three days of talks at Groote Schuur was an enormous breakthrough. They removed an unfounded fear, held for decades by white South Africans, that the ANC is an irresponsible terrorist organization. They began to remove the mistrust the ANC and the majority of black people in South Africa have felt about the National Party as the ruthless regulator of the system, impervious to change.

For me, the talks achieved two main things. The first was the signing of a remarkable agreement which satisfied the main demands of both the government and the ANC. The second was the establishment of an important rapport between the government and its arch-rival, the ANC, which would prove vital in the full-scale negotiations ahead. The Groote Schuur Minute also satisfied de Klerk's demand, committing the ANC to consider suspending the armed struggle, and to work with the government to end the violence.

Minute by Minute: Groote Schuur (May) to Pretoria (August) 1990

Asked about the ANC's position on its 30-year-old guerrilla war against white rule, Mandela said his organization would 'look very hard and earnestly at the whole question of the armed struggle in the light of this agreement.' The ANC found itself in a dilemma on the question of the armed struggle because it could not afford to abandon it too quickly for fear of losing the support of militant blacks. At the same time, the ANC seemed to contradict itself by calling for a negotiated settlement while arguing that the armed struggle and economic sanctions should be maintained. Months prior to the Groote Schuur talks, the ANC had released a working document on future negotiations called the Harare Declaration. The policy document was later adopted by the Organization of African Unity (OAU) and the United Nations. Basically, the document had stipulated a set of demands which the South African government was supposed to meet before any formal talks could start. The major conditions were the unbanning of political organizations, the unconditional release of political prisoners and detainees, the lifting of the State of Emergency, the withdrawal of troops from the townships, and the unconditional right of return for political exiles.

The conditions set in the Harare Declaration did not address the pillars of apartheid, the Population Registration Act, the Land Acts, the Group Areas Act, the Tricameral Parliament and the homelands system. Neither did they address the creation of a mechanism to facilitate the drawing up of a new constitution – a constituent assembly and an interim government.

By the time the preliminary talks were held, the government had met only one condition, namely the unbanning of political organizations. By itself, this concession was not sufficient, since the government still retained draconian security laws which could be used to ban rallies and restrain anti-apartheid activists. The unbanning was also less convincing because it did not mean the immediate sharing of political power. The government had also insisted that a State of Emergency created to curb violence could not be lifted while violence continued. It argued that it could not be expected to release all political prisoners and allow the return of exiles while the ANC's armed struggle was still in force. Although the government acknowledged that its apartheid policies were wrong, the National Party believed that its control over state power was still strong and that it could negotiate a deal favourable to its white constituency. But by the end of the talks, it clearly indicated that it could no longer govern the country alone – that much of the responsibilities it once monopolized had to be shared. Then chief negotiator Gerrit Viljoen indicated that his party had come to accept that it would no longer be the ruling party, but maybe a junior partner in a coalition government.

But even as the two most powerful political organizations were meeting at Groote Schuur, political violence was tearing black communities apart across the country. About 500 had been killed in political fighting since Mandela's release in February.

Three months later, amid murderous township warfare, the government and the ANC held another summit. This meeting, on 6 August 1990, was dogged by recriminations from both sides about the causes of the township killings. The agenda was based closely on the Groote Schuur Minute of 2–4 May. The government saw it as a follow-up, focusing on the report of the joint working group set up in May. Besides a detailed agreement on prisoners and exiles, de Klerk and his team were looking for a reaffirmation by the ANC of a 'commitment towards the resolution of the existing climate of violence . . . as well as a commitment to stability and peaceful negotiations.' The definition of violence and intimidation adopted by de Klerk and his group included rent and school boycotts, thus hitting hard at what the government saw as contradictory statements emanating from ANC leaders who spoke of 'stability and mass action'.

Prior to the talks, the ANC had also indicated to de Klerk that it was concerned about the role played by police in perpetrating violence against blacks and in failing to curtail burgeoning right-wing terrorism and vigilante attacks. For his part, de Klerk was supposed to do all in his power to root out the extremists in the military and the police, to stop his officials sowing suspicion, and to convince blacks that he and his government were sincere in the march towards a new South Africa. In return, the ANC was supposed to realize that a ceasefire would be an act of strength, not weakness; an act that would do much to restore white goodwill and confidence, and help stem the talk of revolution on the white right. History demanded that both parties give these commitments. Neither the return to hard-line apartheid nor the retention of the armed struggle were tenable prospects. Furthermore, neither side could afford to expose itself to international condemnation for allowing the process to falter.

After 15 hours of deliberations, the most stunning surprise of the meeting came when Mandela announced that 'The African National Congress is now suspending all armed action with immediate effect. No further armed actions and related activities by the ANC and its military wing will take place.' It had been a long, hard road from the meeting which had produced 'The Umkhonto we Sizwe Manifesto' to the one which would produce the Pretoria Minute, drafted by the government and the ANC on 6 August 1990.

As the ANC's negotiators later revealed, much to the surprise of their followers, 'we came to the meeting already decided we would declare a ceasefire.' One of the ANC team, Joe Slovo, said: 'We did not go there [to the talks] as part of a cricket cup competition, to score points. We went there to break the logjam and we succeeded 100 per cent.' He added: 'Right at the beginning of the meeting Nelson Mandela made the point that time was not on our side, that the longer the process stretched out, the more time would be given to those who would like to sabotage the process.' However, Slovo later acknowledged that, despite the ceasefire agreement, the ANC and its allies would not abandon underground activities until they were convinced that change was totally irreversible.

To ANC supporters, especially young militants, it appeared that their movement had made more concessions than the government. The main prize for the government was the ANC's announcement that it would suspend the armed struggle. For the ANC, the main achievement was the government's decision to begin releasing political prisoners and detainees and indemnifying exiles and others against arrest for political offences. Why did the ANC give so much at this point to get so little in return? The answer could only be that the ANC valued the prospect of negotiations above all else, even if it meant leaving itself open to attacks from young militants and hard-liners rather than negotiating a ceasefire in accordance with the terms it had set out in the Harare Declaration.

This underscored the fact that, even within the ANC, many leaders had remained ambivalent about the value of the armed struggle. It has been a source of friction between young and old members in the ANC, with attacks on civilian targets favoured by recent young recruits against the older generation's preference for military or government targets. Although ANC bombers bolstered the morale of blacks, attracting them to the ANC, the armed struggle repelled in equal measure whites whose support the ANC also needed. At the Pretoria summit, both delegations expressed serious concern about the general level of violence, intimidation and unrest in the country, especially Natal. They agreed that, in the common search for peace and stability, it was vital that understanding should grow among all sections of the South African population, and that problems should be solved through negotiations.

ANC militants and hard-liners disagreed. They said the government's security forces should set the example by abandoning violence, and that apartheid must be ended totally and democracy established before one could talk about suspending the armed struggle. Without achieving all of the above, thought my radical friends in the townships, who spearheaded sometimes violent opposition to decades of white oppression, Mandela surrendered without dignity and with nothing to show in return. My friends believed the ANC's concession looked like capitulation to the Afrikaner rulers. The government did not lift the State of Emergency in Natal and did not give any firm undertaking to do so. Pretoria did not agree on any moratorium on security legislation, as urged by the ANC. The government gave no undertaking to review other security measures such as detention without trial, but promised to continue reviewing security legislation to give more freedom to political activity. It did give an undertaking to consider repealing certain anomalous aspects of the infamous Internal Security Act.

Hoping to gain even greater concessions, the government went on to urge the ANC to abandon its campaign of mass mobilization, which it considered to be a disguised form of violence, intimidation and instability. Their hopes were dashed when Mandela said the government could not expect the cessation of mass action as long as there were no mechanisms to defuse black grievances. Although it appeared that the suspension of low-level guerrilla warfare would cost Mandela support on the left wing of the liberation movement, the move paid off in the long run because it consolidated Mandela's support among moderate blacks.

Worried that suspending armed action would cost it support, the ANC launched a publicity campaign to emphasize that guerrilla war remained an option. 'The armed struggle has not been abandoned,' advertisements placed in major newspapers proclaimed.

> The people's army, Umkhonto we Sizwe, has not been dissolved; we have not forfeited our right to self-defence . . . continued suspension is conditional on the behaviour of the South African police and defence force. The ANC is committed to the achievement of a united, non-racial, democratic South Africa. We have initiated the process of talks to realize this objective.

After placing the advertisements the ANC began a programme of talks in townships countrywide, both to explain the change of tactics and to hear the people's views.

For de Klerk, the cessation of the ANC's armed struggle was his first real boost since his 2 February speech. It would help him secure the approval of the white electorate for whatever constitutional proposals emerged from the substantive negotiations. He was also equipped with a powerful argument against right-wingers who accused him of making repeated concessions to the ANC without gaining anything in return. Once again, the two men seemed to be working in tandem, each helping to reinforce and strengthen the other against opponents of negotiations. With the Pretoria Minute in August, South Africa came much nearer to peace than anyone had dared hope since the historic February speech first taught them to hope at all.

II

SHADOW OF NEGOTIATIONS

7 Uniformed ANC members form a guard of honour around the coffins of 19 comrades killed in political fighting in Kagiso township, west of Johannesburg. Mass funerals became regular weekend occurrences as political groups fought to influence the transition to democracy.

8 Plainclothes policemen inspect the corpses of two black women killed when gunmen opened fire on people waiting to board trains at Johannesburg's Jeppe station. This was one of many attacks on train commuters, the first of which came on 6 September 1990 when 26 people were killed outright and 100 others hacked and flung from moving trains. More than 350 people were killed in similar attacks over the following three years.

9 *Mandela and Chief Mangosuthu Buthelezi in one of their rare meetings to discuss ways to end fighting among their supporters. Their meetings, which often began and ended with bear-hugs, never succeeded in promoting embraces among their grassroots supporters.*

10 *The corpse of a woman burnt to death by ANC supporters lies on a street in Sebokeng township. The woman admitted giving shelter to gunmen who slaughtered 35 people in one of many massacres in the township. She was hacked, stoned and her body sprinkled with petrol before being set alight.*

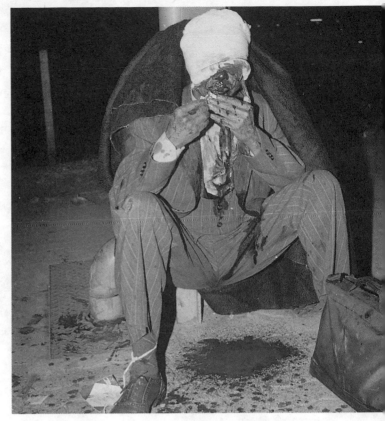

11 *A victim of township political violence waiting for help after an attack.*

12 *'Comrades' armed with clubs and sharpened 'steels' stand over a man who had been stoned, hacked and stabbed to death in Katlehong township east of Johannesburg.*

13 *Mandela salutes residents of Sebokeng at the end of one of many visits to calm residents angered by repeated massacres. Sebokeng, south of Johannesburg, was one of the townships hardest hit by Inkatha–ANC rivalry.*

14 *Zulu migrant workers, wielding clubs and sharpened metal sticks, march through the streets of Katlehong township in a show of force after several hostel dwellers had been killed by residents. The carrying of 'traditional' weapons such as clubs became the focal point of debate as leaders tried to curb political violence.*

15 *Police march down a Soweto street in an attempt to quell township fighting. Their role as peacekeepers was questioned by blacks, who saw them less positively: as butchers, botchers or part of the 'third force' fomenting violence.*

16 *Anti-apartheid campaigner and 1984 Nobel Prize winner Archbishop Desmond Tutu tours a camp housing refugees who fled vicious township fighting in Natal province.*

17 *Armed squatter camp residents gather to ponder the next move after their cardboard and sheet metal homes at the Phola Park shanty town outside Tokoza township were attacked by unknown gunmen. Squatter camps were often flashpoints of township violence.*

18 *A 'comrade' – a militant ANC supporter – proudly brandishes a homemade knife or 'panga' (machete), used against rival members of other groups fighting for township turf.*

Stop Apartheid's War! Defend Natal!

19 *ANC supporters, one with a dummy AK47 automatic rifle, demonstrate in Edendale, a township in Natal where the ANC and Inkatha have fought long and hard for turf. Real AK-47s are now in good supply in Edendale and other townships.*

20 *Zulu migrant workers wearing red headbands to identify themselves as Inkatha supporters stand behind razor wire around their hostel in Tokoza township, east of Johannesburg. The ANC and the government hoped the wire would help stop the feuding between Zulu hostel dwellers and local residents. They hoped in vain.*

21 *A South African soldier guards confiscated weapons such as spears, knives and machetes outside a hostel for black migrant workers. The weapons were used in running battles with township residents.*

5

A TIME FOR WEEPING

> When I looked back, I saw my son being struck with a huge knife. He was then thrown into the flames of our house they had just torched. He was screaming but there was nothing I could do. To this day I can still hear the sizzling sound of the flames as they ate into my child's flesh.

Victim of Natal violence

I was still at high school when I picked up a newspaper one day in 1976 and saw Archbishop Desmond Tutu's letter to Prime Minister P. W. Botha. The letter was to serve as a warning to the nation's rulers.

> I am writing to you, Sir, because I have a growing nightmarish fear that, unless something drastic is done very soon, then bloodshed and violence are going to happen in South Africa, almost inevitably. A people can take only so much and no more. . . . A people made desperate by despair and injustice and oppression will use desperate means.

Botha did not heed the warning. Neither did his successor. Some of the bloodiest violence occurred barely a month after the unbanning of the ANC. Although the killings escalated countrywide following de Klerk's 2 February watershed speech – peaking in April in Natal, subsiding and peaking up again at the end of July with a sudden burst of Inkatha–ANC fighting in Sebokeng – bloodletting around Johannesburg, in the townships of what is popularly known as the PWV (the Pretoria–Witwatersrand–Vereeniging region), began just a week after the signing of the Pretoria Minute on 6 August 1990.

The violence which erupted in Tokoza quickly spread to the other East Rand townships such as my own neighbouring township of Katlehong, Vosloorus, KwaThema and Daveyton. In each case, the scenario was the same: hostel dwellers or squatters fought running battles with residents, while police added to the death count. There were also occasional calculated attacks and counter-attacks by both residents and hostel dwellers. Soweto streets soon resembled battlefields. Within days, some areas of these townships were devastated, shacks razed to the ground, burnt furniture strewn among the rubble, and hopeless people choking from clouds of smoke. Corpses lay amidst the desolation and destruction, some scattered across the townships' open fields which had become battle zones. Horrific scenes of burning bodies became everyday occurrences in Soweto and other townships. Homeless refugees moved from one open patch of veld to another.

In just one month, between August and September 1990, the death count around Johannesburg stood at more than 700, dwarfing the final death toll after four months of the Soweto uprisings of 1976. In the first three months of 1991, more than 400 people died in political violence, 260 of them after the long-awaited and much-applauded Mandela–Buthelezi peace summit. Watching the death count on television and reading about the carnage in newspapers gave the impression that nearly every major South African city, large town, and even outback farming district was experiencing turmoil more fierce than the 1984–6 upheavals. More than 7,000 lives were lost in the 14 months that followed the unbanning of the ANC, and other liberation movements, from February 1990 to April 1991.

It was painfully ironic that, on the same day that the ANC agreed to suspend its armed struggle, more people died in political violence than during the six months following de Klerk's unbanning of the ANC. With political violence at times killing 10 South Africans a day – three times as many as in previous years – many people wondered whether a peaceful transition to a non-racial democracy was possible.

In spite of calls to end the carnage, the death toll kept on mounting and fighting engulfed even townships that had never been affected before. The slaughter moved from one township to another, besieging Johannesburg's industrial heartland and leaving many townships desolated and bitter, drowning in grief, fear and suspicion. As South Africa's township war took on a new pattern and townships went to war with themselves, the realities of apartheid were brought sharply into focus.

De Klerk joined Mandela and Chief Buthelezi in decrying the violence, but little was agreed upon in analysing its cause. Officially it remained 'black-on-black'. The impression was that blacks were not ready to rule and were ripping each other apart as the stakes of political power were stacked higher. But there were strong allegations by residents that Inkatha *impis,* supporters of the party led by Chief Buthelezi, were being used by the police to fuel the violence, and that whites were involved in some of the killings. Vigilante hit squads also left a trail of death and destruction in the townships. In one such incident, 23 people were killed in Tokoza and Tembisa when occupants of a mini-bus drove around shooting and stabbing residents. The ANC accused the government of direct complicity in the violence through a sinister 'Third Force'.

In the months following 6 August 1990, as a journalist who was also a resident of one of the worst-affected areas, I was to report and witness South Africa's time for weeping.

Scenes from My Notebook's Nightmare

A night in the battle zone

The slaughter in my home township of Katlehong began to the sound of male residents whistling from house to house to warn of an impending attack by Zulu hostel dwellers. Whistling is the usual night signal for men to gather in an open area to protect their families and homes. This time it heralded a horrific new eruption of violence in South Africa's township conflict.

The whistlers alerted township residents after they heard that Zulus, mostly supporters of the Inkatha Freedom Party, had just held a meeting in a hostel square at the west end of the township and decided to retaliate for the stoning and burning of a colleague's mini-bus by township residents, most of them supporters of the ANC. Within minutes, men, boys and some women in the township armed themselves with pick-handles, spears, knives, automatic rifles, stones and other weapons. The Zulus emerged from Kwesine hostel on the edge of the settlement of half a million people, and advanced towards the township, where some 50 people had died in clashes two weeks earlier. Shots rang out from both sides and the battle began.

I saw a hostel dweller chop at a youth with a 'panga' [machete], and finish him off with a gun. An unlucky businessman was shot several times while trying to flee the violence in his car, the back of his head torn open and his brains splattered on the car seat. I had gone to the battle zone when my sister telephoned me to fetch her from a particularly troubled part of the township because she feared for her family's safety.

Several lifeless bodies lay strewn on open ground separating the hostel and the township. Township residents led by aggressive youths repelled the Zulu attacks, barricading streets with rocks and sheet metal. The Zulus counter-attacked strongly and the battle intensified as houses and vehicles were stoned, damaged and looted. Police helicopters hovered overhead, aiming searchlights at the trouble spots below. But residents said they were not convinced the white-led police were interested in stopping the fighting. 'They will only do something once whites are victims,' one youth said.

The police did not disarm Inkatha supporters who were brandishing weapons, and instead chased away armed residents. On several occasions police drove residents deep into their own township while giving the Zulus free rein to move around near the hostel. Men wearing balaclavas burnt bodies, some of them beyond recognition. The next day police confirmed that 22 people were killed in the carnage and that more bodies were being found.

The way my friend and his family died

My friend Johannes, unaware that he would find most of his family wiped out and his house torn apart by hostel dwellers, walked towards his home proudly clutching bread for his children. He was about to discover the barbaric slaying of his family when he too was brutally killed by the same assailants. When I arrived six hours later his relatives were still battling to make sense of the attack.

As I approached the house, a chill rolled down my spine when I saw police in the yard taking pictures. Afraid to enter at first, I flashed my press card to the police and went inside the house to see what was going on. I saw the family's vicious dog, Spotty, lying in the yard. It had been shot and stabbed, with some of its intestines protruding from its belly. I entered the house to be met by Johannes's wife's body covered in blood. Terrified, I made my way into the bedroom, where I saw their 14-year-old daughter, Sue, lying next to her parents' bed. The bed had been turned upside down. She had been stabbed on the chest and shot in the eye. She was still breathing, but it was clear she would not live. Her jeans had been pulled down, suggesting she might have been raped.

Inside the cupboard was Sue's 10-year-old brother Tumelo. His throat had been slit and his hand was missing. It had been hacked with a cane-cutting knife before his throat was cut. I found Johannes's mother in the visitors' bedroom behind a pile of clothes and blankets. It appeared the assailants had helped themselves to the family's clothes before shooting the 60-year old Mogau. They stole the family's television set and jewellery, and broke cupboards and furniture.

The attackers were leaving the house when an unsuspecting Johannes arrived from work. He tried to fight back, but was hopelessly outnumbered. Shot in the chest, he fell at the gate and died. They put him the into the trunk of his car which had been parked at the entrance and set it alight. Johannes and his family did not belong to any political organization.

The only person who survived the massacre was Johannes's four-year-old son

Khomotso, who had gone to watch television with the neighbours since the electricity at his home had been turned off following a rent boycott. Like Johannes's relatives, I still cannot come to grips with the way my friend and his family died.

In Tembisa

In Tembisa terrified squatters told me how mini-buses with white and black people arrived at the camp after midnight and randomly opened fire with AK-47 automatic rifles and pistols. Bodies of 14 men were still strewn inside some of the shacks, others lay lifeless between the shacks when I arrived in the morning. Scores of shacks had also been razed.

'I ran away. I heard my room-mate pleading for his life, but they did not even pause before they shot him. I saw black and white people shooting him at point-blank range,' one woman who escaped the carnage said.

'At first I thought they might be plain-clothes police – until I saw the men shooting at us. People panicked and ran into the veld to hide. But those men just waited for them, then opened fire,' one squatter said.

In Soweto

In Soweto knife- and club-wielding men ripped open an 11-year-old boy's stomach. In a frantic bid to save his life, the boy forced his intestines back into his stomach and ran about a kilometre to seek help from neighbours.

The boy, sporting 35 stitches across his stomach, told me afterwards that heavily armed men wearing red headbands stormed into his home and demanded to know where his father was. Before his mother could answer, they hit her with a machete and she collapsed.

'They turned to me. As I tried to get out, they pulled me back and slashed me twice across the stomach. As I fell, they left. I saw them get into a hippo [armoured truck]. I pushed my intestines into my stomach. I ran to my friend's house and collapsed at the door. They called an ambulance.'

In Bekkersdal

In Bekkersdal, my colleagues Juda Ngwenya, William Maclean and I saw a squatter boy die, a neat hole torn in his forehead by a bullet. As his life ebbed away, blood oozing from the back of his head formed a scarlet stain on the mud-path where he fell.

'We do not want to fight. But the police shoot us and protect Inkatha,' said one of a crowd of men who gathered around the body screaming with grief and rage. The volley of gunfire that ended his teenage life was the bloody finale to celebrations by 4,000 Zulu warriors who came from Johannesburg to open a branch of their Inkatha Freedom Party in Bekkersdal township.

The day began with speeches by Inkatha leaders about peace, democracy and tolerance, but ended in a demonstration of the seething aggression behind South Africa's township wars.

And in Sebokeng

In Sebokeng, I watched hundreds of residents gather on the township's main street to march to the nearby Vereeniging town in protest against local councils and high rentals. They never made the 10-kilometre (6-mile) march. Sitting in my car a few metres away from the marchers, I heard no warning. Police opened fire with pistols and shotguns loaded with birdshot and also used teargas. After the volley of shots a burst of laughter came from the heavily armed police.

There was a stampede and screams as the protesters ran for cover. The shooting lasted about one and a half minutes. As the people – men, women and children both old and young – ran for cover, a cloud of dust rose up, mixing with the teargas. People fell like flies being sprayed with insecticide. Some were hit in the head and hip. A teenage girl fell after being shot in the mouth. The injured struggled frantically to crawl to safety amid the laughter of their attackers. Bodies covered with blood splayed on the road. In one case, it looked like police stopped people from coming to help the injured. Afterwards I counted 16 bodies. A post-mortem revealed that they had been shot from behind as they fled.

Two versions of a massacre

In a Sebokeng hostel, four local residents were found dead one August morning. Three died of stab wounds and one was burnt to death. Residents accused Zulu migrant workers living in the hostel of murdering the men. The police were questioning about 150 hostel dwellers about the four murders when I arrived and saw about 1,000 township residents gathering outside the hostel.

'The residents were armed with dangerous weapons and petrol bombs were displayed by many in the crowd. The mob openly declared to the police that they were there to enter the hostel and kill the people responsible for murdering the four men. They stoned the hostel. A Defence Force contingent was called. Shooting broke out. Bloody battles erupted and 36 people were killed by soldiers,' a police statement said later.

The residents' version was quite different. They said soon after the marching and chanting residents arrived to demand the release of the men's bodies, soldiers arrived, got off their trucks, took up positions, and cocked their guns. The crowd came towards them waving their hands, saying 'Peace, we are not fighting.' Some of them even sat down. All of a sudden there was shooting. Many of the people ran. Some of the people fell. When it was all over, 11 bodies were found, some outside and some inside the hostel compound. Hours later the death toll soared past 36.

This was in direct contrast to the statements made by the Defence Force and police. The government immediately ordered a military probe, but the ANC, saying it had been outraged by the shooting, declared that the police and army could not investigate themselves and called for a judicial commission. It was clear to me that police and soldiers were protecting hostel dwellers from rampaging township residents.

'We examined some of the bodies and we were outraged at what we saw. One of the people was obviously shot in the back and his head was crushed. These people have been shot, hit with cane knives and stabbed with spears. This was a very cruel and vicious attack. This only confirms that police conduct leaves much to be desired. We see no reason why live bullets were used because the lives of members of the army were not threatened,' Mandela said. Indeed, Mandela was right.

During the days following the shooting, bloody battles erupted in the township, leaving another 40 people dead. Residents said armed white men, some dressed in dark clothes, were party to the attack. Witnesses said they saw white men running on the roof of one of the hostel blocks, shooting at men fleeing on the ground. They said balaclava-clad men – their white hands visible as they clasped rifles – crouched among a group of men who launched an attack on one block of hostels. White men driving three vans deposited a large group of black men at a hostel entrance several hours before trouble erupted.

Mandela accused the government of using Inkatha to fight its battles in an attempt to undermine the authority of the black people. 'Inkatha members were killing ANC comrades and working with the whites because they had reached a political cul-de-sac,' he said. 'Inkatha leader Themba Khoza was arrested taking AK-47s, pistols and ammunition to his men, so Inkatha cannot deny they are causing the township violence,' Mandela said.

Mourning into mourning

Tears had hardly dried when angry mobs rampaged through Sebokeng township revenging another slaughter. Eye-witnesses said that at about 2 a.m. they saw a mini-bus drive slowly past a house where a vigil was being held for an activist. The mourners, fearful of an attack, quickly erected barricades in the street. Another witness said he saw the mini-bus return and stop. Five men, all dressed in white t-shirts, trousers and berets, alighted from the vehicle and advanced on the tent with rifles in their hands.

The mourners in the tent, as they sang hymns and prayed, never saw their assailants. The gunmen ran forward and opened fire with AK-47 rifles. Two grenades were lobbed into the tent. At least 37 mourners were killed instantly. Five others died in hospital.

Amabontshisi you live, *imbotyi* you die

At first rival factions of Zulu hostel inmates and township residents recognized one another by the red or white headbands and armbands they wore. But as the ferocity of the strife intensified, bizarre password language was used to identify friends from enemies because of the confusion caused by non-Inkatha hostel inmates. This led to Inkatha groups asking people to name things like beans, as a sign of their ethnicity. Beans are called *amabontshisi* in Zulu, but *imbotyi* in Xhosa. The same applied to milk, called *ubisi* in Zulu and *intusi* in Xhosa. A correct answer could mean the difference between life and death.

A person walking by would be stopped, suspected of being a spy. He would then have to undergo a test. If he was suspected of being a Zulu from the remote rural villages, and thus a member of Inkatha, he would be shown a one rand coin and asked to identify it. Most rural Zulus pronounce 'r' like 'l', so a Zulu would pronounce it 'land' rather than 'rand'. If he failed the test, he could easily be killed.

Speaking to some survivors

After marauding hordes armed with clubs, knives and guns went on the rampage, hacking and shooting any unfortunate person who happened to cross their path, I went to speak to one injured victim who survived that massacre of 50 people in Tokoza.

'We no longer sleep at night. We go to bed, but we are listening all the time for the sound of running feet or shots being fired. There is noise in the street throughout the night. When something like this happens to you, it opens your eyes. I do not know what is going to happen tonight, there is always gunfire. So I close the doors and sit down and imagine that they are breaking down the doors. When you are scared you imagine things,' one Tokoza resident told me.

'Just before my brother was shot, I heard him plead for his life. He was saying, "Please do not shoot me. I am not fighting anybody." Then two shots went off, followed by a cry, and silence. I could not come to my brother's rescue for fear of being killed,' one witness of the slaughter said.

Another witness said: 'I was scared for my life, and as I peeped through the hole of my shack, my body shaking, I saw about four figures shooting at anything. What will become of all these children orphaned daily?'

A Zulu-speaking man, part of the rampaging Tokoza hostel mob, told me he did not know why he was fighting. He and scores of others descended on the Phola Park squatter camp, believed to house hundreds of Xhosas who are known to be ANC supporters, and left a trail of death and destruction.

'I came back from work and heard we were attacking the Xhosas living in the squatter camp. I am Zulu, and I joined in,' he said. When Inkatha-supporting hostel inmates were asked why Xhosas and other ethnic groups were targets they simply answered: 'The ANC is a Xhosa organization.' Many of the ANC leaders such as Nelson Mandela, Walter Sisulu, Govan Mbeki and others are Xhosa-speaking. Labelling the ANC a Xhosa organization is intended to give it the same tribalist stigma attached to Inkatha by its opponents.

Random fire

On another occasion, hundreds of mourners in Inkatha attire and colours, brandishing home-made knives, sharpened fence poles and meat cleavers, thronged the stadium in Soweto to attend the funeral of slain Soweto councillor and Inkatha regional leader, Moses Khumalo. Police at the gates and perimeters monitored the crowds. At the end of speeches and obituaries, mourners marched on the nearby houses, hacking at doors, smashing the windows and spearing the occupants to death. Down the street four men were celebrating their reunion with a brother when a rampaging mob descended on them. One was shot several times in the back and hacked with a machete. He died on the steps of the house. Another brother ran to the back of the house and tried to hide in a huge tool box. The mob shot and killed him there. Another brother was shot and killed at the kitchen door as he tried to flee. Even the family dog was shot in the back.

Where were the police? Relatives who hid under beds said the police did nothing to help them except put down the injured dog after the 10-minute massacre of the three brothers. The body count had reached six before the funeral. After the burial, the Inkatha mourners disembarked at a squatter camp and killed five more innocent men, women and children before getting into the bus for traditional handwashing at the home of the deceased.

Following this incident, fighting engulfed the township and 42 people died in the following days. One of them was a mother of five in Soweto's Dube Village who died when a gunman fired randomly at residents. Sindisiwe Motha was killed by a bullet fired through the lounge window as she went to answer the telephone.

Another victim was shot in the leg. He crawled into a nearby house while the gunman tried to finish him off. The gunman then ran into the nearby Dube hostel. Tension rose when residents confronted the police for failing to apprehend the killer despite being a few yards from the incidents.

The two incidents prompted a group of youths to march on Nelson Mandela's home to demand arms to defend themselves. 'It is time the ANC leadership forgot about conferences and meetings and gave us arms to defend ourselves,' one youth said. Winnie Mandela followed the youths to Motha's house, where she comforted the family. 'This is one of the most tragic events. I am outraged,' Mrs Mandela said, fighting back tears. 'People are asking to be armed and they have the right to defend themselves.'

In no man's land

In Kagiso, my colleague William Maclean and I found a man who had been dead for three hours when we saw a chanting crowd approach his lifeless body. In fury, they poured petrol over his badly mutilated corpse and set it alight. There was a hollow sound as a heavy club, like a baseball bat, swung by a youth cracked open the corpse's head. The crowd danced in joy as the man's brain and body burned heavily.

No one seemed to know the dead man's identity. But the location of his corpse, in scrubland beside a migrant worker's hostel, and the anger of the crowd of residents hacking at his body indicated he belonged to Inkatha.

Jikeleza 9436

Train 9436 from Johannesburg to Soweto was on schedule, its arrival awaited by homeward-bound commuters at stations down the line. The coaches usually divided into hymn singers, beer drinkers and those who liked to find a moment of peace to relax, think idly of the day's events, or read newspapers.

One of the peak-hour trains was known as Jikeleza (round-about) because its route followed an easterly arc to collect Soweto's workers from the industrial heartland to the east, south and south-west of the city. From Johannesburg station, it travelled east towards Germiston, past Doornfontein, Ellis Park, Jeppe, George Goch and Denver, and then swung west towards Soweto.

The Jikeleza pulled in at George Goch at 5.12 p.m. The worshippers had just finished a prayer and were about to start a hymn when suddenly a gunman shouted 'Nazi izinja!' (Here are the dogs!) and the coaches suddenly echoed with gunfire as gunmen hacked, shot and stabbed passengers. Passengers screamed, some dropped to the floor where soon there were puddles of blood. Others scrambled for the windows. When the train stopped at Denver station, 26 people had been killed, and 100 injured.

Survivors said the cold-blooded, planned slaughter began when the killers climbed aboard at Jeppe, one of the city's busiest stations. They remained in the last coach, while more attackers, who boarded the front coach, joined them at George Goch. 'I saw about five people with shotguns, pistols and pangas,' one survivor said. 'They just started killing everyone. Then two or three people came from the back, also with guns and pangas. They had trapped us all. I jumped off the train. I think I saw some of the attackers run off towards the George Goch hostel,' he said.

Moving from carriage to carriage, the black attackers shot, stabbed and hacked their way through the passengers. Some jumped for their lives. Others cowered under seats. Some were slain where they sat or hacked as they tried to flee. The killers shouted insults as they carried out the slaughter. When the train lurched to a halt, passengers fled into the night and the killers escaped. Denver station was coated with blood.

The previous night, four gunmen in a mini-bus had unleashed a wave of terror in the Johannesburg city centre, randomly firing on commuters with automatic machine guns as they travelled the city streets, killing three people and injuring 20. The police linked the two incidents.

A Culture of Violence

'Something has gone desperately wrong in the black community. Ultimately we must turn the spotlight on ourselves. We cannot go forever blaming apartheid. Of course it is responsible for a greater deal of evil. But we are human beings and we proved it in the resilience we have shown in the struggle for justice,' Desmond Tutu told me.

Archbishop Tutu was right. Apartheid could be advanced as a mitigating factor, but in 1991, just when blacks were preparing to control their political destiny, it was clear that apartheid at its worst did not induce black people to behave with such barbaric disregard for life. Was it really apartheid that told people to butcher those who disagreed with them politically? Many answered by saying one can present as many theories as one likes, but the buck will always stop at apartheid's door.

Those who blamed the carnage on apartheid argued that it was clear that the children of apartheid were the ones conducting the reign of terror that was tearing the foundations of a new South Africa apart. They spoke of generations of apartheid, steeped in a culture of inferiority, let down by a third-rate system of education, ill-equipped for the challenges of a new South Africa, and forced to live in unbearable conditions in the townships, hostels, and squatter settlements. The children of apartheid were discriminated against, denied their dignity, treated like foreigners in the country of their birth and taught to despise other cultures. Anger and frustration boiled over. Therefore, they said, it was apartheid that caused the carnage.

But then one was tempted to ask: at such a late hour in the history of the country, did apartheid or suffering really account for the brutality of power struggles? This line of enquiry led one to other reasonable explanations such as vengeance, power lust and depravity. Violence had become a new faith – a form of idolatry. Black South Africans seemed to have a death wish. They seemed to believe that democracy only starts after your opponents have been conquered and slaughtered.

Was it really apartheid which forced and intimidated people to participate in boycotts and mass demonstrations? Was it really apartheid which told people to kill and maim those perceived as government stooges and lackeys? It seemed that South Africans had forgotten that violent disorder, once set in motion, resulted in tyranny and not the freedom they have been denied for more than 300 years.

The archbishop also attributed the violence partly to the political transition in South Africa, the government's history of political intolerance, police misconduct and the economic deprivation suffered by blacks. 'But it is not all the truth. A lot of violence is due to political rivalry,' he said. 'Political groups in the black community are fighting for turf and they do not seem to know, or certainly some of their followers do not seem to know, that a cardinal tenet of democracy is that people must be free to choose freely whom they want to support,' he said.

Statements by leaders condemning atrocities were hardly enough. Neither were the ever-growing lists of judicial commissions, inquests and police inquiries that were barely completed before new massacres led to more inquiries. The era of negotiations brought not only the prospect of peace, but heightened political tensions in the complex reality of South African politics. Throughout South Africa, the new political climate opened important arenas of power to contest as the political organizations jockeyed for position. When Archbishop Tutu lamented the loss of respect for human life in the black communities, he touched – perhaps unconsciously – on the heart of the problem, and on the solution.

Why did the violence erupt at a time when de Klerk had sounded apartheid's death knell and the first real prospect of blacks attaining full political rights was nearing reality? One day I asked President de Klerk that question and he said: 'Why are people fighting at the moment? Because their leaders are not talking to each other, because they do not believe that progress is being made, because they feel that there is a grave risk that they might be tricked out of the role that they foresee for themselves . . . .'

But township residents accused white provocateurs, mainly in de Klerk's police force, of trying to preserve apartheid by setting blacks against blacks. Militant ANC youths accused their venerable old leaders of giving up the armed struggle prematurely and leaving their supporters utterly defenceless. Mandela accused the police of favouring Inkatha and also raised the notion of a sinister 'third force' within the security forces bent on destabilizing the ANC. The government blamed a power struggle among different black political factions . . . .

In the midst of all these accusations and counter-accusations, many of us feared that the new South Africa, the one we had been yearning after for years, would not be the bastion of human rights we dreamed of, but just another battleground for power at whatever cost. Despite a commitment to negotiations by the major political parties, events on the ground seemed to be taking a different course that seriously undermined progress towards national reconciliation.

Like many people, my family and friends refused to believe that the sudden eruption of violence was sheer coincidence or fate. For them there was increasing reason to believe that there were alternative forces contributing to the violence. At times an ominous pattern emerged. Men masquerading as soldiers or policemen murdered innocent people with pitiless efficiency. One massacre was followed by another, with sickening frequency. Between February 1990 and September 1992 there were 53 massacres in which 1,500 people died. In some incidents where mysterious deaths occurred, people had noticed a white mini-bus near the scene. Eye-witnesses in Tokoza, and then in Tembisa, Katlehong, Sebokeng and Soweto, came forward with similar descriptions of the occupants of a mini-bus. The trigger for the mysterious attacks seemed to be the renewed promise of peace in the transition process. Whenever peace hovered closer, carnage erupted.

Increasingly, the main flashpoint or source of violence was the migrant workers' hostels. The hostel system was conceived as part of rigid apartheid, along with the homeland system, to enforce South Africa's strict migrant labour system. After being resettled on arid and unproductive homelands, many men were forced to leave their homes in the rural areas to look for jobs in the cities. The Urban Areas Act, an influx control measure, forbade them to bring their families to the cities. This had the effect of denying rural blacks city status, while isolating men in compounds hundreds of miles away from their families. Hostel inmates were forced to live in squalid conditions without day-to-day contact with normal family life. They were caged in dreadful, maze-like, single- and double-storey complexes for 11 months of the year, going back to the homelands to renew their contracts each December.

Their bungalows were filthy and cold and greeted everyone with an unbearable stench. Heaps of rubbish littered the floors. There was no heating system in the cold highveld winters. Rows of concrete bunks served as beds, with personal belongings tucked under them or hung on the walls. As many as 16 men shared one big bungalow. Some hostels had no kitchens or dining halls. Cooking would be done in dark corners and passages on pressure stoves, by the light of candles and paraffin lanterns. Some hostels had no hot water, and some had no water at all. The floors were bare, the walls cracked, and the windows broken. No attempt was made by the authorities to improve these facilities. Until the 1990–1 uprisings no government ministers had even visited the hostels to see how people lived there.

Often separated from other township dwellers by a wire fence, the inmates live in virtual isolation from their surrounding communities, while even their families are prevented from visiting them. It is a life of boredom, deprivation and loneliness. Recreation facilities are non-existent. For many, alcohol is the only form of consolation. Hostel dwellers, who do not see themselves as part of the communities where their hostels are situated, more often develop a sense of being aliens in their own country. 'It is making people live in those dehumanizing conditions, isolating them from the community, that has exacerbated the kind of problems that we have,' Archbishop Tutu said.

This sense of alienation has helped to fuel the conflict between hostel dwellers and township residents. They have been called *iziqhaza* (stupid people), *amagoduka* (migrants), *makontraka* (contract workers) and other stigmatizing names. Residents have accused them of disruption and of inciting tribal warfare. The hostel dwellers, for their part, feel victimized as outsiders. In this sometimes hostile environment, the Zulu migrant workers undoubtedly feel threatened. Their aggressive response to the death of their kinsmen cannot be separated from their feelings of vulnerability. During the height of the carnage, de Klerk paid a surprise visit to Soweto and made a whirlwind tour of one of the hostels. When he emerged from the hostel, he did not wear the same smile he had on when he entered, and he admitted that the hostel system had to be changed.

'Third Force' Tactics?

Rooms in hostels were allocated along tribal or ethnic lines. Tribalism is a dirty word in South Africa because of its association with apartheid, but in every age, in every society, religion and ideology, the call of a tribe has been one of the first loyalties learned. In South Africa, the architects of apartheid used ethnicity to divide the country into minorities in their quest to perpetuate separate development and racial discrimination. When the fighting started in the Transvaal, spreading from township to township and centring on the hostels where many Zulu migrant workers lived, it quickly assumed tribal and ethnic overtones, pitting Zulus against non-Zulus.

Under apartheid, tribalism, culture and ethnicity were used as a means to separate and denationalize black South Africans. A black person's ethnic and racial origin categorized him for all aspects and purposes of life – where he would live, whom he would associate with or marry, and the tribal homeland to which he would belong, regardless of where he was born. South African townships were divided into ethnic regions to accommodate Zulus, Xhosas, Sothos, and others. I lived in the Zulu section of Katlehong. Gradually, ethnicity and tribalism became the basis for political differences. Ethnic sentiments were kept alive by a whole host of other factors deeply embedded in the social, political and economic structure of racially divided South Africa, especially so when identification with one's ethnic group was seen as vital for survival and advancement in a competitive and antagonistic environment.

The Zulus, mostly members of Inkatha, felt denigrated by the ANC's tactic of isolating their party and their leader, Chief Mangosuthu Buthelezi. They felt isolated because most ANC leaders, who belong to the Xhosa tribe, showed themselves more willing to talk to their former jailers and other lords of apartheid than to Inkatha leaders. Furthermore, the ANC had launched a campaign calling for the KwaZulu homeland to be dismantled while not targeting other homelands. The reason was that the other homeland leaders were more compliant with the ANC's demand that they join an alliance against the government.

Responding to the ANC's call for the dismantling of the KwaZulu homeland, Chief Buthelezi also played on tribal loyalties, branding the campaign an act of contempt for the Zulu king, the Zulu nation, and the kingdom of KwaZulu. 'I hope that the Zulu people, whatever their political affiliations, will realize that the ANC campaign of vilification is no longer just against me and Inkatha, but also against the Zulu people, as Zulu people are being singled out by the ANC/SACP/UDF/COSATU [Congress of South African Trade Unions] alliance for vilification, intimidation and killings.'

The Zulus are South Africa's largest tribe and have a proud martial history. Zulus, literally 'people of heaven', live in Natal and Chief Buthelezi's adjoining KwaZulu homeland, where highly structured black tribal life based on mud-hut villages is much as it was centuries ago. Praising Inkatha members as 'Zulu brothers born out of Zulu warrior stock', Chief Buthelezi said modern African states which ignored tribalism had always come to grief. 'Whenever new rulers attempted to rule without traditional leaders, the historical natural leadership that exists among people always surfaces to claim its rightful role.' In one breath he argued that 'Everything had to be done to stamp out ethnicity from politics.' In the next, however, he reminded everyone that 'We will not tolerate attacks on the Zulu nation. We will not be annihilated as a people. These people do not know Zulu history and forget that the warrior blood of kings and war generals courses in my veins. If anyone looking to the future of South Africa expects me to vanish, they had better go and reread their Zulu history.' Thus attacks on Buthelezi are easily equated by rural peasants in Natal with an attack on Zulus and Zulu-ness.

Non-Zulus feared Zulus long before Inkatha was ever established. One can trace the fear back to the Zulu king Shaka and the enormous bloodletting which occurred during the dispersal of African tribes in the nineteenth century. In creating the Zulu nation, Shaka conquered large areas of what is now Natal, driving out tribes who refused to live under him. Many blacks, Zulu and non-Zulu, stereotyped the descendants of Shaka as cruel and bloodthirsty. Whether it was true or not, that was the reality of how many blacks felt, hence the sensitivity to ethnicity and tribalism.

The ANC and other anti-apartheid activists played down the influence of tribalism, saying its importance was inflated by previous white governments who used it to justify racial segregation. ANC membership encompasses all South Africa's nine major tribes, including Zulus, but most of its leaders – like Nelson Mandela – are Xhosa.

The argument that ethnicity was one of the major contributors to the fighting was sometimes misleading. The Natal killings, for example, were Zulu on Zulu. In the Eastern Cape, wars have often pitted Xhosa against Xhosa. Only in urban areas such as the Johannesburg industrial heartland has ethnicity been emphasized. Even there, considering that an estimated 40 per cent of Sowetans or Katlehong residents are Zulu, and the fighting has always been centred primarily around hostels, albeit including Zulus, this could hardly be described as an ethnic clash of any major significance. But this does not mean that the ethnic factor should be dismissed.

How to deal with ethnic feelings has been an excruciatingly difficult problem. Years of enforced ethnic divisions have made many people wary of even acknowledging ethnic feelings exist, lest this be mistaken for racism. Yet ethnic loyalties can unleash enormous political energy. Apartheid itself can be seen as a manifestation of tribal and ethnic hatred of blacks by whites, and Afrikaners in particular. The Afrikaner tribe's urge to survive as a tribe saw it strive to secure the greatest possible share of resources in competition with black tribes by claiming the same fatherland. The Afrikaners constitutionalized tribalism and ethnicity, hence the emergence of KwaZulu and other homelands. Therefore, since tribalism and ethnicity were used to perpetuate apartheid, the township wars can be seen as a direct consequence of the divide and rule policies of successive white governments. The fighting was one of the consequences of a society whites wanted to create; a society of whites united as a single entity and blacks divided into various groups along ethnic lines. As the struggle for power in post-apartheid South Africa intensifies, it is likely that the country will see wider and deeper ethnic cleavages – asserted by or against Zulus, Indians, Afrikaners and all the other groups. We cannot ignore ethnicity when we begin to build a new nation. Let us hope that our understanding of ethnicity will help us build a multicultural society.

During the township political faction fighting, it was clear that the conduct of the police, whether through active collusion or omission, accelerated the conflict: a free hand was given to one group to continue with the reign of terror, while acts of self-defence by the other group were curbed. Township residents believed that even-handed policing could have stopped or at least limited the slaughter. The overall situation had been greatly exacerbated by the fact that law enforcement agencies, such as the police, had long lost the respect and trust of the black community. Police actions on the ground also showed scant regard for de Klerk's attempts to defuse hostilities. The controversial role played by the police and other members of the security forces in South Africa's political violence is dealt with in detail in the next chapters.

Vigilantes were another wing of the so-called 'third force'. In some townships, vigilantes had the tacit approval of the authorities who formerly managed the defunct Joint Management Committees, to help them intimidate and even kill political activists. For example, after the ANC-allied UDF singled out the conservative town of Ermelo for a consumer boycott of white-owned shops to force it to desegregate facilities, vigilante groups emerged to attack the organizers and supporters of the action, most of whom were ANC supporters. One of the widely publicized vigilante activities was the 1986 destruction of thousands of homes in Crossroads, Cape Town, by people who were identified by white headbands. During the destruction and killing, residents said police just looked on, without helping the victims.

State-supported vigilantes played an important role in discrediting black organizations, creating the impression that the state and the security forces were playing a peace-keeping role while blacks were tearing themselves apart. Most of the vigilante attacks on black communities have gone unpunished, leading communities to lose faith in the criminal justice system and legal institutions for curbing township violence. Loss of faith in state legal institutions carried with it the danger of people taking the law into their own hands, which in turn contributed to the spiral of violence.

As the legal pillars of apartheid crumbled, arguments ensued whether the government was serious about change or whether it had a hidden agenda. The debate was further fuelled by the government's allocation of more than R5 billion each year for what it called 'covert operations' and special forces. Was de Klerk's objective real power sharing or was it his intention to strip the ANC of its allies and let political faction fighting cripple the organization?

The ANC believed de Klerk had a double agenda. He wanted to negotiate with the ANC but he also wanted to weaken it. In many instances, even outright attacks by Inkatha supporters escaped criticism by the government. Yet the ANC never escaped verbal attacks even for a small outburst from its supporters. Many people thought the government and Inkatha had a keen political interest in the fighting, as they both stood to benefit from a weak and demoralized ANC. De Klerk denied this charge, saying he would not have started the process of dismantling apartheid and replacing it with democracy if it was his intention later to wreck the new structure. Chief Buthelezi said his repeated calls for non-violence down the years would speak for him.

But despite de Klerk's denial, Nelson Mandela, his supporters and other anti-government organizations said de Klerk and his ruling National Party benefited from the violence. They said de Klerk's party was able to maintain control of its traditional white support base, as the violence remained almost exclusively concentrated in black areas. As a result of the violence, the ANC found it difficult to recruit additional black support and strengthen its membership base in the townships. This was compounded by the inability of the ANC to respond to calls from township residents for weapons with which to defend themselves against attacks. The ANC's major focus shifted from political recruitment to organizing funerals and assisting people displaced by the fighting, while the National Party maintained its political initiative.

Mandela and other leaders, and many victims of political violence in the townships, condemned de Klerk's apparent unwillingness to restrain Inkatha, including his refusal to impose a ban on its traditional weapons. Despite being aware that Zulu cultural weapons such as spears, sticks and knobkerries provoked violence, de Klerk issued a proclamation making it legal for Zulu-speaking people to carry such dangerous weapons. Despite repeated calls to rescind his proclamation, adequate measures to control the public carrying of weapons were not instituted. If they were, they stopped short of an ultimate ban.

Nico Basson, a disgruntled former major in the South African intelligence branch, became one of the first white former officials to accuse the government of seeking to destabilize the ANC. He said the government was providing aid to members of the Inkatha Freedom Party to attack and weaken the ANC. The South African military, said Basson, paid about R50,000 ($22,800) a month to run a similar secret operation in Namibia in 1989 to discredit the South West African People's Organization (SWAPO), which has run Namibia since March 1990 after gaining independence from South Africa. He said the whole process started years ago and was designed to destabilize southern Africa. By destabilizing the region, the government wanted to prove to the international community that blacks could not run a country. 'The operation was found to be quite successful [in Namibia] and it was decided to apply it in South Africa,' Basson said.

Basson provided further details:

The government decided that black-on-black violence should be one of the strategies, and a confrontation between Zulus and Xhosas should be encouraged because the two ethnic groups were the largest in the country. The army recruited people, especially youths, from outside South Africa, mainly rebel soldiers – trained them in game reserves and sent them to specific areas to start paramilitary units, protect hostels and start violence. At these camps the youths are also trained to destabilize communities. The strategy is also aimed at neutralizing the ANC's visibility, such as discouraging the wearing of ANC t-shirts and promoting Inkatha in its place.

Not surprisingly, the government denied these allegations.

Basson's revelations, if proved, would have corroborated a belief held by some blacks, and especially by the ANC, that a 'third force' had been operating within the white-dominated government's security forces to instigate conflict between black organizations. The government confirmed that Basson once served in the military, but said he was doing intelligence work, adding that his assertions were unsubstantiated. Chief Buthelezi dismissed Basson's allegations, saying they were part of a campaign to smear Inkatha.

The ANC's hands are not clean, either. For one thing, it has initiated plans to destroy the Zulu homeland. Its cadres and supporters have been involved in clashes with Inkatha, the PAC and AZAPO. Members of its guerrilla army have been suspected of killing dissidents from their own ranks and black people deemed to be informers, such as black municipal councillors. Despite the ANC ceasefire, its mass action campaigns have sparked violent confrontations with the police and rival groups. In an open competition for power, both sides wished to see their opponent diminished. It was an open secret that de Klerk would be only too happy to enter into negotiations and the transition to democracy with a disorganized and weakened ANC.

Although he said he did not condone the violent transition, de Klerk was often quick to point out that one need only look around the world to see that societies in transition experienced some form of instability. He was right. Studies of societies in transition show them to be characterized by instability and frequent periods of unrest. The motives for violence are often multi-faceted. There is usually no single cause. Among the many causes of instability are rapid change, high levels of expectation which cannot be met in the short term, poor socio-economic conditions, the competition for political power, the competition for other resources, class conflict, tribal/ethnic/ religious cleavages, rapid urbanization and societal alienation or a lack of sense of belonging. In South Africa, the rival groups are playing for high stakes and there is no second place. The winner takes all.

Indeed, a combination of these factors constituted the issue of ethnic identity in the lives of the protagonists. Appalling conditions in the migrant workers' hostels and the squatter camps, the dearth of employment and education opportunities, and a volatile and militant youthful population all increased the likelihood of an outbreak of violence. Political bitterness and socio-economic grievances growled in the background. In the foreground, claims of complicity and partiality were directed at the police.

At times the example of transitional societies such as Romania and the Soviet republics taught us lessons. In our own backyard, the seeds of instability were always going to find very fertile ground. South Africa's history of intolerance and the total absence of a true democratic culture only made violence more inevitable. South Africa's politics has mixed confrontation, anger and fear for centuries. In the process of transition the country was moving away from apartheid towards an unknown non-racial democracy. It could not escape the problems of transition which include uncertainty, instability, violence, heated exchanges and sudden crises.

The moment one steps back from our culture of violence, its causes as numerous as its injuries, one notices again the enormous shadow cast by the most fundamental social and economic problems. Millions of blacks are caught in a spiral of landlessness, homelessness, unemployment, and poverty. Add to that a clash between modern political structures and traditional tribal ones. Mix in a struggle for hegemony in the region between major political players. Stir in the security forces in all their guises: South African Police, KwaZulu Police, South African Defence Force, Umkhonto we Sizwe, Azanian People's Liberation Army, (APLA/PAC), Azanian National Liberation Army (AZANLA/AZAPO), Ystergarde, WenKommando. Add faceless, apparently trained killers such as the 'third force', etc. Sprinkle all that with ancient and recent political or social grudges and you get a deadly brew.

One should not forget the question of time. One of the reasons South Africa is going through such a violent transitional period is that the leaders are working against time. Without a rapid political settlement, violence will probably escalate. Sadly, even after the rival factions have agreed on a model for a non-racial democratic constitution in South Africa, the country is still likely to experience turbulent times.

As all these theories were being bandied around to try to understand the causes of violence, the world watched in horror. South African communities were tearing each other apart just as prospects for democracy became brighter. Many people doubted whether we blacks, the hardest hit in the carnage, had the right to tell the world that our struggle for liberation was just, or whether we understood what democracy meant or would mean once apartheid had been defeated.

6
LEADING THE 'PEOPLE OF HEAVEN'

There is an orchestrated plot to culturally and ethnically castrate the Zulu people through intimidation and provocation. . . . We are not a creation of apartheid. Any history student will tell you that this area has always been KwaZulu. We have faced the British and Boers defending KwaZulu, and we will do so again, with our lives if necessary.

Chief Mangosuthu Buthelezi, October 1992

As the structures and forces of apartheid disappear under the continued reforms of F. W. de Klerk, those forces of repression are only to be replaced by a new terror. . . . The Zulu people are bracing themselves for a direct onslaught from the ANC and its allies. We are tired of the intimidation and provocation against the Zulu people of South Africa.

King Goodwill Zwelithini, October 1992

Chief Mangosuthu Gatsha Buthelezi often doffs his tailored pin-stripe suits to don the leopard skins and feathers that are the garb of his Zulu ancestors. On ceremonial occasions, before he addresses his followers, the chief is often preceded by his praise singer, who raps out an intense monotone, often 30 minutes long but sometimes an hour, extolling the heroism, wisdom and courage of his prince in lyrics such as: 'We will follow Shenge [his clan name] to death.' 'Shenge has said that Ulundi [capital of KwaZulu homeland] will be defended with the last drop of blood, and we also say this.'

At one of the Shaka Day ceremonies I attended in Nkandla, a dusty settlement in the heart of Zulu territory not far from the grave of Cetshwayo, the Zulu king who resisted British invaders, Buthelezi compared his fight to preserve Zulu interests in the modern-day homeland of KwaZulu to the battles his ancestors fought against the British in 1879. With a shield, a stick and a spear in his hands, he warned Zulus that their foes plan to wipe KwaZulu and Zulus 'off the face of the earth'. These foes include the ANC, which he describes as an alien force in KwaZulu, adding that those who support it are traitors, like the 'loyal natives' who stood with the British against their own Zulu kinsmen a century earlier.

These annual Shaka Day festivities seek to revive the former glories of the Zulu empire by proclaiming loyalty to the past and solidarity for the future. Under the guardianship of Buthelezi, those Zulus who still cling to the nationalism Shaka forged in the 1820s, when he wanted to transform them into the mightiest tribe in Africa, throng to the ceremonies. The crowds were made up mostly of men from the rural areas attired in traditional regalia and brandishing spears, axes and round-headed clubs. Joining them was a sprinkle of ululating, bare-breasted women who would occasionally burst into singing and war dancing.

Beside him at the Shaka Day ceremonies was his cousin, King Goodwill Zwelithini, who looked just as imposing in his leopard skins, headpiece and royal peacock plume. Venturing into the political fray amid the foot-stamping of his spear-carrying warrior subjects, the king warned that any post-apartheid constitution had to be big enough to accommodate Zulus. The king has often criticized the ANC for 'sowing seeds of discontent and division' among black South Africans, 'as they pit Zulu against Xhosa and brother against brother.' 'The ANC has been abusing my name and accusing me of political partiality merely because I do not endorse their wrong policies, which are costing us as Zulus such a high price when human lives are lost,' he said. At the end of the speeches, Buthelezi and the king left the tented podium and strode down to their subjects, uttering battlecries and kicking their feet in the air in a show of solidarity, before getting into their German-made limousines.

Angry Spoiler or Guiding Spirit?

As the head of the KwaZulu homeland, Minister of State, Minister of Justice, head of the KwaZulu Police, and president of the Inkatha Freedom Party, Chief Buthelezi is one of the most powerful black leaders in South Africa. Many people believe he is the most powerful leader after de Klerk and Mandela. But many of his fellow South Africans say he accumulated his power by serving in an apartheid structure, his homeland government. They say his homeland was one of those created to keep black communities isolated within South Africa and to provide a pool of labour for white business.

But Buthelezi is not bothered by the criticism. He says he has used his prominent position among seven million Zulus to fight apartheid from within. When other black anti-apartheid leaders refused to have anything to do with the white government, he established a relationship with the government sufficient to permit a dialogue, but refused to be drawn completely into the white camp. He spurned substantial negotiations with the government while Nelson Mandela was imprisoned. While the ANC ran a guerrilla war against white rule and many of its leaders served long jail terms for anti-apartheid activities, the Chief stuck steadfastly to his belief in a negotiated settlement.

Despite the fact that his power derives in some measure from apartheid structures, Chief Buthelezi says he is not just another homeland leader like those to whom he has been linked. He says that as a major regional figure in Natal, he has a unique claim to a degree of federal independence based on Zulu history and geographical location. He assures his followers that KwaZulu, far from being a construct of apartheid, has its own historical sovereignty which it will fight to preserve.

Buthelezi has been hailed by some as the guardian of democracy and reviled by others as a tribal despot. In the view of others, he is simply the angry spoiler of South African politics. But to his Zulu supporters he is the guiding spirit behind the Zulu nation and a political philosopher of our time. Albert Mncwango, spokesman for the king's royal regiment, says: 'South Africa is fortunate that we have such an outstanding leader as Mangosuthu Buthelezi. If it weren't for his moderation, the Zulu people, because of the many deaths, would have risen long ago against the ANC.' Nevertheless, many people believe that, under Buthelezi, hundreds if not thousands of Zulus are in a state of war-preparedness, ready to be mobilized against their enemies. 'The Zulu people have been unified as never before in the more than 113 years since our humiliation by the British at the battle of Ulundi,' Mncwango told me when he heard that the ANC was planning to march on the capital Ulundi to protest against the lack of free political activity in the territory.

Elsewhere across urban South Africa, there are many Zulus who dispute Buthelezi's claim to be a spokesman for the Zulu nation. They are largely urbanized, educated and westernized. They think of themselves as South Africans first and Zulus second, although they have not forgotten their roots, brave ancestors and the fighting spirit of King Shaka. These Zulus believe Buthelezi has hijacked Zulu nationalism to boost his image and that of his party. To them, being a Zulu does not necessarily make one an Inkatha member or a supporter of the organization's activities. To them, the Shaka Day holiday I attended in Nkandla is a cultural day, not a political event. They want Zulus to be proud of their culture and wear *amabheshu* (leopard skins) during this day, instead of singing Inkatha songs.

Man of Peace, Heritage of Blood

The founder of the Zulu empire, King Shaka, had ambitions to extend the Zulu nation through conquest. He brought together different tribes to form one Zulu nation. Before Shaka, some of these tribes were living under tribal authorities of their own. After Shaka's death and after his successor's failure to consolidate the empire, several tribes went back to the authority of the old or obeyed new rulers; today, the people of these tribes cannot be regarded as Zulus *per se.*

The difficult history of the Zulu nation was explained to me and the readers of *New Nation* newspaper (23 October 1992) by Natal academic Mary de Haas. 'Historically, the Zulu nation was a political entity under a king. It was all those people who gave allegiance to the Zulu king. After the civil war in Zululand, the Zulu nation started falling apart. Two rival factions emerged. After that war, the British colonizers demoted the King of the Zulus to the status of a paramount chief.' De Haas maintains that the Zulu monarchy only reemerged in the 1960s, reconstituted by South Africa's apartheid government when the homeland policy was introduced. 'What they did was to constitute something for KwaZulu, which is not the same as the Zulu nation.' KwaZulu – like any other homeland – was based on reserve land, land reserved for African occupation.

KwaZulu today is very different from Zululand historically. Therefore, according to de Haas, 'It would not make sense . . . for the king (or Chief Buthelezi) to claim land which he knows does not historically belong to what was supposed to be Zululand.' The homeland is made up of pockets of land on the peripheries of so-called white land. Moreover, says de Haas, the present king has no power. All the political power in what is supposed to be the territory of the Zulu nation rests with the KwaZulu legislative assembly led by Buthelezi. The assembly was a creation of the architect of apartheid, Hendrik Verwoerd, and his successors.

With the only real power in Buthelezi's hands, even the Zulu monarchy is in decline. Many years ago many Zulus respected King Zwelithini because they believed that the authority of their ancestors resided with him. He was their ombudsman. But many of them in the urban and rural areas of Natal are now beginning to lose faith in him. They are beginning to realize that nothing derives from him. Many people are disturbed by his close association with Buthelezi and Inkatha. They believe that belonging to one nation should not mean toeing the same political line. People want the king to be seen as clearly above party politics. Some are strong Zulu nationalists, but would resist being put in the same basket as Inkatha supporters simply because they support the king. Even along cultural and linguistic lines, the Zulu tradition is changing. My uncles and aunts used to define the Zulu nation on the basis of those who speak Zulu. But with so many non-Zulus now speaking Zulu, this definition makes it no longer a sufficient indicator of the shared values on which to establish a solid nation.

Previous Zulu leaders sought to expand the Zulu nation rather than regroup it as a clan, as Buthelezi and King Zwelithini are trying to do. One of these outward-looking leaders was Chief Albert Luthuli. In October 1992, *New Nation* recalled how Luthuli, one of the first presidents of the ANC, used to say: 'From the beginning our history has been one of ascending unities, the breaking of tribal, racial and credal barriers.' Luthuli had a vision of one South African nation: 'There remains before us the building of a new land, a home for men who are black, white, brown, from the ruins of the old narrow groups, as a synthesis of the rich cultural strain we have inherited. [This] remains to be achieved through our integration with the rest of the continent.'

Initially, Buthelezi, who was said to be Luthuli's disciple, agreed with him. But he no longer goes along with Luthuli's approach to nationalism. 'I shared his dream for black fulfilment. I shared his patriotism which transcended just Zulu horizons. I was, like him, an African nationalist, who, however, did not try to erase one's ethnic background, in order to be seen as an African nationalist par excellence,' Buthelezi said in 1976 as he consolidated his power in KwaZulu and within Inkatha. When Buthelezi was challenged in the 1970s over his participation in the KwaZulu homeland, he even acknowledged that KwaZulu was an apartheid creation. But now he proudly proclaims that KwaZulu is no longer a creation of apartheid, but the property of the Zulu nation.

Citing the positions of his great-grandfather and his father as 'prime ministers' to the Zulu kings Cetshwayo and Solomon Dinizulu as precedents for his own prominent role, Buthelezi has defended his right to speak on behalf of the Zulu nation. 'From the beginning of the Zulu kingdom, my family has been very close to the Zulu king. My great-grandfather was of course prime minister of King Cetshwayo and commander-in-chief of the Zulu army. Even if there was no KwaZulu homeland that would still be my position,' Buthelezi said, referring to his father's succession in 1953 and his election as chief minister of the homeland in the early 1970s. But even some members of the Zulu royal family dispute his claim to speak on their behalf. Prince Mcwayiseni Zulu, of the Zulu royal family, says it is a 'gross misinterpretation' to regard Inkatha as representative of the Zulu nation: 'I am a Zulu, but I am a member of the ANC and so was my grandfather King Dinizulu. Inkatha cannot claim to speak on behalf of Zulus.'

Despite his controversial status, almost everyone agrees that Buthelezi is not just another homeland leader. The fear is that Buthelezi could lead Zulus to a war similar to the one fought by the Afrikaners against the British for their independence. Buthelezi's power base, Inkatha, was originally founded in 1922 by King Solomon Dinizulu to promote Zulu culture and advise him on political matters. It became moribund soon afterwards. Half a century later, in 1975, it was revived as a national cultural movement by Chief Buthelezi and other senior officials in the KwaZulu local government service, with the encouragement of the ANC. Although Inkatha was one of several anti-apartheid organizations, it had a strong conservative image in rural areas and appealed mostly to Zulu nationalism and pride. During the 1970s, Inkatha appeared to enjoy mounting support when other black organizations were banned. In its early stage of development, it enjoyed cordial relations with the ANC. No objections were raised, publicly at any rate, over Inkatha's adoption of ANC colours.

The ANC confirms that it encouraged Chief Buthelezi to form Inkatha to keep the home fires of the struggle against apartheid burning while it was banned. It said it had hoped Chief Buthelezi, as a former member of the movement, would help mobilize the black masses in the fight for a non-racial, democratic and united South Africa. 'We failed to mobilize our own people to take on the task of resurrecting Inkatha,' ANC president Oliver Tambo told delegates at the organization's national executive meeting in exile. 'The task of reconstituting Inkatha therefore fell on Gatsha Buthelezi himself, who then built Inkatha as a personal power base, far removed from the kind of organization we had visualized.'

Over the years, Buthelezi's once close alliance with the ANC has withered into a fierce competition, leading to angry recriminations and outright war. Buthelezi has long objected to the ANC's choice of weapons to fight apartheid. He staunchly rejected international sanctions and guerrilla warfare as effective weapons against apartheid. In his view, sanctions cost blacks jobs while the armed struggle cost black lives. 'Because I did not support the armed struggle, I am portrayed as a traitor to the cause. In fact I am the only one who is at the centre stage. I have stood there for a long time and I do not have to move at all,' he has said.

According to the ANC, 'Gatsha Buthelezi dressed Inkatha in the clothes of the ANC, exactly because he knew the masses to whom he was appealing were loyal to the ANC and had for six decades adhered to our movement as their representative and their leader.... Later, when he thought he had a sufficient base, he used coercive methods against people to force them to support Inkatha.'

Fighting back, Chief Buthelezi responded: 'I had to form Inkatha because the ANC was doing nothing for my people.' He says his relations with the ANC turned sour in 1979 after he declined to recruit young Zulus for the ANC's guerrilla wing or to subject Inkatha to its control. 'They thought I could be a surrogate organization. The ANC proclaims itself the sole and authentic representative of the people. It aims at the total takeover of power and control. It is ruthless in its dealings with those who are not its supporters,' he declared.

With the formation of the UDF in 1983, an ANC-allied federation of anti-apartheid groups, and increased black resistance against apartheid in the 1980s, Buthelezi found his support base being increasingly undermined. Serious differences between the Zulu leader and the ANC began in September 1983 when the UDF mobilized support against the government's creation of a tricameral parliament for whites, coloureds and Indians, to the exclusion of the black majority. The UDF was joined by a coalition of the country's trade unions, the Congress of South African Trade Unions (COSATU).

Chief Buthelezi accused the UDF of acting as an ancillary of the ANC, by striving to fulfil a mandate from the ANC to make the townships ungovernable and trying to destroy and discredit his political standing by presenting him as a mere homeland leader. His argument has been confirmed by ANC documents. In one paper entitled 'Commission on Cadre Policy, Political and Ideological Work – Commission on Strategy,' the ANC said:

> The openly counter-revolutionary role that Chief Gatsha Buthelezi has turned is noted. Buthelezi, unlike Mphephu [a deceased former leader of the Venda homeland], cannot be dismissed as a mere puppet of the racists. He projects the illusion of autonomy from the enemy and pretends to pursue national aims. His counter-revolutionary role must be exposed and we must work to win over his supporters and deprive him of his social base.

A position paper from the ANC's union wing, COSATU, stated: 'The onus is on us to neutralize Gatsha once and for all. The snake that is poisoning South Africa needs to be hit on the head.'

Verbal conflicts between Inkatha and UDF supporters soon led to open warfare. One of the first serious incidents was the killing of five students at the University of

Zululand by stick-wielding members of Inkatha, who accused the student population of attempting to prevent Chief Buthelezi from officiating at the university's graduation ceremony. After that, the battle lines were drawn and a struggle for the allegiance of the Zulu people began. The UDF and COSATU undertook aggressive recruitment drives, establishing their areas of control village by village and street by street. As a result, all townships were forced to take sides, leaving no room for fence-sitters or neutral parties. The UDF and COSATU presented a strong, aggressive anti-apartheid image, directed at both rural and urban communities. Their supra-ethnic stance clashed head-on with the ethic of Inkatha, which emphasized Zulu identity. Inkatha's methods were seen by many people as regression to the worst aspects of tribal life.

The sudden proliferation of AK-47 automatic rifles brought a grave new dimension to the conflict. Inkatha loyalists and leaders warned their followers of a sinister attack by members of the UDF/COSATU alliance whom they claimed were intent on undermining the Zulu nation. Fighting between the UDF and Inkatha reached frightening proportions well before Mandela's release, with thousands of people killed. In a letter to Buthelezi from prison, Mandela wrote in 1989:

> In my entire political career, few things have distressed me [as much] as to see our people killing one another as is now happening. As you know, the entire fabric of community life in some of the affected areas has been seriously disrupted, leaving behind a legacy of hatred and bitterness which may haunt us for years to come. It is a matter which requires the urgent attention of all the people in the country.

With the unbanning of the ANC on 2 February 1990, the war intensified. Inkatha feared a rapid loss of support to the ANC, which threatened Inkatha leaders. Buthelezi denies that his party has been responsible for the murderous violence in Natal. However, he himself says he 'would not dismiss the possibility of people revenging themselves.' The ANC argues, however, that Inkatha has used force in Natal to demonstrate its strength in an attempt to secure a powerful place for Buthelezi in negotiations for a future non-racial constitution. They argue that Buthelezi tried to establish a one-party state among Natal's blacks. To them, Buthelezi's claim to be leader of seven million Zulus has more to do with power politics than a romanticized cultural or ethnic revival. To them, his emphasis on the Zulu nation is an appeal to a narrow, ethnic chauvinism for the purposes of commanding a significant number of blacks by appealing to their emotions rather than seeking their votes. For this reason, the ANC likes to question Buthelezi's legitimacy since there has never been an election among Africans in Natal. Consistently, meanwhile, opinion polls show larger support for the ANC than for Inkatha.

Nevertheless, at the launching of the Inkatha Freedom Party (IFP) in July 1990, Buthelezi made it clear that Inkatha wanted to prevent the ANC from monopolizing black politics by claiming to represent the black majority. The chief says he champions not just the interests of the Zulus, but those of other groups that risk being excluded by the ANC from a political settlement. 'There is going to be a new South Africa with or without the ANC. We will not allow the ANC and its South African Communist Party partner to crush all opposition and emerge as the only viable party,' he said.

Buthelezi constantly portrays himself as a man of peace on whom violence is often forced. He says his followers in the townships are the victims of violence and only retaliate when attacked, or occasionally stage 'pre-emptive violence' to ward off attacks. He claims that his opponents would like to drive him into a corner where he would have no option but to submit or fight. He, of course, has chosen the latter path, declaring: 'If people think the future of the country can be determined without an impact by Mangosuthu Buthelezi, they need their heads read. I am a powerful man, I cannot be wished away. . . . The Zulu people are forged in violence, we are forged in blood. We are welded together as a powerful nation through bloodshed,' he said in 1992.

Buthelezi told a meeting of chiefs called to discuss the Natal violence in 1990:

> We must now declare ourselves to be at war with these developments which wish to threaten us, and the people who lead it. Going to war against that which threatens us is something which we as Zulu leaders understand and it is something that brings out the best in us. . . . Our forefathers wrote many such chapters into our illustrious history, and we have the blood of our forefathers running through our veins. We feel right now this blood giving us the courage to move quickly against that which must now be defeated.

This threat is not new. In a letter written to ANC president Oliver Tambo in 1984, Chief Buthelezi said: 'In this part of South Africa [Natal], we come from warrior stock and there is a resilient determination in KwaZulu and in Inkatha which even the full might of the state will never be able to flatten. Do your colleagues really think they can flatten us on the way to their intended victory?'

For years, the ANC and its allies made no bones about their intentions to marginalize Buthelezi and Inkatha. They forged alliances with other traditional and homeland leaders. 'They say they are going to marginalize me. They say Inkatha must be smashed and finished. It is not possible. They say all kinds of things of me, including that they are going to kill me, not by shooting me, but politically.'

Chief Buthelezi's political challenge to the ANC has been welcomed by many whites who consider the ANC too radical. Unlike any other black liberation movement, Inkatha is acceptable to many whites because it has said that it supports a multi-party democracy and the free enterprise system, and that it rejects winner-takes-all politics, marxism, socialism and many ANC policies. Like the National Party government, it also opposed the imposition of sanctions against South Africa and foreign intervention in domestic issues. On many issues, its position is closer to that of de Klerk's National Party than it is to most of the anti-apartheid organizations.

This relationship or alliance has brought Buthelezi many benefits, chief of which is the flow of funds from the government to the KwaZulu homeland government. These funds have enabled the IFP to develop a well-oiled publicity department in South Africa and abroad. The party says it has 1.8 million members, 300,000 of them recruited a few months after it became a political party. However, this relationship has severely damaged Buthelezi's credibility in the black community. The eruption of the Inkathagate scandal, which clearly demonstrated that the government was taking sides in Inkatha's feud with the ANC, did much to discredit the Chief.

Inkathagate

As in the Watergate scandal that led to the resignation of US President Richard Nixon, the Inkathagate affair involved the use of state funds or taxpayers' money to fund Inkatha's anti-ANC activities. As the full extent of the scandal was unravelled, it was alleged that the money funnelled to Inkatha passed through the hands of two top men in de Klerk's team: Foreign Minister Pik Botha, the most senior man in the cabinet after de Klerk, and former Law and Order Minister Adriaan Vlok.

The *Weekly Mail* was the first to offer evidence of security force complicity with Inkatha. The newspaper published top-secret documents which told of police payments to Inkatha to help it oppose the ANC. The documents showed extensive discussions between Chief Buthelezi and a senior Durban policeman about ways of preventing the

ANC from eroding Inkatha's support in Natal. The top-secret documents revealed that Buthelezi was concerned about the declining membership figures in Natal at the time of Mandela's release. The documents also said that Chief Buthelezi was very emotional and expressed gratitude for the extent of the financial assistance provided.

According to reports, at least R250,000 ($90,000) was paid into an Inkatha bank account by the security police for the purpose of organizing rallies and other anti-ANC activities shortly after Mandela's release from prison. One of the rallies sparked an upsurge of civic violence that came to be known as the 'Maritzburg War'. Monitoring groups issued statistics which illustrated that violence escalated shortly after the police funded Inkatha. At first these shocking revelations were denied outright by the government and Inkatha.

But within 24 hours of the *Weekly Mail* article, the government admitted it had channelled funds to Inkatha as part of covert operations to fund organizations that opposed sanctions. Chief Buthelezi denied that he had any knowledge of government funding of Inkatha activities. He emphatically denied that he had spent 'one cent of government money' on undermining the ANC and had not known that government money had been used to fund an Inkatha rally. 'I do not know who arranged for government money to be channelled through the security police to an Inkatha bank account in Durban,' he said.

The government said the funds had not been drawn from a special account of the police, but 'from funds earmarked by the government for the combating of sanctions.' It said the funding had been 'non-party political'. The funds were used for 'visual anti-sanctions banners, advertisements, transport, hire of stadiums, and other facilities'. Vlok offered this explanation: 'Due to the special circumstances applicable in South Africa before February 1990, it was essential to launch covert projects in order, *inter alia*, to promote order and stability and to combat South Africa's isolation.' He disclosed that the Inkatha-allied United Workers' Union of South Africa (UWUSA) had received more than R1.6 million ($600,000) during the previous six years. The union was also receiving a monthly stipend from the government until the end of July 1991.

His colleague, Foreign Minister Pik Botha, spilled more beans. He announced that the government spent at least R100 million ($35 million) in 1989 in a vain attempt to stop SWAPO coming to power in neighbouring Namibia after a long war against South Africa. 'Yes, yes, the South African government did provide funds. . . . In a quiet way, in a secret way we assisted them. . . . The sum was considerable, well over 100 million,' he said.

With regard to Inkatha, Botha said there was nothing to apologize for and the money had been meticulously audited. 'I am not feeling sorry for it,' he said. 'I'll do it again, just like that.' Seven anti-SWAPO organizations had been assisted with money for education and training. The anti-SWAPO Democratic Turnhalle Alliance admitted it had received government funds. 'We welcome that this has come about. There is nothing wrong. Why worry?' the party said. It was also revealed that the government funded scores of other organizations, most of them run through government-created structures or by conservative blacks. But despite government's attempts to play down the scandal, the story of Inkathagate further weakened Buthelezi's credibility.

Defending the Lawful Authority: Inkatha and the Kwazulu Police

The government's admission that it had meddled in extra-parliamentary politics followed months of accusations from political organizations that the security forces were favouring Inkatha in its battle against the ANC, and claims that the government was involved in sophisticated clandestine operations to erode the ANC's power base.

An affidavit by a constable in the KwaZulu Police said senior police officers headed a hit-squad whose targets were supporters of the ANC, usually called 'comrades' in the townships. The affidavit said all members of the KwaZulu police force were obliged to join Inkatha. There has always been an unwritten law, especially in Natal, that members of Inkatha should not be arrested by the KwaZulu Police. When an Inkatha person is arrested, a phone call is made to Ulundi (the capital of KwaZulu) and, soon after, orders for that person's release are issued.

'We tell the police we are defending Inkatha and when we get arrested, we produce Inkatha special cards to confirm that we are members of Inkatha. We are then released,' said Bheki Mvubu, a member of an Inkatha gang who said ammunition and guns were supplied directly from KwaZulu police to Inkatha members. In a detailed affidavit, Mvubu confessed he had taken part in the killing of more than 40 people since 1987 and burnt down a number of ANC homes in Durban townships. In the eyes of ANC supporters, the homeland police effectively act as the agents of apartheid in suppressing the growth of opposition groups. It became clear that a bid to oppose apartheid in Natal was tantamount to opposing Inkatha. 'We support the lawful authority, which is the KwaZulu government. To the extent that Inkatha is part of the lawful government, I suppose you could say we support Inkatha,' KwaZulu Police commissioner Jac Buchner said. 'But when we encounter armed people gathering, we act against them no matter who they are. These things happen at night and it is impossible to tell which side they are on.'

My investigations also showed me how the fighting has corrupted both sides. I met 15-year-old Zondani while touring Natal townships with Nelson Mandela in March 1990. He told me he had abandoned his education to defend his neighbourhood. Zondani said he could not stop fighting unless his enemy, Inkatha, had been defeated. He could not remember how many people he had killed, but that he had used his home-made gun extensively to repel attacks.

Every time we go to combat, I think this could be it. I have seen many people killed and many hurt. On one occasion we came across a burning body of an attacker, killed by one of our groups. It was the worst experience of my life seeing this guy burn. I just felt cold. Each time I think of the incident, I just want to vomit. He was totally burnt, and the fire was getting to his bones, which were turning to ash. The police arrived and we ran away. When the police come we run into the houses. They do not chase us because they are scared, we have lots of guns, they could get shot.

Betting on Zulu Nationalism: Buthelezi Looks to the Future

Since the slush fund scandal, Inkatha and the KwaZulu leadership have continued their attempt to secure a role for themselves in a post-apartheid South Africa. But the idea of creating a niche for Zulu nationalism in Natal has been seen as the survival strategy of the conservative élite in the KwaZulu homeland. Inkatha is faced with a dilemma about its future. While it claims to be a national political party, its major source of strength is in KwaZulu. Thus it cannot abandon this homeland, and cannot attract non-Zulus for whom national liberation cannot be based on tribalism. The Zulus that Inkatha talks about are essentially Inkatha members and supporters, camouflaged as 'the Zulu people' in an attempt to mobilize support. Buthelezi thus has no right to speak on behalf of the Zulus, let alone contemplate secession from South Africa on their behalf.

Although only an election will reveal the true strength of Buthelezi, he takes issue with those who say that Inkatha is losing support even in Natal, its traditional power base. Some say it has lost many followers to the ANC since 1987. Inkatha has a loyal following among rural Zulus, but many others in the cities support the ANC. In some places, the conflict is generational: parents join Inkatha, children join the ANC. Statistics show that between 1977 and 1988, Inkatha's support in the industrial heartland of the Transvaal shrank from 30 per cent to 5 per cent, with support for the ANC rising to 70 per cent. The same trend applied in Natal.

But when I spoke to Buthelezi about this, he did not appear to be bothered. He assured me he knows that many Zulus in ANC areas are 'Inkatha at heart' even though they may carry ANC cards for expediency. He says non-political Zulus who are daily harassed by the ANC in Johannesburg for being Zulu are coming into his party fold. Many others, sick to death of ANC violence in the name of revolution, are looking towards Inkatha, which they perceive to have strong leadership.

Many ANC foes, from black homeland leaders to far-right Afrikaners, have put secession on the agenda as a last desperate option, and Buthelezi is no exception. KwaZulu possesses institutions such as a police force, army and government, which could make a go-it-alone drive an exciting adventure. And if Buthelezi seceded from South Africa, other anti-ANC leaders such as Lucas Mangope of Bophuthatswana, or Ciskei's Brigadier Oupa Gqozo, might try to follow his example. But since KwaZulu is a scattering of enclaves within the province of Natal, for secession to have any chance of success − or for the threat of secession to carry any weight − it would have to comprehend the whole of Natal, and not his KwaZulu homeland only. Buthelezi would have to weigh up his support in the region before seceding. KwaZulu's capital, Ulundi, is also very remote from the economic and political hub of the port city and industrial heartland, Durban, where Inkatha support is negligible, and the provincial capital of Pietermaritzburg, where most of the clashes with the ANC have occurred.

The fighting in the province must serve as a reminder that any attempt by Buthelezi to lead Natal into secession would undoubtedly lead to an all-out civil war. Such a conflict might engulf the whole country and make the death toll since the ANC was unbanned seem insignificant. The consequences of secession are not to be contemplated by the faint-hearted. But since he is betting on Zulu nationalism, secession could be the last card Buthelezi can play politically.

Buthelezi's insistence on a federal system of government in the post-apartheid era has been seen as a desperate move to secure some role for himself in Natal, his traditional power base. 'During apartheid the National Party government gave [Natal] little because the [provincial] administration was by English South Africans. The ANC will do the same because most of us here do not support them,' he says. If Chief Buthelezi and his followers become embittered and are driven into a corner, there is a danger that they will elect to fight.

While it is difficult to predict where Buthelezi would fit in a post-apartheid South Africa, he has said he would be prepared to serve under de Klerk or Mandela if Zulus and Inkatha played a significant role in shaping the future. He has challenged them to make a similar commitment. It is hard to envision a peaceful settlement without him, however ephemeral his critics portray him as being.

These people [his critics] do not know Zulu history and forget that the warrior blood of kings and Zulu war generals courses in my veins. If a man sticks out his hand to shake my hand, I will shake his hand. If a man swears at me, I will swear at him. If a man hits me with his fist, I will hit him with my fist. If he uses a knife on me, I will use a knife on him. History demands no less than this. We dare not be weak.

The Zulu factor threatens to become more intractable than South Africa's white–black years of anti-apartheid struggle. Much of the recent conflict has been a struggle to command the allegiance of black people in Natal, in which both sides have committed atrocities. Chief Buthelezi's distrust of the ANC is such that he fears for his own life and the continued existence and security of his party.

'I have worked all my life for peaceful change in this country but, of course, if one is forced to lead my people through the dark water of war, I'll be there,' he told me. 'The reality is this. KwaZulu will not disappear. At least not without a bloody fight.'

7

BOTCHERS BUTCHERS OR 'THIRD FORCE'?

You will no longer be required to prevent people from gathering to canvass support for their views. This is the political arena, and we want to take police out of it. We do not want to use you any more as instruments to reach certain political goals. I want you to make peace with this new line.

F. W. de Klerk, 1990

Over the years we have been drilled with 'The ANC are terrorists,' and this and this and this – and now all of a sudden, we got to accept them as cadres, colleagues, which I find it hard to accept. I mean, I won't accept that.

Sergeant Gibson, BBC documentary, 1991

Black South Africans will never forget Colonel Pieter Goosen who kept Steve Biko, the famed leader of the Black Consciousness Movement, naked in a cell for two weeks in September 1977, refusing him medical treatment in the city of Port Elizabeth where he was being detained. Instead, he chose to send him to Pretoria, one thousand kilometres away. Goosen used a Landrover to transport Biko to Pretoria and had him manacled at the back of the van during the entire trip. Biko died from his injuries while in police custody, though the police claimed he committed suicide.

After the Biko debacle, Goosen was promoted to a senior position. Goosen's colleague, Captain Danie Siebert, who remarked that he thought the injured Biko was shamming during interrogation, was promoted to colonel. The district surgeon who issued an incorrect death certificate was promoted to become a chief district surgeon, and the inquest magistrate found that nobody was criminally responsible for Biko's death. Many blacks have died in similar circumstances. Of the hundreds who have experienced detention, none will forget the torture and humiliation they endured, which often left them depressed, irritable, and emotionally distanced from family and friends. No black person was safe while in police custody.

The Permanent Removal of Matthew Goniwe

Even those who were not in detention were at risk. In June 1985, eight years after Biko's death, came the assassination of Eastern Cape activist Matthew Goniwe and three of his comrades. Until May 1992, Goniwe's death and the identity of his killers remained shrouded in uncertainty, amid murmurs and suspicions of 'state involvement'. The original inquiry found that Goniwe and his colleagues were murdered by a 'person or persons unknown'. But this finding became almost laughable from May 1992 in the light of evidence which heavily implicated the state security establishment and the clandestine operatives it had been using.

Devastating evidence of the state's role in the murder of Goniwe and his colleagues was provided by Transkei military ruler General Bantu Holomisa when he released to the media a document recording a military signal made on 7 June 1985, ordering the 'permanent removal from society' of Goniwe and others. General Holomisa said all members of the State Security Council, including President F. W. de Klerk, attended a meeting in Port Elizabeth just a few weeks before the signal was sent to Pretoria allegedly arranging for the elimination of the Cradock Four. Members of the State Security Council at the time also included ministers Foreign Minister Pik Botha, Justice Minister Kobie Coetzee and then Law and Order Minister Adriaan Vlok. The 'top-secret' document had made it 'very clear that the current unrest situation cannot be permanently stabilized through the current conventional methods of the state of emergency.' This meeting of security heavyweights preceded the signal to permanently remove Goniwe and his colleagues. The 'top-secret' document was signed by Colonel Lourens du Plessis, then in command of the Eastern Cape. It recorded a conversation in which Joffel van der Westhuizen told a Major General J. F. J. van Rensburg, a former member of the State Security Council, of the order to remove Goniwe. After the revelations of the Holomisa Files, which the military ruler said were sent to him anonymously by someone in the Eastern Cape, de Klerk reopened the inquiry.

For many South Africans, the pivotal importance of Holomisa's revelations was whether they would uncover sufficient evidence to explain not only the Goniwe assassination, but also the fates of scores of other political activists who have gone missing without trace. It became apparent that 'permanent removal' as a way of controlling political development was not limited to the Goniwe incident. More specifically, the authenticity of the controversial military signal, sent by Colonel du Plessis on the order of his superiors General van der Westhuizen and General Janse van Rensburg, was no longer in dispute as a record of conversation between them to 'permanently remove' Goniwe.

What *was* in dispute, and still unclear to the legal eagles, was the meaning of the key phrase 'permanently removed'. Van Rensburg testified that it meant to detain indefinitely; du Plessis averred that it meant assassinate. Glenn Goosen, du Plessis's lawyer at Goniwe's inquest, said terms such as 'remove, take out, eliminate, cause to disappear' were commonly understood in the security establishment to mean 'kill'. General Janse van Rensburg said: 'That may be so but it is not professional terminology we would use at the intelligence secretariat.'

On the night of 27 June 1985, twenty days after this message was sent, Matthew Goniwe, Fort Calata, Sparrow Mkonto and Sicelo Mhlawuli disappeared after attending a United Democratic Front (UDF) meeting in Port Elizabeth. Their badly burnt bodies, riddled with bullets, were found near Blue Water Bay, on the outskirts of Port Elizabeth. Goniwe's body had 27 stab and bullet wounds and his face was burnt beyond recognition. Goniwe's death unleashed unprecedented anti-government defiance by the now disbanded UDF and its then banned affiliates, the ANC and SACP. Black communities were convinced Goniwe and his colleagues were killed because of their role in the formation of street and area committees in defiance of apartheid structures in the Eastern Cape. The day of Goniwe's funeral was the day on which then President P. W. Botha declared the first State of Emergency. What followed was a rehearsal for the oppression and bitter opposition which epitomized the rest of the decade.

'Hammer'

It emerged that van der Westhuizen had set up a clandestine civilian unit called 'Hammer'. According to one of its former members, it was this unit that intercepted Goniwe's car in a roadblock on the night he disappeared. Colonel Gert Hugo told journalists that Hammer was 'a bunch of cowboys calling themselves Special Forces'. He said its origins lay in the early 1980s under the protection of President Botha's powerful State Security Council, and that it was now out of control. Jennifer du Plessis, another former agent, told the ANC that Hammer member John Scott told her the Goniwe killings were a joint operation involving the South African Police and the South African Defence Force, including Hammer members. Scott said he had been instructed to pack special weapons for the operation. Among them was a Gevarum .22, a rare sniper rifle found to have been used to shoot Mkonto.

It also emerged that the military establishment, and more particularly Joffel van der Westhuizen, the general who gave the order for the permanent removal of Goniwe, also advocated permanent removal of all enemies of apartheid. This must raise the question – were the scores of activists so far unaccounted for, or slain by unknown assassins, also 'permanently removed' on the orders of the security establishment?

In the townships, particularly among the families of the victims, Goniwe's brutal death and the subsequent inquest would serve as the sword to cleave open and expose some of South Africa's murkiest military secrets. His death assumed far larger importance that the question of who his murderers were. It became the springboard from which South Africa's first Nuremberg-style trials may be launched.

'We want to believe things are changing, but you have to have pointers and see concrete things. We do not trust the government, we do not trust the legal system. It would be nice if the government finally admitted and took responsibility for what they did. Matthew's death, and especially the manner in which he was killed, made us very angry and bitter. The government must take responsibility for sins of the past,' said, Matthew Goniwe's widow, Nyameka. To date there are no less than 80 activists who remain unaccounted for. Many others were found killed under mysterious circumstances.

More Holomisa Files: Operation Katzen

Linked to Goniwe's permanent removal from society were other Holomisa Files, some of them in General van der Westhuizen's own handwriting, revealing a master plan called 'Operation Katzen'. It showed the General and his colleagues as the cutting edge of strategic thinking in the Defence Force. Operation Katzen was a boldly calculated spider at the centre of a tangled web of political intrigue, deception and violence with broad national implications.

The plot was hatched in 1984, during the countrywide upheavals caused by the introduction of the tricameral constitution and parliament which included coloureds and Indians as junior partners in the white-dominated parliament but excluded the black majority. Operation Katzen was an ambitious plan to secure lasting regional security and stability by overthrowing then Ciskei leader Lennox Sebe and installing a strong, conservative regime to be controlled covertly by the South African security forces.

One aspect of the plan bore a striking similarity to the mobilization of Inkatha against the ANC in KwaZulu/Natal. It proposed securing South African public funds to establish a covert Xhosa Resistance Movement which could replace Sebe and form an organization opposed to the ANC throughout the Eastern Cape province. The plan also anticipated the unification of Transkei and Ciskei, both Xhosa homelands, and the eventual incorporation of a White Corridor between the two states in order to develop the Eastern Cape into an independent power bloc. An attempt was made on Sebe's life at the time, but it was never established who was responsible.

The plan contained such far-reaching implications that one has to doubt whether it could have been set in motion without the knowledge of the State Security Council. What was surprising was that the aims and objectives of Operation Katzen were not compatible with de Klerk's reform process and the unbanning of the ANC and other movements. Government spokesman Dave Steward conceded that the government previously used what it termed 'unconventional strategies', but denied the State Security Council ever approved murder or any other crime – or Operation Katzen, for that matter.

Steward never attempted to rebut the documents, showing that the National Party was seriously embarrassed over indications that some of its prominent personalities knew of plans to eliminate black leaders and set up pliant governments regarded by the black majority as stooges. Without doubt, the documents prove – and their authenticity has not been challenged or questioned by the government – that the South African Defence Force and senior ministers were involved directly in political shenanigans.

The questions which then issue from the Holomisa Files are: Was General van der Westhuizen the instigator and architect of the plan, and was it carried out with the approval of the army chief? Or was it approved at ministerial level? Was the general a loyal soldier, or was he, like the US's Oliver North, who was grilled by his country's highest court for supplying weapons to Iran, merely a pawn in a political game?

Some observers might agree with Dave Steward that every country in the world has its clandestine security operations, and that the full extent of such activities seldom emerges. But the epitaph of white rule in this country will surely have to include the chilling deeds of many operatives who defended it in the name of what they saw as state security.

We remember that when de Klerk took over – as I explained in Chapter 2 – he disbanded P. W. Botha's National Security Management System (NSMS), a giant security octopus with tentacles reaching every corner of daily life. Under the auspices of state security, the NSMS, the vigilant custodians of peace and political power, served on a myriad of committees with mandates that permeated every level of our society. At the apex of the NSMS was the State Security Council, chaired by the President, to advise the government on the formulation and implementation of a national security policy to combat any threat to South Africa, and to determine intelligence priorities.

Holomisa, Mandela, white liberal politicians and millions of South Africans believe these revelations exposed an agenda which has resulted in the deaths of tens of thousands of other people. They say the plan explains to all why the black communities were plagued by internecine civil strife, costing thousands of lives. These, they say, were plans which destabilized black communities.

Black South Africans do not mince their words about who was to blame for township violence, the third force which the government denied existed. 'It is a case of pitting Xhosa against Xhosa, Zulu against Zulu, Xhosa against Zulu and vice versa – and then white supremacy is guaranteed and given another long lease of life,' Holomisa said.

The Gluckman File: Steve Biko Won't Lie Down

Reminded of the way Biko, Goniwe and many others died, most blacks still find nothing good to say about the South African Police or the South African Defence Force. One afternoon, almost 15 years after Biko's death and eight years after Goniwe's, and in the middle of negotiations on the transition to democracy, Simon Mthimkulu and three of his friends were arrested as they walked past a stolen car in a stretch of open veld in the township of Sebokeng. Police bundled the youngsters into a truck, drove to an isolated spot and beat them, then took them to the local police station. One of Simon's friends told the story to the *Weekly Mail*'s Phillip van Niekerk:

> At the police station there was blood on the floor, but I could not tell whose blood it was. Simon was taken to the toilet by five policemen. They forced us to do squatting exercises. Simon was unable to perform the exercises. He looked like he was injured or he was too tired. He asked for water and they refused and instead kicked him in the ribs. They asked me to cover my face. When I peeped through my hands, I saw a policeman pick up a rock and throw it on Simon's ribs. The policeman did that three times. When they realized I was watching they forced my head into the toilet basin. Another black policeman entered the room and started beating me. I tried to pick up Simon. He was lying on his back and blood was dripping from his nose. He was still breathing.

Meanwhile Simon's mother looked for her son without success until the next day, when she visited the police station. 'One of the policemen told me four youths had been brought to the station and let go. They advised me to look for my son at the local hospital. When I could not find him at the hospital I went back to the police station. I was asked to bring his photo,' said Mrs Mthimkulu. She finally found her son in the mortuary and she never heard from the police. 'Simon was my pillar of strength. I would have preferred to die first than see him go like this,' she told me.

A state pathologist reported that Simon died from heavy blows to his head and ribs. In anguish, his mother referred the matter to human rights lawyers, who in turn asked Dr Jonathan Gluckman, an independent pathologist, to perform a second post mortem on the body. Gluckman had become internationally renowned as the pathologist who had examined Steve Biko's body, but he had been exposed to hundreds of lesser-known cases in which South Africans in police care had met a fate like Biko's.

Examining Mthimkulu was the last straw for Gluckman. He decided to make public more than 200 files on people he said were killed by police while in custody.

> Simon Mthimkulu had injuries all over his body. The injuries were entirely consistent with the stories of witnesses as told to me by the lawyers. I could not stand it any longer. I got sick at heart about the whole affair. It was the last straw that broke the camel's back. This was a young boy of 19. Not charged with an offence. Tortured, ill-treated and killed. He could have been my son. I have constant evidence of police handling people in a vicious manner. My impression is that they are totally out of control. They do what they like.

Gluckman said 90 per cent of the 200 people he had examined were killed by police. 'The lower rungs of the police are totally out of control. Tragic case after tragic case goes on and on,' he said. The pathologist said de Klerk and his Minister of Law and Order Hernus Kriel had failed to respond to past pleas for action against policemen involved in these killings, and this prompted him to go public after he examined Simon Mthimkulu.

> I am convinced this is the last thing the government wanted. I just feel they are not doing enough to stop the killings. When I sat in front of Hernus Kriel and Adriaan Vlok at Correctional Services and told them about this, they were shocked and said: 'What do you think we should do?' I said, 'You must have an inquest in every case, in an open court and preferably in front of a judge.' In almost all post mortems I have conducted there has been no inquest. I do not know why no inquests have been called. I have not been called to give my evidence.

The Biko case will never lie down. Everybody who was involved in it has thought about these things ever since.

Yet, despite this history, Gluckman said the stand that he had chosen to take was not really his job.

I am an objective scientist, I report to lawyers – they are officers of the court. But when I came to realize the extent of this problem, I became progressively more worried. I continuously thought about what I could do about it. It was not my job but when nothing happened I decided to address the State President.

His letter to de Klerk led to meetings with Kriel and Vlok where he presented his cases of brutality.

You Are Gonna Get Stuffed Up, My Man: Policemen Face the Future

My father used to tell me there was a time when judges and magistrates would compliment police and members of the security forces for their diligence in investigating cases. That was the time when they hunted down Nelson Mandela and other anti-apartheid activists with zeal. After sending Mandela and countless others to jail, they continued harassing, torturing, and even killing political prisoners. I grew up believing that the police were ruthlessly effective, and absolutely painstaking in tracking down their targets. After 1990, I also learned the depths of police subterfuge, duplicity, and corruption.

While the de Klerk initiatives have gone some way towards improving race relations, the goodwill he has earned has been damaged by the police force and the Defence Force. Recruited in the main from the poorly educated and economically vulnerable whites on the lowest rung of the Afrikaner community, most of the force consists of people who have imbibed from childhood onwards the Afrikaner myth of God-given superiority.

For decades, police and soldiers were charged with executing unpopular, unjust racial laws, traditionally making themselves part of the privileged white establishment and giving themselves a stake in maintaining the *status quo*. Instead of functioning as a neutral professional force, combating crime and protecting all the country's citizens, the security forces became an extension of the ruling National Party, enforcing apartheid laws. Police targets were mainly anti-apartheid protesters who were regarded as the political enemy. Since most were black, racial animosity permeated the force.

There was no black person in the townships who was not a potential target of police brutality. In order to obtain convictions, the security forces extracted their information by resorting to brutal tactics, torture and intimidation. Blacks saw the police as a harsh and cruel force, serving an illegal master to perpetuate racial oppression. They cited several reasons: members of the security forces simply did not appear to act against the perpetrators of certain crimes, took sides in conflicts between various political groups, ignored warnings of impending attacks, covered up investigations to protect their colleagues and demonstrated lack of enthusiasm in investigating political crimes.

Successive white governments covered up for the police and denied all reports of police abuses. They even made laws to prevent any publication of materials about police activities without their approval. It amounted to telling the police that they could get away with anything. There was no doubt that for many white policemen, whose racial hatred was encouraged in the force, the mere fact that a group of black people behaved defiantly was an affront to their white superiority. Police and soldiers were told that all their powers must be used to halt black advancement to national liberation. To some members of the security forces, that was a licence to kill or torture suspects.

Thus, until 1990, police and Defence Force policy in South Africa was predictable. They acted as instruments of the state to crush black liberation movements and to give protection to white lives and property. They did these jobs well. Suddenly, after 1990, the official enemies of the state, the ANC and other black liberation movements, were given a clean bill of health: overnight, the bad guys became good guys. The same people that the police had arrested not long before for not having their passes were now using once-segregated facilities, living in white areas, and freely denouncing the government. When de Klerk began the process of dismantling apartheid, the police were expected to adapt to these changes.

Not surprisingly, many policemen refused to be drawn into political debates for fear of exposing their depth of resentment against de Klerk's reforms. Those who did express their feelings openly were deeply anxious about the future, trying to resist change and still convinced about white supremacy. Most of them feared a climate of revenge should the ANC come to power.

'Everyone has certain reservations, and I have one for certain, and that is I am not prepared to serve under a communist government. And I think I can speak on behalf of most of my colleagues if I can say that,' Colonel Chris Loedolff told a BBC television documentary. In the documentary Sergeant Herbie Johnson said he believed that black people were lazy. 'Like animals in the wild who come to rely on being hand-fed. They are unsuited for leadership. They do not have an understanding to rule. It's been proven throughout Africa, wherever they have got independence and taken over the reins of the country, the country's gone to rack and ruin due to the fact that they do not have the expertise to run a country,' he said.

Johnson's colleague, a man named Sergeant Gibson, believed the policies of apartheid were the best the country has ever implemented. 'I do not think apartheid itself was a mistake, because you cannot mix the black culture with the white culture. That will not mix because they have their way of doing things and we have our own way of doing things,' he said.

Sergeant Geoff MacMaster could not hide his anxiety:

Ninety-nine per cent of the policemen, if they want to give you their honest opinion, they are worried if the ANC government had to take over here, what is going to happen to them. And I can tell you one thing, there is only one way – you are gonna get stuffed up, my man. You as a policeman, you were the oppressor, you were over-reactive, you were this and that, you were everything that blacks did not like.

Informal surveys suggested that 60 per cent of the junior officers of the Defence Force and 50 per cent of its senior officers were supporters of the pro-apartheid Conservative Party and strong opponents of de Klerk's negotiation initiatives.

Assuming these figures to be correct, it should come as no surprise that de Klerk and his cabinet had a limited influence on the security establishment. De Klerk seemed to lack the executive and operational muscle to contain police excesses and the security forces escaped effective control. Whatever reservations the reformist president had about the security establishment, he could not afford to antagonize it. There was fear that if his vision of power sharing in South Africa failed, he might not only have to rely on them, but could also end up being ousted by them. De Klerk faced a huge dilemma: he would have liked to establish political control over the security forces but, on the other hand, he needed them as an insurance policy in case negotiations failed.

Rumours started circulating that de Klerk was in a sense a hostage to the arrogant officers. He felt he could not act against maverick elements in the security establishment because he risked a backlash. He could not allow officers promoted to the top echelons during the Botha era to embarrass the government. At times there was speculation that de Klerk and his cabinet were not getting the cooperation they needed, suggesting a split within the security establishment between those who were still geared to P. W. Botha's 'iron fist' rule and those who saw a prosperous future under a non-racial government. This lent credence to a growing perception that some members of the security forces regarded themselves as above the law or, effectively, beyond state control.

In interviews, Colonel Gert Hugo, a former senior intelligence officer in the Defence Force, described the existence of a 'third force', calling it a 'headless force out of control'. Hugo said he knew from direct experience that such a network operated within the country's security forces. He witnessed the force being born and nurtured in the early 1980s under the protection of former President P. W. Botha's powerful State Security Council. It operated on the basis of minimal political accountability.

Communist chief Joe Slovo described these elements in the security forces as a 'Frankenstein that has been created by a racist set-up.' His explanation for police excesses also suggested that de Klerk was to blame for exercising little control over his forces. 'Very often people acting on the ground have got more power than those who are supervising. The perception of our people is that it is de Klerk who is acting, who is killing,' Slovo said. Mandela said police had been trained to regard demonstrations by black people as a declaration of war on white supremacy, and that the police were directly involved with some organizations in attacking innocent people. Mandela, whose initial attacks were less scathing on de Klerk, felt that 'The government has either lost control of the police or the police are doing what the government wants.' The ANC said the government's complicity was evident from its failure to act against members of the security forces, or to protect witnesses, and from its use of censorship to prevent the publication of evidence of security force involvement in violence.

To be sure, years after police death squads and security forces unleashed a reign of terror in the townships, few people have been charged for the carnage that has left thousands dead and others maimed for life. Before 2 February 1990, men carrying automatic weapons in a car could not travel far before being hunted down and arrested. People merely suspected of being ANC members were rounded up and detained. The police force that uncovered sophisticated political operations in the past, and acted with precision and speed when the victims were either white farmers or white policemen, could not display this level of efficiency when the victims were black. Less than 80 arrests have been made in connection with more than 6,000 deaths in townships around Johannesburg between July 1990 and August 1992. For example, in Tokoza I saw a man being shot in full view of the police, just 100 metres away from them. They made no attempt to disarm or arrest the assailant.

According to Hugo, not only was there a third force stoking violence and undermining negotiations, but there were contingency plans for a military takeover if the government appeared to be losing its grip on the ANC and its communist allies. He said de Klerk was severely constrained in acting against officers involved in the third force because the generals had so much dirt on his cabinet that they had become virtually untouchable.

Blood Brothers

Evidence of police abuses in the townships could fill volumes. In 1988, my colleague Ruth Pitchford and I covered the case of two South African policemen on trial for murder. They told of blood brother oaths and a drunken foray into a black township. Eight members of a riot squad turned witness against their chief, Warrant Officer Leon de Villiers, and Constable David Goosen, describing a night of random arrest and assault in Lingelihle township a few weeks after former President P. W. Botha declared a nationwide State of Emergency. Other squad members made rare admissions of arresting and torturing blacks with no proof that they were involved in the anti-government violence then erupting everywhere. The two men, appearing in the remote Cape Province town of Graaff-Reinet, pleaded not guilty to two murders, two assaults and seeking to defeat the ends of justice by urging their colleagues to lie.

Ben Loots, an assessor assisting the judge at the trial, asked Constable Michael Neveling what the squad did if the people they had arrested did not want to talk. 'You make them talk . . . as we did, assaults, plastic bags [placed over their heads],' Neveling said. 'You mentioned a water method,' said Loots. 'Yes, you hold them under until they talk,' said Neveling. 'How did you expect them to talk when you did not even speak Xhosa [the local African language]?' asked Loots. 'If you take them far enough, they speak Afrikaans,' said Neveling.

Neveling and other squad members then described how they were sent from their base in the Eastern Cape city of Port Elizabeth to monitor the funeral of a man killed in political violence in Lingelihle, outside the market town of Cradock. They said they drank brandy, seized from township drinking dens on the journey from the coast, made stew over a camp fire, then swore secrecy and loyalty to the squad by cutting their forearms and mixing the blood together. In the early hours of the morning they drove on an 'unofficial operation' to Lingelihle where Goosen stabbed 25-year-old Andile Plaatjies to death with a diver's knife.

When daylight came, the 10 went into the township again, arresting four men, including one who was lying asleep in the sun wearing a t-shirt saying 'Forward to People's Power'. Three of the four were freed after interrogation, the policeman said, but de Villiers said of 18-year-old Wheanut Stuurman: 'This boy must be taken out. He is too badly hit to detain.' His colleagues said Goosen took Stuurman to the banks of the Great Fish River – the frontier in the nineteenth-century battles for land between white settlers and Xhosa-speaking blacks. Goosen came back and told his colleagues: 'I shot him from behind, through the neck. . . . The boy fell like an ox. I grabbed him and threw him in the river.'

Informal Repression: The Police, Inkatha and the Violence

One of the recent tragedies that illustrated police complicity and partiality in stoking the violence in Natal was the Trust Feed massacre. Convicting a police captain and four black policemen of 11 murders, a judge said the 1988 massacre was the final event in a planned security force operation to disrupt the community, oust an established ANC-aligned residents' association and give Inkatha control of the area. In the Trust Feed case, the judge showed that a senior policeman, Captain Brian Mitchell, worked with Inkatha members to plan and execute killings, and later engineered an elaborate cover-up. It became clear that such evidence was coming in from townships across South Africa, showing that police fuelled political violence, assassinated government opponents, bolstered Inkatha and sowed seeds of division. One shocking aspect of the Mitchell trial was that a man who held the position of station commander believed he was doing the state's bidding by siding with Inkatha and killing 'ANC-aligned' elements.

It all began on 13 November 1988, when Captain Mitchell had a meeting at the Inkatha headquarters in Pietermaritzburg with the Inkatha chairman of Trust Feed,

Jerome Gabela, and another high-ranking official, David Ntombela. On 2 December, Mitchell took four black policemen to Trust Feed and placed them in the care of Gabela. Members of the Trust Feed Residents' Committee were targeted and detained. That night a curfew was imposed and their houses were burnt down. The next day Mitchell fetched the four from Gabela and took them to a house where a family and its relatives were holding a vigil before the burial of an elderly relative. He opened fire and ordered the four to follow suit. The judge described in detail the groaning and screaming of the women inside, the shouts by the attackers to finish those still alive. Two of them went inside and, with a powerful torch, went from room to room finishing off the occupants. Innocent women and children were slaughtered as they sat in mourning at the side of a dead relative. The aim of this operation was to blame the residents' association for the massacre, thus creating something of a blood feud which made it impossible for members of the association or their supporters to enter the region. Captain Mitchell and his colleagues did not know that most of those slaughtered were actually Inkatha supporters, the group they wanted to put in control of the area.

After four years of intense investigation, punctuated by allegations of police cover-ups, Mitchell was sentenced to hang in August 1992 and his four black colleagues were given long jail terms. The ANC said the case proved that police actively sought to stimulate violent conflict between the ANC and Inkatha. People in the townships saw the outcome of the trial as having confirmed a long-held suspicion that the police were not only involved in fanning the violence, but also perpetrating acts of violence. Mitchell's case also proved that the police could not be trusted to investigate themselves. The judge said it was mere luck that Mitchell and his colleagues were arrested, given the evidence of an attempted cover-up.

A detailed dossier on political and tribal violence compiled by the Independent Board of Inquiry into Informal Repression (IBIIR) confirmed there was growing evidence of collusion between the police and Inkatha, in spite of strong denials by both. The Board, a watchdog group that scrutinizes underground political activity, concluded that alleged police collusion, if true, might be aimed at protecting the interests of right-wing elements in the police force. The objective, it said, would be to sustain the level of black-on-black violence as a means of driving whites further to the right.

The IBIIR detailed several incidents of police collusion as recounted by witnesses and victims in statements to its lawyers, which were supported by corresponding reports in the South African media, including the government-supporting press. The IBIIR said police vehicles accompanied Inkatha members armed with assegais, pangas, clubs and other weapons before violence broke out in Sebokeng and no attempt was made to disarm them. The Board said township residents made statements claiming that police committed unlawful acts, including the destruction of property, theft and assault, during a massive search operation for hidden weapons days after the violence. While shots were fired at a squatter camp in Tokoza by Inkatha members, police were parked only 200 metres away and failed to act or disarm the attackers. The group also said that police at times escorted Inkatha members preparing to attack, watched them attack without intervening, disarmed them only after the attacks had taken place, and fired teargas at opposing groups of township residents, but not Inkatha *impis*.

In the fighting in Natal between UDF supporters and Inkatha members, many people accused the police of siding with Inkatha. While most observers believed that violence was caused by political rivalries, some did not believe it was being perpetrated by ordinary township people acting alone, but by faceless professional hit men. 'When it began in Natal there was indeed conflict between the UDF and Inkatha,' said PAC president Clarence Makwetu. 'But now there is a force of well-financed, well-trained hit men who do these things and then disappear without trace.'

Sipho Madlala said he worked for military intelligence in Natal. He was seconded to the security police and then began taking part in hit-squad killings of senior ANC officials. When the killings moved to the Transvaal, a hideous routine emerged. Two young men who came from Natal said they had been lured to Johannesburg by an Inkatha leader with promises of employment. When they arrived in Johannesburg, they were given spears, axes or guns by Inkatha leaders and told to attack local residents because they were all ANC members. The first of countless massacres began in Sebokeng, where 36 people were killed at once. From then on, the carnage spread to other black townships as hordes of Inkatha supporters in red headbands rampaged through the communities from their bases at the single-men's hostels. This was the precise pattern of violence witnessed by tens of thousands of townships residents. The government called it black-on-black violence. The ANC blamed police partiality towards Inkatha. Inkatha blamed the ANC's hunger for control of all black townships.

A Catholic priest told how he saw Inkatha members being protected by armoured vehicles travelling on either side of the marching column. A Kagiso woman told how Inkatha supporters had been brought to her house in a police van before they killed her husband, a 60-year-old pensioner. It was hard for many South African policemen to adjust to the fact that the enemy, the ANC, PAC and other organizations, had been unbanned. It seemed unlikely that many members of the police force would have adapted to the new South Africa in just a few months. 'The government may have tried to persuade the police force not to use these methods, but it has created a monster and it will be difficult to use the same police for the transformation to democracy,' said Nelson Mandela. South Africa's Law and Order Ministry disagreed with Mandela's assessment. According to the ministry, 'The police enforce the law and serve the government of the day. The South African Police is firmly under control and performs apolitical and impartial policing to the best of its ability.'

In July 1990 the Congress of South African Trade Unions (COSATU) compiled a dossier and presented it to the Commissioner of Police and the Minister of Law and Order. The dossier warned them that Inkatha had held meetings in hostels around Johannesburg at which plans had been laid to hold a rally in Sebokeng and thereafter attack supporters and members of the ANC and COSATU. The union also sent a letter to the Inkatha head office in Ulundi, informing the movement that they (ANC allies) would be the subject of attack after an Inkatha rally in Sebokeng on 21 July. The dossiers gave details of where and when the Inkatha meetings were held and the substance of COSATU's concern that township residents who were not members of Inkatha, and certain officials of the ANC and COSATU, would be attacked after the rally. COSATU's dossier also said that Inkatha supporters catching trains and buses would be armed and that police should disarm them at the station before they got to Sebokeng in order to prevent violence.

The police and the Law and Order Ministry replied that they had investigated the contents of the dossier and were unable to confirm them. They said they had been informed of the Inkatha rally and would monitor the proceedings in the normal line of duty. On the day of the rally, violence flared in Sebokeng and 19 people were killed by Inkatha supporters. Without any doubt, police failed to intervene despite a warning by COSATU that Inkatha members were planning to attack township residents. While President de Klerk and then Law and Order Minister Adriaan Vlok defended the police as having acted impartially, black South Africans were sceptical.

In the Heart of the Whore

The police were not the only ones allegedly fuelling township violence. According to evidence in several court cases, both the SADF and the police trained hit squads that were used to assassinate government opponents. One of the well-known cases was that of self-confessed hit-squad member Almond Nofomela. In a hard-hitting statement to a court, Nofomela said: 'I am a member of the Security Police seconded to a police assassination squad. In late 1981, I was instructed by Brigadier Schoon to eliminate a certain Durban attorney, Griffiths Mxenge.' In this way the case of Griffiths Mxenge came back to haunt de Klerk in 1990 as he was dismantling apartheid. Mxenge's death was one of about 80 unsolved murders and about 100 disappearances of anti-apartheid activists.

Nofomela became the first policeman to reveal the existence of South African Police death squads. He told a packed Pretoria courtroom that he and scores of other black policemen killed government opponents on orders from their superiors. In a detailed statement to the court describing Mxenge's killing Nofomela said: 'We then all stabbed him several times. He immediately died, and we all carried on butchering him badly.' Nofomela was condemned to death for robbing and murdering a white farmer in 1987. The murder was not politically motivated. His statement that he helped to kill Mxenge and eight others won him a last-minute stay of execution, while his allegations were being probed. He said he made the statement because police associates had promised to halt his execution but failed to do so.

One of his superiors, a retired policeman named Dirk Coetzee, backed Nofomela's allegations in an interview with an anti-apartheid newspaper, *Vrye Weekblad*, in which he confessed to having commanded the death squad. 'I was in the heart of the whore. I was the commander of the South African Police's death squad. My men and I had to murder political and security opponents of the police and the government. I knew all the secrets of the unit which was above the law,' said Coetzee, who admitted that he had carried out several killings. Coetzee made the confession from a foreign country after fleeing South Africa soon after Nofomela's story was publicized. The other policeman mentioned was Willem Schoon, a senior officer who had retired from the force.

Civil Cooperation: The Killing of David Webster

The revelations shocked the South African public and provoked widespread demands for a judicial inquiry into dozens of murders of opposition activists that remain unsolved. Since Nofomela's confession, a number of secret military networks have been uncovered, the most notorious being the Civil Cooperation Bureau (CCB), whose tasks included harassment and elimination of enemies of the state.

South Africans got to know the CCB after the assassination of Dr David Webster, a lecturer in Social Anthropology at the University of Witwatersrand, a friend, and the man who secured my university study loan. On 1 May 1989, Webster was returning from a trip to the local garden centre to buy plants. As he walked to the back of his van to let out his dogs, a white sedan with darkened windows sped down the road, the snout of a shotgun appeared through the back window, and a close-range shot blew a huge hole through his chest.

The evidence led in the David Webster inquest shone a torch into the murkiest period of South Africa's history, when government warlords reigned supreme over parliament and when members of the security forces lied brazenly whenever they were challenged by the courts. The CCB was said to have been established by the South African Defence Force during the supremacy of the military under P. W. Botha's presidency. What emerged from the Webster inquest was that senior police officers took steps to inhibit the investigation into Webster's death, and that senior CCB members authorized the assassination of activists within South Africa. In the words of the judge in the inquest, 'the truth was not told on who killed Webster because many of the suspect witnesses were professional liars who made their living in deception and who were unblushingly resourceful in building up tissues of conflicting falsehoods.' The inquest ended without reaching definite conclusions, with the judge saying police investigations would remain open. But the more the public heard about the activities of the CCB, the more appalling what they heard became.

South Africa's armed forces have also killed exiled opponents in raids on African countries as part of the onslaught on opposition groups. Inside the country, Mxenge's wife Victoria was murdered four years after her husband's brutal assassination. The South African government has admitted that until 1990 it employed sabotage units in neighbouring black states to assassinate its opponents, mainly South Africans from anti-apartheid groups which were outlawed from 1960 to 1990. Government agents, in many cases with the full knowledge of government officials, used all kinds of dirty tricks to ensure the survival of apartheid.

In addition to the police and the SADF, South Africa had a sizeable informal military sector: foreign mercenaries, veterans of other African wars and right-wing reservists trained in commando units, and other special forces such as Koevoet, a counter-insurgency unit used during the Namibian war, and Battalion 32 from the Angolan war. These elements, in the main, ran the destabilization campaigns in the neigbouring states such as Namibia and Angola. Many were suspected of involvement in the carnage that continued after Namibians attained their independence and Angolans declared a truce.

Judge Goldstone Uncovers Some Risky Business

Perhaps the major source of revelations exposing military dirty tricks against government opponents was the Goldstone Commission's raid in November 1992 on the offices of a front company formed by senior army officials. The Commission was a statutory body headed by Judge Richard Goldstone to investigate and expose causes of violence. A credit card receipt in the records of a hotel led to evidence of military intelligence's dirty tricks. It also exposed the continued existence of a unit of military intelligence staffed by murderers, prostitutes and drug addicts, whose purpose was to blackmail top ANC officials.

It all started with claims to *Vrye Weekblad* newspaper by a Mozambican army deserter that he had been recruited by military intelligence to spy on, and even kill, ANC activists and officials. Mozambican immigrant Joao Alberto Cuna, alias Malefetsane Johannes Mokoena, who deserted from the Mozambican army in 1987 and entered South Africa illegally, said he had murdered seven ANC members in a Durban township on the instructions of the South African Police.

The police, seemingly stung by these charges, interrogated Cuna and came out with a different story: that he had lied to the newspaper for money. Certain that their name would be cleared by Cuna's evidence, they handed him over to the Goldstone Commission. They were satisfied he had lied on all counts. But they were soon to realize they had made a grave mistake. When in the hands of Goldstone officials, Cuna reverted to his original story that he had been taken to Pietermaritzburg by two men who identified themselves as Joseph Schultz and a Mr Smith, whom he described as a 'Boer'. There he had been booked into a hotel and the next day he was driven to a township where he and another black man killed ANC members. During exhaustive questioning by Goldstone commissioners, Cuna mentioned a piece of information that was to become an important clue to military dirty tricks – that one of the men paid the account at the Hilton Hotel with a Diners Club card.

Investigators went straight to the hotel, searched through the counterfoils, and found what they were looking for – a Diners Club counterfoil signed by the Mr Smith Cuna had named. He had paid for three rooms. They telephoned Diners Club and requested the name and address of this Mr Smith. Pleading client privilege, Diners Club at first refused to provide the information. Judge Goldstone telephoned Diners Club attorneys and insisted he be given the details, otherwise he would institute legal action. After they had been given the details they required, Goldstone's men discovered that the account was a corporate one, with 48 other people buying on the same account. The amount spent daily by all the card holders was about R25,000.

What had begun as a search for one man now looked like a conspiracy. The Commission traced the name of the company which held the credit card account to plush offices in Pretoria. They found it to be a front company for Military Intelligence, operating under the name Africa Risk Analysis Consultancy. Goldstone's men went straight to the address given. On arrival they presented their credentials and encountered no resistance. They then realized they had just stumbled into the nerve centre of military intelligence. Indeed, they were about to crack the army's deepest secret – a military task force called the Directorate of Covert Collection, specializing in dirty tricks against political opponents. Brigadier Tolletjie Botha, director of the front company, offered them his full cooperation.

Brigadier Botha watched the Goldstone investigators cut telephone lines, search the 50 or so staff members, and then begin the huge task of sifting through files. During the first eight hours they found four files pointing to military dirty tricks. Twelve hours into their work they made the most significant find – a fifth file, code-named Baboon. It was about the work of Ferdi Barnard, a convicted murderer suspected in at least two political assassinations, including that of David Webster. Barnard was a former member of the Civil Cooperation Bureau, by this time disgraced and disbanded.

Investigators found that Barnard headed a unit whose aim was to use prostitutes, homosexuals and drug dealers in dirty tricks operations to blackmail ANC leaders. The file showed that the Defence Force's Military Intelligence approved the plan submitted by Barnard to subvert the ANC's Umkhonto we Sizwe by linking it to criminal acts and crime syndicates. Barnard himself boasted to journalists about the effectiveness of his plan: 'The ANC is deeply infiltrated by the security forces. From my experience, I would say the ANC has been infiltrated very much, all departments, including the intelligence department and at the very high level. I recruited certain MK commanders as informants of mine. I started strengthening links again with Mandrax smuggling networks operating between here, Zambia, and Maputo, which had very good contacts with certain MK commanders.'

Goldstone's findings were chilling indeed. They came just a few weeks after newspapers exposed another Military Intelligence secret operation called Project Echoes, whose objective was to discredit the ANC by linking it with the Irish Republican Army (IRA). Echoes was authorized by the head of the army, General George Meiring, noted for his vigorous political utterances. More chilling was that this time the Goldstone Commission found that the dirty tricks operation originated at a high level, with Chief of Staff of Intelligence Lieutenant-General Witkop Badenhorst. It was even more chilling to realize that the operation began only in 1991, the year in which the people of South Africa were supposed to begin the process of reconciliation. *Sunday Times* editor Ken Owen was right when he said in June 1992: 'This is President de Klerk's difficulty; everytime he tries to move forward, the past reaches out to ensnare him. He is entangled in lies, subterfuges, deceits, cover-ups, and cover-ups and cover-ups, and he never knows when the National Party's evil past will catch up with him.'

Goldstone was ambivalent when journalists asked whether he had discovered an official 'third force', but said there was some evidence. To millions of blacks, his revelations provided irrefutable evidence of moral corruption and depravity at the highest level of the South African Defence Force. It confirmed that there was a distinct possibility that dirty tricks operators not too far removed from inner government circles would seek to impose their will on vulnerable members of the ANC's armed wing. The revelations also shortened odds on the involvement of the security forces in 'third force' activities primarily aimed at sowing terror in black communities.

It was not surprising that black people should draw these conclusions. In the townships, they knew that South Africa's security forces were allowed too much rein, usurping the very laws they were supposed to uphold, protect and enforce. The army ended up terrorizing neighbouring states and conducting undeclared wars against them, while the police, through its secret branch, conducted a ruthless Gestapo reign of terror against opponents of apartheid. As people in the townships saw it, a boil had been lanced and the ugly truth was beginning to come out. They knew that the security establishment had been blackmailing de Klerk, fearing that his reform programme would expose its activities in the bad old days when destabilizing black organizations was the order of the day. The result was that Military Intelligence had made a mockery of de Klerk's statements that he was negotiating with the ANC and other political groups in good faith. Widows and widowers, the orphans and the disabled, the people who had borne the brunt of 'third force' activities for almost a decade, were crying out for justice. Political organizations were now operating above ground, yet the government's close allies were still hell-bent on covert attempts to destroy them. How did the government expect blacks to believe that it was levelling the political playing field when Military Intelligence molehills continued to surface with undiminished frequency?

Chasing Shadows? De Klerk Purges the Generals

After Goldstone's revelations, de Klerk placed all army intelligence services under the control of Lieutenant-General Pierre Steyn and ordered him to conduct an urgent investigation into the shadowy Directorate of Covert Collections. A month later Steyn briefed de Klerk on his findings. We do not know what the general told the president, but we believe he dropped a bombshell which eventually prompted de Klerk to dismiss 16 senior officers and suspend seven others for alleged involvement in illicit political activities, including murder.

De Klerk himself admitted that members of the South African Defence Force had been involved in illegal activities – some of which even led to civilian deaths – and that they had attempted to impede the country's movement towards democracy. He said the revelations left him 'shocked and disappointed.'

> However, I am also resolute. I always said if there is a sore, I want to cut it to the bone and I think we are finally on our way to doing so. We will use every effort to attain that goal. I do not think one can say that the relatively limited number of people involved in any way could constitute a third force. That term has become something to denote a sinister force behind all the political problems of South Africa. There is no evidence of such a force in the security forces.

De Klerk said there were indications that some individuals were trying to sabotage the negotiation process, but added that there was as yet no evidence that anyone had been aiming to overthrow the government violently.

This was the biggest shake-up in the South African military in 70 years. Some of the senior officers de Klerk axed were Major-General Hennie Roux, chief of staff of the army, and Major-General Chris Thirion, deputy chief of staff of intelligence. Brigadier Tolletjie Botha, director of the Directorate for Covert Collections, was also among those axed. But de Klerk failed to act against General Kat Liebenburg, the highly controversial chief of the army, Lt-Gen George Meiring, head of military intelligence, or General Joffel van der Westhuizen, linked to the security signal to 'permanently remove' Goniwe and his colleagues.

'Bring me the evidence,' had been de Klerk's stock response whenever confronted with allegations about a shadowy group of security force personnel thought to be deliberately subverting the reform process. He now had some evidence, and his axing of the 23 senior army officials was the most dramatic and stunning development since he took office. He had ended the careers of a group of hitherto powerful men, who under his predecessor had been given free rein. Although he still denied the existence of a third force, his announcement removed any remaining doubt that the military had been playing its own political game. His purge of the military was the closest his government had come to admitting the existence of conspiracy in the security forces aimed at derailing the negotiation process. His acknowledgement that members of the security forces were engaged in illegal activities designed to hinder the transition to democracy confirmed what many had for some time suspected: that networks within the security services set up during the reign of P. W. Botha were pursuing a private agenda in a changed national and international political environment.

The ANC said de Klerk's action vindicated their fears of a 'third force'.

The acknowledgement by de Klerk that serious malpractices and activities that undermine organizations and events originates from the security forces confirmed what the ANC has said for a long time. There is clearly a third force operating within the security forces and it was exactly because of such a third force that the ANC suspended negotiations in 1991. It is sad that it has taken so long for de Klerk to respond to a situation that has been glaringly apparent. If President de Klerk could have acted then, many lives could have been saved. The current revelations are only the tip of the iceberg.

While the disclosures left de Klerk shocked and disappointed, the country was enraged. People in the townships did not believe the 23 security officials were a few putrid flies in an otherwise pure ointment. To the masses, to deny the existence of a 'third force' was to indulge in sophistry. Daily, there were calls that de Klerk should submit the country's security forces to supervision by an international force and resign his own position to make way for a democratic government.

Serving the Government of the Day

Brigadier Jaap Venter, head of the Johannesburg's Internal Stability Unit, a section formed to curb political violence, believes policemen and soldiers occupy a tenuous position in the townships, caught between the authority of the government and the political hatred of township residents.

We find ourselves in the middle of conflict and crisis situations and in which we have to act against those doing wrong and protect those under attack. When things do not go the way of the party in the wrong, the easiest thing in the world is to use the police as a scapegoat. Look, all policemen are not angels. We have faults and are not always in the right. Where there have been cases where policemen overstepped the line, the South African Police have taken prompt and effective action.

Venter said the police had come to expect that whatever they did would be criticized. 'We get very little credit for the countless incidents we have prevented and lives that have been saved at the risk of our own lives. How do you protect a community that is all times telling you it does not want your protection?' he asked.

It is true that policemen and soldiers daily brave the censure of anti-apartheid campaigners. Since anti-apartheid groups were unbanned, close to 250 policemen have died in the line of duty, though according to SADF spokesman John Rolt only one soldier has died. Most of those who were killed were black policemen on duty in the townships. Since 1984 militant youths have burned down the homes of more than 3,000 black policemen. Some were compelled to leave the force. Researchers and social workers say policemen were nine times more likely to commit suicide than civilians. They were increasingly becoming targets themselves, and long hours, low salaries and low morale added to the problem. 'They are reminded of death every day. Not only that, but it is death in its most gruesome form,' said Johannesburg police liaison officer Henrietta Bester.

Of the 120,000-strong police force, at least 60 per cent are black. Black policemen have a double burden to carry in that they are seen as defenders of apartheid, while as blacks they are also apartheid's victims. The government has admitted that black policemen have been discriminated against. The élite circles of the South African Police remain predominantly white, male, and Afrikaner. By March 1993, only 94 black male policemen were senior officers, whereas over 4,000 white policemen held senior positions. In attempting to correct the wrongs of the past and give the South African Police a new image, the government acknowledged there should be a wholesale restructuring of the force in the future.

Brigadier Magabole Tsoka, who became South Africa's first black major-general, said the country would have a better future if the police and the black community could develop a mutual understanding and tolerance. Tsoka, who joined the police force in 1956, now heads the newly created community relations unit in Johannesburg. He admitted that black policemen had been tasked with enforcing unpopular laws for years and that this had caused difficulties for policemen in their communities, prompting threats from all directions. Black policemen felt that police ineffectiveness could, at times, be blamed on liberation movements who called on residents not to cooperate with the police because they were an extension of the ruling party. They complained that the ANC, while it criticized the police for failing to protect black lives and property, was actively preventing police from doing their jobs properly.

Joseph Ngobeni, Soweto Police liaison officer, also lamented the lack of understanding between public and police. 'The public is not interested in reporting incidents of crime. Given such a scenario, police cannot achieve their goal of preventing crime and violence,' he said. Ngobeni and his colleagues do not agree that black policemen should be viewed as part of the apartheid system. He said police only enforce existing laws. 'The police are neutral and apolitical. They do not take sides. We serve only the government of the day. I do not understand why we should be attacked,' he said.

Ngobeni denied police were excessively brutal, adding that they had a right to use force within the limits of the law. 'We do not support brutality. We are only allowed to use reasonable force. Policemen have to implement the law. That is not something confined to a black policeman. This is the function of the police all over the world, even if they personally do not agree with the laws they are enforcing.'

Ngobeni's sentiments are not shared by most blacks. 'A policeman is supposed to serve his community. But these guys are not serving us. They are killing, harassing and terrorizing us. Our people live in constant fear. These uncouth and rude people seem to regard themselves as above the law,' a Soweto resident said.

A Part of the Problem

Bowing to internal and external pressures to discipline the security forces, de Klerk called in international and local experts to identify, examine and address the problems of South Africa's security establishment. One of the first tasks has been to expose obvious cases of incompetence, poor judgement, and excessive force which resulted in unnecessary deaths.

The Goldstone Commission, investigating the shooting of more than 30 Sebokeng protesters in March 1990, found no indication that the marchers had acted so provocatively as to warrant the use of firearms and live ammunition by the police. The Commission found that the police opened fire on a peaceful and disciplined marching crowd, without proper warning. The report said the fact that many of those killed and injured were shot in the back showed that they running away. It said police officers confronting the crowd had loaded rifles without the necessary orders, and 'there was a complete lack of discipline in the police line. At the most, the behaviour of the crowd had justified the use of teargas, and only after a proper warning.'

The International Commission of Jurists, which completed an independent investigation into violence in Natal and Transvaal, confirmed some of these views in its report. 'The strain on police resources is compounded by serious police misconduct. There is no confidence in the police force, which is seen as partisan. There is a lack of determination among senior police officers to put matters right.' According to the jurists, this still applies in parts of the Transvaal and Natal.

'Perhaps after decades of enforcing apartheid laws, the South African Police must learn afresh how to cultivate relationships and adapt their tactics in order to achieve public responsibility,' said a study by Peter Waddington. Waddington, a British criminologist, was asked to probe police conduct during the Boipatong massacre in the summer of 1992 in which 45 people died, 24 of them women and children. 'If effects are to be addressed, it will require thorough reappraisal of the entire organization, backed by the political will to ensure sufficient funding,' he reported.

Waddington identified several problem areas in his findings: lack of internal and external accountability; poor police–community relations; discrimination in favour of hostel dwellers; the failure to gather information which would have enabled the police to prevent the massacre; failure of police leadership and command; incompetent investigations; shortcomings concerning command and control intelligence and contingency planning; investigative procedures; and a lack of awareness of the importance of sound community relations. Waddington found no political bias within the police force during the Boipatong massacre, but lambasted them for sheer incompetence on the day of the killings.

For the ANC, 'the manifest incompetence and failures of the police as confirmed by the report is evidence, at best, of the neglect and indifference of the police to the plight of township residents and/or a conscious refusal to address the serious nature and consequences of violence in our townships. At worst, it is symptomatic of a more sinister involvement in the massacre.' In township eyes, Waddington's diagnosis confirmed the sickness affecting the entire South African security forces. The police complained, however, that such negative reports only served to undermine confidence in them.

Waddington underlined the need to place the police and other security forces under interim multi-party control and for the urgent monitoring of the security forces by international and independent local bodies during the transition to democracy. Anti-apartheid parties have long demanded the same thing. It is also crucial that planning for a new police force should not wait until the new constitution has been drawn up, since policing is a vital and ongoing task. With violence ravaging South African townships all over the country, political parties should insist on restructuring the police force even while the political process stumbles along.

Forces to Face the Future

In one form or another, the integration of the various armed forces is inevitable. Neither the government, the ANC, nor any other party has the strength to ensure its army is installed to the exclusion of the others. So far, no programme has been implemented to retrain the security forces, who have been taught that it is their duty to defend apartheid and wage war against anti-apartheid campaigners. In the long run, however, the police force must be dismantled and reconstituted with a completely new command structure, philosophy and training regimen.

It was naïve to believe that de Klerk's watershed speech on 2 February 1990 was sufficient to reorient the security forces. As South Africans grapple with the task of nation building and democratization, the police are uniquely placed to strengthen or destroy these delicate processes. An impartial force is a priority. Violence in our society cannot end until the police culture of violence has been brought under civil control.

Expert opinion is that policing will be devolved to regional and local levels, partly because that is the best way to make police responsive to the needs and concerns of local communities. Local and regional authorities would be required to finance the police in their area of jurisdiction. This is the advice Harvard University criminologist Professor Phillip Heymann gave at a press conference in July 1992. Heymann thought that devolution of policing could meet some of South Africa's special problems, especially if minority representation was built into whatever authority controls the local force.

> At one extreme the local police organization can be hired, organized and paid out of the funds of a local community – that is the general practice in the United States – but that is not essential. The minimum conditions for local control are either that the top leadership of the police organization can be chosen or removed by representatives of the local community, or that those representatives control the amount of resources made available to the police in their area.

Either of these minimum conditions could be consistent with a centralized administrative structure. The central point, however, is that black communities will not shed their distrust of the police and the army until they can exercise substantial control at a local level. Another alternative would be to make key police offices elected positions, with each commanded by an elected chief constable who would be the supreme police authority for a region, with the right to appoint his own deputies and to recruit and dismiss staff within an overall national policy framework that defines regional police powers and accountability. This would allow constables to be swept from office if their performance failed to satisfy the public at large. Furthermore, elected police chiefs could be subject to recall in the event of major abuses of police power. That might remove some of the stigma attached to a force which for decades was better known for enforcing apartheid and frustrating the ruling party's political opponents than for law enforcement.

Ideally, regional and municipal police forces might be used for petty crime prevention, while a well-trained and politically independent national force should be retained with clearly demarcated powers that do not infringe on the police functions of the regional force. Accountability and credibility should be the cornerstones of effective policing. South Africa's police force during the dark days of apartheid lacked accountability. Credibility would be easier to achieve if the security forces were accountable to the communities they serve.

As for the army, instead of expanding and adapting the SADF, a new and smaller professional defence force must be formed. The new army would be representative: certainly, it would have to incorporate members of Umkhonto we Sizwe and the homeland armies. The new defence force would have to be apolitical, with loyalty to the country and its citizens, not the government of the day. The country's arms industry should be dismantled, and the billions spent daily on defence rechannelled to economic development and black advancement. The same energy and commitment which was used to protect white interests should now be used for developing the townships.

In the future there is no doubt that the new South African force will consist of soldiers who once faced each other in battle. What is uncertain is whether some soldiers will subscribe to the new order or choose instead to launch a destabilization campaign against the new government.

8
PEACE HOPES STILLBORN

> If it is the scheme of the government and its black allies to rise to power on the corpses of our people, they must not count on my support.

Nelson Mandela, April 1991

> The ANC and the South African Communist Party originally played a dominant role in unleashing the violence now threatening to consume the entire country. It is their creation of a culture of intolerance and the use of violence, especially to eliminate political opponents, which has cheapened human life. They realize that they are losing their power-base, have a divided leadership and are uncertain about their future role in the new South Africa. Frankly, I do not think disarming the people or banning cultural weapons will solve any problem.

Adriaan Vlok, April 1991

Hundreds of bare-breasted Zulu men and women, wearing leopard skins, chanted war cries and waved war axes as they lunged at each other in mock combat, smacking their ox-hide shields with spears. The demonstrators, making a sound like distant staccato gunfire by banging sticks and spears together, marched past police armoured vehicles. An armoured car kept watch on the protesters while a police cameraman video-taped the proceedings. Johannesburg's city centre streets, normally packed with Saturday shoppers, were sealed off by police in camouflage-painted armoured vehicles to allow the marchers right of way on one of the main streets. 'I will be a Zulu in the new South Africa and I will die a Zulu,' a protester declared in one of the many placards.

The weapons, brandished under the gaze of police, appeared to be in breach of the spirit of key clauses of the National Peace Accord due to be signed by 24 organizations, including the government, the ANC and Inkatha, later that Saturday afternoon. The Accord of 14 September 1991 demanded that political parties 'actively contribute to a climate of democratic tolerance, refrain from intimidation, and agree that no weapons . . . may be possessed, carried or displayed at any political meeting.' As their war chants soared from street level through fourth-floor conference windows, accompanied by fearsome foot-stamping and shield-smacking, the ANC and its allies seethed over what they saw as deliberate provocation. 'This demonstration speaks for itself. Any appearance of this kind generates tension,' said ANC official Gill Marcus. 'These are not weapons,' said Inkatha official Musa Myeni, gesturing at a forest of spears, sharpened steel spikes, lead pipes and clubs. 'They are cultural accoutrements,' he said.

When Mandela and de Klerk later clashed on live, prime-time television, against the backdrop of spear-waving and war-dancing Zulus, it illustrated the fragility of the Accord. Within minutes, Mandela, de Klerk, and Buthelezi had had their first public falling out, televised to an expectant nation. The relaxed bonhomie of the signing ceremony switched to sharp exchanges when de Klerk defended the Inkatha demonstration and show of force. Mandela, who had often accused the government of siding with Inkatha in the township wars in order to maintain white supremacy, angrily declared that if the demonstrators had been his followers, they would have been disarmed and dispersed as ruthlessly as they had been many times before. In a series of rapid interjections watched by fascinated local and international journalists, diplomats and television viewers, de Klerk indignantly denied bias and Chief Buthelezi charged Mandela with lying.

The demonstration of muscle by Inkatha supporters dramatically illustrated the main problem facing South Africa's peacemakers: translating paper accords, resolutions taken at summits and high-level meetings by the top leaders into reality at the violent grassroots level.

Traditional Weapons vs SDUs

To carry a spear or not to carry a spear emerged as the centrepiece of discussions between the ANC, Inkatha and the government. The spear, the traditional weapon with which South African Zulus won their reputation as fearless fighters, was one of scores of issues at the centre of a critical dispute between the country's key political players as they debated how the township slaughter could be ended. The ANC, striving to end the internecine war, demanded that the carrying of cultural weapons in public should be prohibited. The Zulus replied that the carrying of such weapons was obligatory on cultural occasions, which they defined as events at which a cultural leader was present, whether the occasion had political significance or not.

The government accepted Inkatha's view that traditional or cultural weapons were safe for public display – a position which dismayed many who questioned the government's motives. For, in a little noticed proclamation in August 1990, the government had legalized traditional weapons just a month after Inkatha transformed itself from a cultural movement into a political party. For a century before the change, Zulus in Natal were prohibited from carrying virtually any instrument, even sharpened sticks. Even walking sticks were prohibited to all but the old and infirm. Only persons engaged in *bona fide* hunting or travelling at night in rural areas were allowed to carry sharpened sticks or spears. Police tested the legality of knobkerries by seeing if the club's head fitted in the carrier's mouth. If it did not, the carrier was prosecuted.

But after political faction fighting broke out in Natal in 1987, police stopped enforcing the bar on traditional weapons, particularly against Inkatha supporters. When fighting moved to Johannesburg in August 1990, traditional weapons, carried in rallies mostly by Inkatha supporters, helped to turn Johannesburg townships into killing fields. The role of the official peace-keepers emerged clearly enough in their response to fighting in Alexandra before and after Good Friday of 1991. After clashes between hostel inmates and running battles in the streets of the dilapidated township, security forces belatedly raided a hostel inhabited mainly by Inkatha members and confiscated lethal traditional weapons, some still bloodstained. A week later, police handed them back. Most South Africans wanted these glaringly dangerous weapons outlawed.

There were other such incidents. One Sunday afternoon police intercepted trains at three Soweto stations and found what they described as the largest weapons haul yet confiscated. They took 2,000 traditional weapons, 30 handguns, 10 AK-47s and more than 300 rounds of ammunition during a search of trains ferrying Inkatha supporters to a rally in Soweto. Other weapons included axes, spears, pangas, sjamboks, and sharpened wooden and metal sticks. Residents gathered on overhead bridges of the stations and cheered as police searched the commuters. When the first AK-47 was discovered, a white police officer raised it triumphantly above his head to wild cheers from spectators. A day later, police dumped the haul back at Inkatha offices, stressing they were only returning their traditional weapons, excluding the AK-47s.

Inkatha dismissed the call to ban traditional weapons, saying most victims of political violence were those killed by people brandishing AK-47 automatic rifles than those displaying cultural weapons.

As the debate about traditional weapons raged on, the ANC revealed its own plans to launch armed paramilitary self-defence units to safeguard its members from Inkatha and vigilante attacks. The movement called for one in ten township residents to be trained in the use of various weapons. It recommended purchase of licensed weapons, intensive physical training, and training in the use of weapons. The defence units would be trained by the ANC's military wing, Umkhonto we Sizwe, and would involve all members of the community, 'even small boys'. 'Umkhonto cadres, particularly ex-prisoners and those due to return from exile, must play a leading and active role in the establishment of the defence structures,' the ANC said.

Nelson Mandela, announcing the formation of the units, said they would not attack anyone, but were necessary for self-defence.

I have seen people hacked beyond recognition. I have seen women with their breasts cut open and men with their heads split open and their brains dripping out. If it is okay for whites to have neighbourhood watches and civilian guards, it should be equally acceptable for blacks to have their own defence units.

Among the duties of the defence units would be barricading streets during attacks on residents and slowing down or delaying 'enemy vehicles'. Training of defence unit members would also involve the 'surveillance of red-headbanded vigilantes [Inkatha] with whom members of the community would not cooperate.' Mandela also said that the ANC would implement the defence units regardless of what the government, police or Inkatha thought.

The government condemned the ANC's plans, saying people should seek under-standing rather than confrontation. 'We do not agree with this and we will try to reason with the people. It is unnecessary . . . we cannot allow people to form private armies, alternative security forces,' it said. 'They do nothing but polarize the situation further. It is a recipe for violence, bloodshed and civil war.'

The ANC's call to arm the people was not the way to democracy; it was more likely the path to chaos. The ANC's assurance that the defence units were not designed as elements of a private ANC political army was less than reassuring. Even accepting it at face value, the township fighting showed starkly that all political organizations, including the government, have been unable to instil discipline among unruly members, let alone control them. It was not surprising that, a few months after the formation of the units, there were reports that its members were running amok in the townships, conducting kangaroo courts, killing opponents and even fighting among themselves. Some were arrested for crimes such as armed robberies.

But in one way the ANC was justified in taking the law into its own hands. The following comparison often crossed my mind. Imagine a group of armed men wandering in any of the Johannesburg white suburbs slaughtering white residents at random. The response of the white public, the media, the security forces, and especially the government would be strong. White residents would demand quick action and they would get it. The white-led security forces would storm the suburbs and flush out the killers. They would even conduct house to house searches, seize weapons and arrest suspects. The courts would quickly punish the guilty. Indeed, something like this has happened before. There have been cases where the killing of a lone white farmer by black robbers precipitated the descent of hundreds of police, soldiers, helicopters and dogs. They would comb the area and arrest the suspect, who quickly would be brought to court.

Why didn't the horrifying outbreak of violence in the black townships bring this kind of reaction? Why did the government and the security forces appear helpless to stop it? Overwhelmingly, the victims of both the everyday and the political violence were black. Black people were dying not just because they were the majority in the country, but because they were black. In this sense, there was a chilling accuracy to Mandela's accusation that the South African state was guilty of the genocidal slaughter of black people. My feeling was that the government response to the violence was clearly racist. It would not have been this way if the victims were white.

The Killing Routine

As politicians manoeuvred for power, a horrifying similarity in the killings was emerging. A single attack prompted a chain reaction from township to township; this would be followed by a lull, supporting a widely held view that the violence appeared to be switched on and off at strategic moments.

We were becoming inured to violence. The ugly, ungainly sprawl of dead bodies on the front pages of newspapers was becoming a norm. Killings which used to shock were downgraded to routine newspaper items: Two Massacres in a Week – Peace in the Balance as the Season of Violence Returns! Slaughter: 78 Killed in Township Massacre! 55 Dead in Tokoza, 8 in Tembisa, 9 in Katlehong, 5 in Sebokeng, 1 in Bekkersdal – Killers had Death List! Unrest Death Soars to 82! 6 Killed in Taxi Rank Attack! Mob Rampage after 35 Die! Sebokeng Slaughter! Massacre at ANC Vigil!

South Africans – black, brown, white, coloured – were mesmerized into a kind of confused paralysis. All of us, of whatever colour or political persuasion, had become so brutalized by the grotesque violence in our country that it no longer shocked us to hear of the gruesome deaths of people like my friend Johannes (see Chapter 5). Herein lay a terrible danger for the future. We had become blasé about the wholesale slaughter of innocent fellow citizens. Because we were no longer greatly surprised to hear that bloody battles were raging in other townships, we implicitly let the politicians off the hook. It was unimaginable that in countries like Britain, the United States and France such civil carnage could occur without urgent intervention at the highest political levels. Obviously there was no quick fix, but the country had reached a stage in which atrocities had become so regular that they had lost their power to shock. The violence had created a climate in which people were more concerned with finding weapons to defend themselves than with ending it.

A Brief Embrace: The Mandela–Buthelezi Meeting, January 1991

There was a growing belief that a meeting between Mandela and Chief Buthelezi could minimize the fighting between their supporters. With no end to the carnage in sight, many thought that if the ANC could control its followers, if 'Comrade' Mandela and Chief Buthelezi could get together and swear peace, the violence would stop.

Chief Buthelezi was at the forefront of those demanding such a meeting: 'The ANC wants everything ... they will fight for what they want, and people will continue dying. I say to Dr Mandela, have the courage to put South Africa first and help me act against the violence instead of fanning the flames of violence by refusing to enter into any peace agreements with me.' As the spectre of charred corpses continued to haunt the nation, calls for a Mandela–Buthelezi meeting grew louder. It was felt that a symbolic meeting between the two leaders would send a signal to their supporters to cease fighting. Even the ANC-supporting *New Nation* declared: 'It may well be that a meeting between the ANC and Inkatha and between Chief Buthelezi and deputy president Nelson Mandela may have an important bearing on curbing the rampant violence that is destroying the soul of the people.'

Their friendship dated back to the days when the young Buthelezi followed in Mandela's footsteps at the University of Fort Hare and both were members of the ANC's Youth League. It continued even when Mandela was in jail serving a life sentence, during which time Mandela praised Buthelezi for his anti-apartheid stance. 'He was my friend before I went to prison and he and the king [King Goodwill Zwelithini of the Zulus] gave tremendous support while I was in prison. Also the stand taken by Chief Buthelezi was one which I admired a great deal because he told the government he was not prepared to negotiate while I and my colleagues were in prison, and that is something for which I am greatly indebted to him,' Mandela said.

Attempts to convene a meeting first faltered over the choice of a venue. Other attempts also failed because of differences over issues such as dates, strategies, and accusations and counter-accusations as to who was the source of the violence. Mandela's supporters saw Inkatha as a violent organization responsible for hundreds of deaths in Natal and later in the Transvaal. The UDF and COSATU in Pietermaritzburg said Inkatha attacks on their homes amounted to the most systematic, coordinated and concerted onslaught undertaken in many years. Although Inkatha and the ANC both wanted majority rule, they had different visions of the future and neither appeared ready for concessions that might have stopped the bloodshed between their supporters. Therefore, soon after his release, Mandela was advised against such a meeting with Chief Buthelezi by ANC leaders in Natal who sought to isolate and marginalize Buthelezi. Mandela was forced to go along, issuing the following statement: 'Mr Buthelezi has attacked the ANC in very unacceptable terms and when he did that, of course he angered the people and it became understandable that they felt the time was not ripe for me to meet him.'

As the violence intensified, Mandela shuttled back and forth in a series of meetings with government officials, discussing measures to curb the fighting first with de Klerk, then with Law and Order Minister Adriaan Vlok and Justice Minister Kobie Coetzee. But Mandela's refusal to meet Chief Buthelezi made him appear dangerously detached from the real fray. He had an obvious dilemma. He had taken a risk in opening negotiations with the government in opposition to his radical followers, and he was preparing for full-scale negotiations for a non-racial constitution even while some of his followers were still in jail or in exile. Now he was being urged to meet Chief Buthelezi, whom many ANC followers regarded as a government stooge. Another dilemma was that if the meeting failed to produce peace, as did Mandela's appeal to his supporters to throw their weapons into the sea, Mandela's credibility would be tarnished.

The ANC said a meeting between Chief Buthelezi and Mandela could only occur once structures to achieve peace had been established on the ground, and once both sides had made it absolutely clear that they were committed to peace. Unless this happened, leaders of the ANC felt that the meeting would just be a jamboree to give Inkatha political clout. The ANC said it was not convinced that Buthelezi was urging his grassroots supporters to stop the violence. They said Inkatha was losing support and was using violence as its only weapon to force the ANC to recognize its power. If Buthelezi was granted a meeting, they said, it would show that violence was a lever that could be used whenever Inkatha wanted something.

Chief Buthelezi was quick to capitalize on the ANC's reluctance to meet him. 'People are actually dying because the ANC will not talk with Inkatha and Mandela will not talk to me,' Chief Buthelezi said. He blamed the ANC for creating a culture of violence inside the country. 'It is the ANC which declared the armed struggle as the primary means of bringing about change in South Africa and it was the ANC which moved from hard military targets to making soft targets of the public. It is now sordid to drag me into the political arena as the man most responsible for violence in Natal when I have done more to stop violence in this region than any other black leader,' he said. 'I have gone to the areas worst hit to hold rallies, to gather the people together to tell them to rally together for peace,' he said.

When Buthelezi was invited again to tour Tokoza, one of the hardest-hit townships east of Johannesburg, by the South African Council of Churches, white liberal politicians, editors, businessmen, church leaders and ambassadors, he declined, saying he was not informed in time. But, on the same day, he toured the township with Vlok.

On 29 January 1991, almost a year after Mandela's release and hundreds more deaths, the ANC announced that the two leaders would at last meet. The announcement gave rise to much euphoria that the factional strife might soon end. Belated though it was, their encounter nonetheless held a promise of peace, even though their spokesmen were careful not to build high expectations. 'It is one thing for leaders to meet and shake hands, another to transfer the reconciliation down to the grassroots level. Without grassroots support, it will be impossible to stop the violence,' said an ANC spokesman. Inkatha's Themba Khoza said: 'That does not mean to say the meeting will stop the violence or that it will bring completely a clean page, but as far as I envisage, it will be a contribution towards the lessening of violence.'

The question facing the ANC and Inkatha presidents was whether their supporters could bury their festering enmity and restore the fraternity which once characterized the Mandela–Buthelezi relationship. Giant strides were made during the eight hours of talks. The parties jointly agreed to cease hostilities, they agreed to stop calling each other names or what Chief Buthelezi called 'killing talk', they agreed to cease coercion and intimidation, and they even agreed to work together on certain political campaigns. The organizations also recognized each other's right to exist – and differ.

In a joint statement, the two leaders said, 'We call on all of our people . . . . as well as our allies to cease all attacks against one another with immediate effect and to promote the quest for peace in our community.' A peace plan hammered through at the meeting called on their supporters to stop vilifying each other's leaders and stated that the two leaders would meet from time to time as the need arose. It was also agreed that Mandela and Chief Buthelezi would go on a joint tour of all the areas hit by violence and that a 24-member committee (12 per side) would be established to monitor violations of the new accord. The group also called for development programmes in deprived areas, for an effective and impartial peace-keeping force, and agreed that persons with authority over public facilities should make themselves available to all people irrespective of their political affiliation.

What strides were made were soon overshadowed by their inability to produce a formula for eliminating violence by clearly defining the roles of members of joint committees, for example, by bringing in third parties to help, or by setting out a timetable for achieving specific goals. This failure made it more difficult to communicate the positive aspects of the agreement to the grassroots level. For Mandela and Buthelezi to have embraced at an exclusive hotel was an achievement, but no sooner had they met than their failure to implement their undertakings rendered the summit ineffective.

Another meeting during the Good Friday weekend of 1991 also failed to restrain the level of violence on the ground. This prompted other leaders to oppose further meetings between Chief Buthelezi and Mandela to discuss violence. 'Such a meeting must relate to the people themselves and it must enjoy the support of the comrades on the ground if it is to be successful,' said ANC Natal Midlands leader Harry Gwala, a man known for his Stalinist beliefs. 'We have had so many peace efforts in the past and they have always been scuttled. Inkatha has embarked on a full-scale war against our people and have reached a stage where they cannot go by promises alone and the shaking of hands,' Gwala told me.

Among preconditions laid down by the ANC before any summit could be successful were: the banning of traditional weapons; free political activity in all areas, especially those controlled by the KwaZulu goverment; and the fencing of hostels regarded as springboards of township attacks. 'These are practicalities that could bring peace. If any meeting between Comrade Mandela and Chief Buthelezi goes ahead without these preconditions being addressed, that meeting will be a farce and will be nothing more than mere window dressing,' said Gwala, whose region had been the hardest hit since 1987.

Near the Edge: Ultimatum Politics

When the Mandela–Buthelezi meeting failed to produce results, the ANC launched what was later to be known in South Africa's political lexicon as 'ultimatum' or 'deadline' politics, as every political party tried to do something to absolve itself or demonstrate its abhorrence of the way people were dying in droves. The ANC sent an open letter to de Klerk on 5 April 1991, threatening to break off the power-sharing talks if he did not end the violence. 'In no other country would the government keep ministers whose departments were responsible for the death of thousands of people . . . no democratic government would allow it,' Mandela told us in a news conference. He said the figure of more than 12,000 dead represented deaths caused by death squads, faction fighting and security force action since 1984.

From that day, political violence shadowed the negotiations. The ANC also demanded that the government dismiss police and army officers responsible for covert action against anti-apartheid activists, and dismantle all special counter-insurgency units. It demanded legislation banning the carrying of all weapons, including the 'traditional' sticks, clubs, spears and assegais used by Inkatha members during rallies and fights in the townships. It wanted assurances that security forces would use civilized crowd control measures; that single-sex migrant worker hostels, where much of the township violence has erupted, would be closed; and that an independent commission of inquiry into allegations of misconduct by the police and the army would be launched.

In its ultimatum, the ANC cited two possible reasons for the continuing violence, saying it was either a result of the government's 'cynical irresponsibility,' or alternatively its 'connivance in acts of organized terror aimed at destroying or seriously crippling the ANC'. It said the violence had assumed a more organized and systematic character despite an Inkatha–ANC peace accord.

It was clear that the organization was becoming aware that negotiations could no longer be driven only by the apparent friendship between de Klerk and Mandela or cosy talks about the democratic future while townships were on fire and people continued to die. At the moment when violence devastated the black neighbourhoods, the bond, chemistry and understanding between the two main players no longer seemed enough. Whereas previously a great deal of confidence had been placed in de Klerk's goodwill and his relationship with Mandela, there was now a strong sense that de Klerk was duplicitous in his dealings with the ANC. He was accused of watching in comfort as the violence took its toll on his opponents. Whereas, a few months earlier, de Klerk had been seen by many South Africans, including the ANC and its allies, as a man dedicated to a new South Africa, now he was being depicted by others as a crafty and ruthless rival, prepared to give free rein to elements within the state security apparatus which sought to destabilize the government's opponents.

Empty as the ANC's threat seemed to some South Africans, especially the white community, it would have been suicidal for the organization not to have conveyed the feelings of its constituency. ANC branches in affected areas were reporting dismay from members that the ANC could not protect them and were increasingly horrified that they were being asked to place their faith in de Klerk's *bona fides*. It was clear that, for as long as the violence continued, the ANC would be under pressure from its township constituency, which saw negotiations with the government as meaningless while the townships were burning. A further drawback for the ANC was that 'This cycle of violence has raised the risks entailed in being a member of the ANC . . . this has proved a far more effective means of political repression than the legal measures previously employed by the state.' As a result, many former supporters were returning their membership cards to protect their lives. This weakened the ANC's credibility, and limited its scope for growth among blacks and whites.

ANC militants welcomed the move, saying it represented a dramatic shift away from unproductive peace talks and accords, which had done little to end the carnage. They said the ANC's hardline stance signalled an end to simple rhetoric and political posturing. The militants believed that apartheid ensured that whatever legal space was created by the unbanning would promptly be closed off through a programme of violent destabilization. They said the violence had virtually paralysed the ANC and threatened to reduce it to a political formation that would be able to do no more than issue threats and engage in political theatre. Evidence of how effective the violence had been was most vividly illustrated in the fears and reluctance expressed by ANC members when approached to participate in the organization's activities, such as signature campaigns launched to demand an interim government and a constituent assembly, or even pro-democracy marches.

De Klerk was quick to reject the ANC's demands. He insisted that he had moved steadily to fulfil the pledges his government made in the Pretoria summit in August 1990, to release all political prisoners and ease the return of exiles by the end of April, thus opening the way to negotiations. De Klerk accused the ANC of issuing the ultimatum to cover up division among its ranks. 'This is a matter which nobody should use to gain political advantage,' de Klerk said. 'Now that we are entering the straight of removing obstacles, new demands are being made and the goal posts moved in order to cover up serious problems within its own ranks.' Adriaan Vlok, taking the same line, called the ultimatum the ANC's desperate response to loss of support in the townships.

'They are only stalling, they are only lengthening the process of coming to the peaceful solution. They will have to come to the negotiation table eventually. This is posturing, trying to position themselves.' Chief Buthelezi also denounced the ANC's demands as unreasonable and provocative. 'The ANC is . . . making the kind of demands which would precipitate . . . civil war,' he said.

As relations between his government and the ANC worsened, de Klerk announced a three-pronged plan to end the bloody political faction fighting. He convened a summit of all political leaders to end the violence, appointed a permanent commission of inquiry to probe the causes and solutions of the fighting, and increased township policing and military action to stop the carnage. 'We cannot do it alone. The real solution lies in the leadership in all spheres in this country taking hands and . . . using all their influence and power in regard to their own supporters,' he said. The ANC said the proposals did not address the question of violence as raised in its open letter. It said it wanted an independent commission of inquiry that would have full powers to deal with the violence. 'De Klerk has not demonstrated any willingness to end the violence. His proposal for a Mandela–de Klerk–Buthelezi meeting, and his proposal to convene a multi-party conference on the violence, are a diversion from the issues raised in the open letter and subsequent information released,' the ANC/SACP/COSATU alliance said. 'De Klerk is trying to build a smokescreen to conceal his own reluctance or inability to take immediate and effective action. We therefore reject his proposals.'

Announcing more concessions, de Klerk promised to deliver more funds for reform programmes. He said the government would sell oil reserves to raise up to $770 million for job creation, economic stimulation, and an emergency aid fund to provide food, clothing, and blankets for violence-hit communities. 'The time has come for men of peace to gather. If we stand arm in arm, we will be able to turn the tide of violence. Let us act in such a way that history will never be able to say that we failed as responsible peace-makers.'

Although de Klerk was careful not to be seen to be giving in to the ANC's ultimatum, he announced a further ten-point plan to end the violence. He said he would strengthen police manpower and added that police and soldiers would continue 'firm and impartial' action, with special action from time to time. He also established a standing commission under a judge to investigate complaints of violence and advise the government. Responding to calls to ban traditional weapons, he said he planned to intensify the control of dangerous weapons. De Klerk added that victims of the violence would benefit through a special aid fund. Hostels, the flashpoints of most of the fighting, would be upgraded and converted into family units.

De Klerk's proposals were generally regarded as statesmanlike. They also allowed him to continue occupying the political high ground because they suggested a course of action which would maintain the impetus of the peace process. But inevitably, given the mood in the ANC, they were dismissed by the liberation movement as designed primarily for the purpose of winning applause from the outside world while continuing to do nothing concrete about the violence at home.

(Another) National Peace Accord (14 September 1991)

Just when many thought the ANC was bluffing, the organization officially suspended constitutional negotiations on 11 May, a month after their 5 April deadline. 'Until such time as progress is made in regard to these demands, the ANC will not involve itself in constitutional discussions with the government or in any all-party congress to discuss mechanisms for drawing up a new constitution.' But the ANC did not slam the door on all contacts with the government. Talks on constitutional matters, including the proposed all-party congress, were suspended, not terminated. Discussions between the government and the ANC on how best to end the violence would continue, as would joint working committees on the release of political prisoners and the return of exiles. The ANC also said it would continue discussing its demands without touching on constitutional matters. At the same time, the ANC announced a nationwide mass action campaign to pressure the government. The plan included nationwide boycotts by millions of black consumers, mass demonstrations, and a general strike. The decision marked the lowest point in the government's relations with the ANC since it was legalized.

Gerrit Viljoen, then the government's chief negotiator, said the ANC's decision was 'unjustifiable and irresponsible'. 'The planned mass action announced by the ANC cannot contribute to peace, but must inevitably aggravate violence by leading to further confrontation and conflict,' he said. Inkatha leader Mangosuthu Buthelezi said: ' The ANC is playing games with the people of South Africa.' He had told de Klerk that 'the ANC would throw its toys out of the cot every time it became frustrated and would then go to the street corners to play brinkmanship with violent disaster.'

The movement's decision to suspend constitutional discussions was a bargaining ploy in the tough negotiation process, as well as a tactic by its leadership to gain the support of militant members. But it could also have sent wrong signals to some of its more impatient cadres, eager to hit back at what they believed to be connivance by the government in the township slaughter. There was a danger that hardliners in the ANC would interpret the suspension of constitutional talks as opening the way for the resumption of the armed struggle.

One of the frustrations of the impasse was the delay the unrest was causing in implementing programmes crucial to the improvement of black living standards, such as the provision of low-cost housing. The money was available, including R1 billion set aside by government for social upliftment. Administrative delays were only part of the problem. The real difficulty was that construction work could not begin while the townships were in turmoil. So the social benefits of a stable environment were denied to thousands of people, and a major job-creating scheme, with all the economic benefits that would flow from it, was postponed.

After refusing to participate in the first government-led summit on violence, among other objections because it was organized by one of the 'belligerents', the ANC and its allies finally settled for another convention sponsored by churches and big business on 14 September 1991. After exhaustive negotiations spanning almost five months, about 24 organizations – led by the three major political rivals, the ANC, government and Inkatha – signed a 33-page National Peace Accord to help end political violence which had claimed 12,000 lives since 1984.

With the slogan 'Peace Now, Not Another Death Later', the Accord called for the establishment of five committees to monitor a code of conduct for political parties operating in townships and for police and the army forces deployed there. Another was supposed to monitor socio-economic programmes for black areas, while the remaining two would implement and monitor other peace initiatives. The Accord called for the establishment of a peace secretariat which would have legal powers, a permanent directorate, a multi-party peace committee to act as a watchdog, and a code of conduct which would lay down enforceable rules to prevent provocation and intimidation.

Multi-party working groups approved the appointment of a statutory commission to be headed by Judge Richard Goldstone to investigate and expose causes of violence, and of a police board with equal representation from the force and members of the public to advise on future policing policy. The Accord recommended the setting up of a special police unit headed by a general to investigate allegations of misconduct by members of the force, and the appointment of regional ombudsmen to ensure the proper investigation of all complaints against the police. It also called for the creation of special courts to deal solely with cases of political violence.

'No language calculated or likely to incite violence or hatred, nor wilfully false allegations should be used at any political meeting. No pamphlets, posters or written material containing such language can be prepared, printed or circulated, either in the name of any party or anonymously,' the Accord said.

The test now was whether the desire for peace was strong enough to prevail over factionalism and the shadowy forces which brought the country closer and closer to chaos. A year after the Accord was signed, only the white businessmen and professionals (who chaired almost all Accord structures) and leaders of parties to the Accord still championed it as the answer to the endemic violence gripping so many areas. The violence was as bad as it had ever been. Whole communities were being torn apart, leaving thousands homeless and community infrastructures destroyed. In dozens of areas countrywide, violence, or the threat of it, was ever present.

In one of his findings a year after the signing of the accord, Judge Goldstone blamed most of the violence on the rivalry between Inkatha and the ANC.

'It remains clear that a primary trigger of violence and intimidation remains the rivalry between and the fight for territory and the control thereof by the Inkatha Freedom Party and the African National Congress,' he said in one of his reports on violence.

He has also said that contributory factors in the violence continued to be socio-economic conditions, suspicion and negative perceptions of the security forces, and the availability of sophisticated weapons and explosive devices.

In Natal, Goldstone said, violence could only be curbed if there was agreement by the parties on free political activity in all areas, the role of tribal chiefs, investigation by police of political deaths and injuries, and the cessation of attacks in breach of the National Peace Accord. 'If elections or referenda are to be held in South Africa, it is obviously a precondition that the parties contesting such an election or participating must be free to carry on political activity,' he said.

Violence is ingrained in the political facts of life in South Africa – those economic and political issues such as unemployment, homelessness, crime, ethnicity, the third force, the behaviour of the police, the fight for political turf and a great range of ideological differences. Only an acceptable political solution and greater prosperity for all will do much to combat, contain and reduce the conflict.

III

AT THE CROSSROADS

22 *Pro-apartheid supporters of the neo-Nazi Afrikaner Weerstandbewiging (Resistance Movement) standing to salute the arrival of their leader Eugene Terre'Blanche. They have vowed to fight for the self-determination of the Afrikaner nation and to resist any majority government.*

23 *Barend Strydom salutes supporters who attended his trial for murdering eight blacks because, he said, they were endangering the survival of the white nation. He was sentenced to hang but freed under an amnesty agreement between the government and the ANC. He has said he would kill again if necessary.*

24 *AWB leader Eugene Terre'Blanche saluting supporters after one of his fiery speeches calling for a racially pure white South Africa without blacks.*

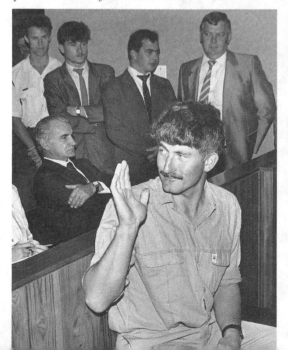

25 *Winnie Mandela and South African Communist Party chairman Joe Slovo walking away from the steps of the Union Buildings, the seat of white power, after one of many ANC marches ('rolling mass action') to back demands for majority rule.*

26 *Mandela and Slovo give the 'Amandla!' (Power!) salute under a Communist Party flag. The ANC acknowledged that its relationship with the SACP was costing it the support of whites opposed to communism.*

27 *Cyril Ramaphosa, ANC chief negotiator tipped by many as one of the contenders for the ANC presidency after Mandela.*

28 *An ANC supporter with a portrait of Nelson Mandela sits unperturbed in front of police watching the organisation's leaders address a rally protesting against township violence.*

29 *F. W. de Klerk and Chief Buthelezi addressing the media after a meeting to discuss political violence. The relationship between the two soured after Chief Buthelezi accused de Klerk's negotiators of striking a deal to share power with the ANC after South Africa's first non-racial election.*

30 *Inkatha Freedom Party supporters chant songs in support of their leader Chief Mangosuthu Buthelezi at a rally held in Soweto's Jabulani Amphitheatre. Chief Buthelezi is one of the most powerful leaders after Mandela and de Klerk.*

9
ADAPT
OR DIE

OUR PEOPLE DEMAND THE RIGHT:
To exist as a people; to be free; to rule ourselves in our own fatherland without intervention from outside; to protect our identity; to protect our existence with all means at our disposal; to establish according to our choice an own community life and educational system.

Manifesto of white right-wing parties, 1990

We in the CP are adamant that there is a territory which belongs historically and otherwise to the White nation. While we accept that there are whites who are prepared to live under an ANC government in a unitary state, there are others – we believe, the majority – who will never submit themselves to a Communist terrorist regime. . . . Unless any future constitutional dispensation addresses the problems of ethnicity and self-determination, it is a waste of time and a recipe for discord.

Andries Treurnicht, CP leader, 1991

A parcel bomb blew up in the face of a young white computer consultant involved in work for black political organizations, virtually decapitating him. Police issued an all-points bulletin for two 'nice-looking' white men. . . .

A van careered through central Johannesburg and gunmen inside, firing indiscriminately, killed two young black men and a middle-aged black woman. Before she died, the woman said she saw a white man shooting at her. . . .

In a statement filled with racist language, the White Liberation Army claimed responsibility for placing a bomb at a taxi rank frequented by blacks in central Johannesburg, which injured 27, three seriously. . . .

In the conservative town of Louis Trichardt, a group of 40 white right-wingers terrorized and beat up a group of 200 black Sunday School pupils for attempting to relax in a public park once reserved for whites only. Wielding sticks, fan belts and clubs, they told the youngsters they did not want to see blacks playing or relaxing in the park. . . .

In Welkom, a small mining town south-west of Johannesburg, white khaki-clad vigilantes, charging that police were unable to contain crime, established night patrols to chase blacks from the town's neat suburbs and leafy avenues. Armed with shotguns and Magnum pistols, vigilantes headed out in groups of 12 in unmarked vans to patrol the uneasy streets of Welkom. Organizers said that most night patrols were uneventful, with routine checks on properties of elderly people and women living alone. But Welkom's black residents said the vigilantes were more concerned with 'black bashing' and terrorizing law-abiding residents than maintaining law and order. . . .

In the centre of the country, in scenes reminiscent of clashes between the Ku-Klux-Klan and black civil rights workers in the American South, whites roamed highways at night beating and shooting black travellers. In one of many such incidents, four black friends driving home on the outskirts of Pretoria one Saturday night were forced off the road by four white men. In the style of a Mississippi civil rights slaying, they were shot at point-blank range. Three of the four died instantly. One survived because he lay on the ground pretending to be dead. Bleeding profusely and slowly losing the use of his left hand, he crawled and hid in the tall grass near the road. . . .

A seven-page section of the weekly newspaper *Vrye Weekblad* told of assassination squads across the country. It contained an affidavit by Jannie Smith describing the transcripts of up to 10 tapes of conversations in which right-wingers discuss plans to kill senior officials of the ANC and white cabinet ministers. Smith, a police spy, swore in papers which were later handed to the police that he had been approached by AWB members to assassinate Mandela. He further said in an affidavit that the AWB planned to bomb power stations, dams and a football stadium in Soweto. Assassination targets included de Klerk and his senior cabinet colleagues. 'I believe that the respective members of the AWB are deadly serious and are busy carrying out their plans. In my opinion, drastic action has to be taken against them to prevent a bloodbath. . . .'

In an extraordinary confession, Conservative Party parliamentarian Koos Botha spoke of frustrations at the thought of power slipping away from the Afrikaner and of the dismal prospect of a one person, one vote election. What was important for him was that the Afrikaner should not concede the moral high ground, and to achieve that he blew up a school to be used by children of the ANC's returning exiles. In his defence, he said he resorted to violence only because other avenues were closed, meaning that de Klerk was proceeding with constitutional negotiations despite right-wing protests. . . .

On Christmas Day in 1991, as South Africa and the world debated the pros and cons of CODESA, a white couple living on a smallholding south of Johannesburg accosted a black labourer, 60-year-old Molatu Lebeta, on a neighbour's plot. Lebeta's wife said there was an argument, after which the couple returned with six other whites. They beat Lebeta, and the next day he died in hospital. What was the argument about? 'The white woman said she did not want her dog mating with a kaffir's [a derogatory term for blacks] dog,' said Lebeta's wife Maria. . . .

C. J. de Waal, 21 years old, said everything went black when his girlfriend refused to accept him back. 'That is why I zapped so many kaffirs.' De Waal's rampage began in a white suburb in the conservative town of Middelburg and ended in the nearby Mhluzi black township when he was hit by five police bullets after killing one black man and wounding five others. His arm was later amputated. Swathed in bandages, de Waal described how he cracked when his former girlfriend rejected his pleas to return to him. 'She left me just before Christmas and I could not handle it. I was at her house and she said I must go. I begged her. Everything went black. That is why I zapped so many kaffirs, but probably not enough,' he said.

The Rise of the Right

A disparate collection of forces, ranging from neo-fascist zealots to the church-going members of the Conservative Party, are preparing for a revolution they say will come no matter who's in power in a democratic South Africa.

In the months following de Klerk's 2 February speech and Nelson Mandela's release, it was the white right-wing extremists who planted bombs in city streets, government buildings and other targets to scuttle the apartheid reforms. They bombed synagogues, the offices of anti-apartheid groups, and the homes and offices of liberal politicians. To vent their anger at the unfolding transition to democracy, some whites just killed blacks for the fun of it. White terrorism was the most dramatic manifestation of the growing right-wing resistance to de Klerk and his policies for ending white minority rule.

Today's right-wingers consider the prospect of black domination an even greater threat to their survival than British hegemony in 1914, when the First World War, and the German presence in neighbouring South West Africa (now Namibia), brought die-hard Boer resentment – simmering among the *bitter-einders* (bitter enders) since the Anglo-Boer War – back to the boil. In 1915, most whites sided with the government, especially in the fight for the occupation of South West Africa, and the rebels were in the minority even among the Afrikaners, although over 10,000 took up arms against the government. While the catalysts were different, the motive for rebellion was the same in 1915 as in the 1990s: to protect cultural sovereignty and retain power. Then, the danger of being swamped by blacks was far from the minds of whites. After the fight for survival against British oppression, Afrikaner nationalism reached its peak with the institutionalization of apartheid in 1948.

Since the far right gained momentum in the early 1970s, culminating in the founding of the Afrikaner Weerstandsbeweging (AWB) in July 1973, more than 80 right-wing organizations have sprung up. Since 1990, white gunmen and bombers have staged as many as 80 attacks (which killed five people) – as many as black guerrillas managed in the first four years of their armed struggle against apartheid rule. Intelligence sources say rightists could make up as much as 60 per cent of the police and army. Highly trained policemen, military servicemen and ex-servicemen are among thousands recruited to join right-wing paramilitary groups. Highly skilled instructors lend their services at weekend training camps. Trainees are instructed in the use of handguns, shotguns, automatic rifles, batons and knives. Some paramilitary groups like the AWB's Ystergarde (Iron Guards) are training openly for war. There is a call by right-wing groups to arm one million whites, or one in five. 'A white man without a gun in Africa is a dead man,' according to neo-Nazi leader Eugene Terre'Blanche.

Orangeworkers, White Wolves and the Pure Blood of Boere

Since 1990, I have travelled throughout the country interviewing white farmers and reporting on court cases involving white pro-apartheid rightists. In the farming areas of South Africa, I found few who supported de Klerk and many who longed for the good old days of apartheid. I visited white Utopias such as Orania and Morgenzon, created by white separatists who argue fiercely for their right to self-determination. Their vision of a future democratic South Africa is one which has been parcelled up into separate racial states.

Support for right-wingers is rooted among poor whites, the population group most likely to suffer from black advancement. White nationalism runs deepest in the Afrikaners, who forged their identity as a nation early in the nineteenth century when they rejected British rule of the Cape Colony. They laid claim to most of the interior, defeating black tribes; these victories, they believed, were granted by God. They fought the Anglo-Boer war in a vain bid to prevent their land being overrun by the British Empire, and right-wing Afrikaners still say they need their own state to guarantee their survival. Right-wingers see white farmers as the most potent of the forces which could be readied for armed action at short notice. South Africa has about 50,000 full-time white farmers and another 20,000 part-time smallholders. Reportedly, all farmers have undergone military training and most are members of commandos and paramilitary units.

The CP, the AWB, and several smaller extremist groups also enjoy considerable support from within the ranks of the police and armed forces, although exactly how much is difficult to assess. Right-wing leaders believe that if it came to an armed struggle by whites, the security forces would either split or come out in support of the right. Most rightist groups have seen a massive surge in membership and are attracting a younger and more sophisticated segment of the white South African population. There has also been a significant growth in the number of English-speaking right-wing supporters. These groups comprise a mix of white supremacists, miners, and ex-Rhodesians embittered by the bush war that led to the liberation of Zimbabwe. A further source of recruits is a recent influx of right-wing immigrants from Eastern Europe, among them Janusz Waluz, the fanatical anti-communist who killed Chris Hani.

Wim Booyse, a Pretoria-based political risk consultant who spent months studying the right wing, identified 70 groups: 15 cultural/political organizations, two women's groups, seven churches, four political parties, eight paramilitary groups, 28 fundamentalist groups, four trade unions and two dormant organizations. He divided them into three broad categories: the fringe groups, the neo-Nazi groups, and the assorted reactionary groups with names like the Order of Death, the White Wolves, the White Liberation Army, the World Apartheid Movement, the White Freedom Army, the Transvaal Separatists, the Flamingos and the Jackals. Police have said that the fact that there are so many groups makes it difficult to monitor or even arrest right-wing extremists.

The growth of the white right wing must also be set in an economic context. With inflation running at 15.8 per cent at the height of apartheid reforms in 1990, most whites are struggling financially. According to economists, their personal disposable incomes will continue to fall in the years ahead. Many right-wingers blame the de Klerk government. Their bitterness is strengthened by their suspicion that the government is in cahoots with big business, a suspicion encouraged by the rising share of revenue obtained by the government from personal tax and the falling share of revenue from company tax.

Their financial worries were compounded by political anxieties. They do not know what the future holds. They fear that de Klerk was ushering in black rule without adequate guarantees. However irrational they may seem, their fears have been implanted insidiously and effectively since 1948 by the National Party's manipulation of religious doctrines and history. Now that the NP wants to ring the changes in South Africa, it is faced by the monster it has created, a menacing right-wing group that is prepared to resist change at all costs.

The Conservative Party is the voice of this disaffected white minority. The CP says it is opposed to violent methods of achieving its political objectives, but there would be circumstances in which it believes violence might be forced upon South Africa. Such circumstances include a situation in which the majority of the electorate reject a new dispensation in a referendum, while those in power try to force a new dispensation on the country. Alternatively, violence could result if a black government tried to force whites off their land through its policies of nationalization or other types of land reform.

The CP's plan of action to thwart the government's reform initiatives includes the collection of millions of signatures in protest against apartheid reforms, the establishment of a conservative newspaper, creating their own financial institution and moves towards the establishment of a white homeland. Koos van der Merwe thought the CP's civil disobedience options were numerous: 'Suppose we start to paralyse certain services in the country? Suppose we really use our muscle to bring traffic in the PWV [Pretoria –Witwatersrand–Vereeniging, Transvaal province's industrial heartland] to a standstill for a day? Suppose we ground South African Airways for a day? Suppose we cut off ESCOM's power for a couple of days?' Van der Merwe was later kicked out of the Conservative Party.

The CP established a committee to look at ways to oppose the government, including the possibility of whites withholding their taxes or television licence fees. Another ploy was for right-wing whites to take over towns which have a small black population, where even if a system of one person, one vote was introduced, the white population would be large enough to command an overall majority. However, the die-hards publicly said they were prepared to fight – and their determination to thwart black majority rule should not be underestimated. 'You do not have enough jails to keep Afrikaner nationalism imprisoned,' Treurnicht said in a warning to de Klerk. He said the CP would resort to all possible democratic, constitutional ways to fight for the retention of apartheid. 'But if all channels are closed to us, we would regard ourselves as an oppressed *volk*. Then we would have no choice but to take the path of an oppressed nation, to fight for our freedom.'

Shortly after Mandela's release, Treurnicht announced the beginning of the *Derde Vryheidsoorlog* (Third War of Freedom, the previous two being the Anglo-Boer Wars of 1880–1 and 1899–1902), a struggle to return the country to the days when Mandela was still in prison, when it was an offence even to mention his name or that of the ANC, to the days when a black was forced to call a white *baas* (boss), and when blacks were forbidden to walk on city pavements.

To the right of Treurnicht, Eugene Terre'Blanche, the leader of the AWB, has fought a kind of Boer *jihad* for several years now. For him, because of the ANC alliance with the South African Communist Party, whose members are viewed as the anti-Christ, the right-wing struggle in South Africa is a fight between good and evil. His fiery speeches are often sprinkled with religious rhetoric, but contain the threat of civil war. 'We did not kill or trample anyone – we brought civilization, we brought life where there was death into the dark heart of Africa and created a model state. We have never been forgiven for bringing God's light into dark Africa. Our nation is hated because we have a contract with God. We are the smallest nation with the richest, widest country. We possess the riches of the world contained in dunes and rocks,' he said. Stirring his supporters into hatred, he has often declared: 'If the ANC wants bloodspilling we'll give it to them.' He has also said, 'If uncivilized blacks want to kill and maim white people, we will level them with the gravel.'

Terre'Blanche has vowed his organization will use all available means to prevent an ANC government taking office.

> No one dares take the land that God gave us. They [the blacks] know very well how to make crosses. And if they make their crosses [in a one person, one vote election] they will take our country away from us. If the government capitulates, we will refuse to live under an ANC government. That day there will be war in South Africa. That day we will fight like our forefathers and we will fight until we win.

If the ANC wanted South Africa, he has said, it would first have to get rid of the whites, as had been the case in the rest of Africa. And 'if the ANC wants a war it will get one. There will be bloodshed if the ANC wants to take over the country.'

The AWB launched self-defence units for whites in direct response to the legalization of black political organizations. According to AWB sources, membership of the defence units has increased by 365 per cent. 'The AWB's central infrastructure and communication system are now in place and our units are being trained countrywide in self-defence methods such as . . . handguns and shotguns and karate,' revealed Servaas de Wet, national commander of the AWB commando system. According to Terre'Blanche, 'If the South African Police and South African Defence Force are prepared to play this role, there should be a guard at every AWB home because the ANC has said they are going to kill. If they do not defend us, we will do it ourselves because we are policeman and soldiers.'

It is not always clear whose side the police are on. In one of the worst confrontations, popularly known as 'the Battle of Ventersdorp,' the South African Police clashed with AWB members trying to prevent de Klerk from speaking at a local rally in an area the AWB considered the stronghold of right-wing politics. The AWB vowed that the president would not speak. De Klerk vowed he would. Terre'Blanche called on his followers to turn up in large numbers and bring along their licensed firearms. The president ordered a police escort.

Half an hour before de Klerk arrived, street lights went out, plunging the town into darkness. More than 2,000 angry right-wingers led by AWB leader Eugene Terre'Blanche marched on the main street in a bid to try to storm the meeting. They were blocked by police. Teargas was fired and shots rang out. AWB members, some armed with pistols, crossbows and hunting rifles, jeered and spat at police before the battle erupted. It was the first fatal clash between the police and the far right since de Klerk launched the reforms that die-hard defenders of apartheid regard as a traitorous deal with the black majority. 'If they had left me alone, nothing would have happened. Instead an officer sprayed teargas in my face and ran off. They set their dogs on us and shot at my people,' Terre'Blanche said.

Terre'Blanche admitted advising his followers to bring licensed firearms to the meeting. 'A disarmed white man in this country, this unsafe country of the National Party, is a dead white man. If a man has a licensed gun, then he may carry it,' he said. Incensed white extremists pelted police with an assortment of missiles. The angry mob set upon two mini-buses carrying blacks, baying for their blood. Both drivers managed to force their way through the crowd to safety behind the police lines.

A van with passengers and a coffin at the back did not escape the wrath of the mob. Cries of 'Kill the bastards!' rang out. Armed police forced the right-wingers back and stood protectively over the wounded blacks. When the battle was over, two right-wingers and one black lay dead and scores more were injured. . . .

The pure blood of Boere has soaked into the ground. By their deaths you are now part of the blood pact. What has happened today will reverberate through history. There will be more death on the road to freedom. The land is ours. We got it through fighting. If they want to take it back, they are going to have to fight. We will fight them to the end. We will not surrender.

Terre'Blanche's declamatory response to the episode was issued on the steps of a police station after negotiating the release of some of his disciples.

The CP and AWB were the most vocal organizers of rallies and marches. One of the biggest right-wing gatherings was held on 26 May 1990 when about 70,000 supporters gathered at the Voortrekker Monument to launch the Third War of Freedom. Boosted by a host of other rightist movements and cultural groups, the rally was a culmination of efforts to raise a million signatures petitioning the government to call an election or referendum to test de Klerk's reforms. The crowds were stirred by a host of diatribes against moves towards a non-racial democracy.

Treurnicht said the new South Africa would rob whites of their political rights and their identity as a white community. In the end they would lose everything.

People must realize that the South African reality is one of multi-nationalism and multi-ethnicity. Any thought of a non-racial democracy based on supposedly non-racial population is in total contradiction of the basic human realities of South Africa. The best way to accommodate the political and social rights of the various communities or peoples is not by an effort to safeguard their rights and interests through checks and balances, minority veto or proportional representation in a unitary system, but by a dispensation of separate freedoms, own jurisdiction in own areas and self-determination for all people.

Carel Boshoff, an Afrikaner academic and the son-in-law of Hendrik Verwoerd, the architect of apartheid, believes strongly in white self-determination. He recently finished designing a white homeland in the arid desert of the Northern Cape and the Kalahari. Boshoff and his followers have taken the first delusionary steps to self-determination by buying Orania, a small farming town in the Northern Cape province, which they dream will one day become the capital of a white homeland called Orandia, or Orandee in Afrikaans. At present, it is a dusty ghost town 150 kilometres south of the diamond-mining town of Kimberley on the banks of the Orange River.

According to Boshoff,

Time is running out for Afrikaner identity and self-determination in this new South Africa. An independent Afrikaner state would have as uncertain a future under a black majority government as other whites have had in the rest of Africa.

For an individual to survive when he is not in his own cultural circumstances, that is possible. But for a nation to survive, for what we call a *volk* to survive, it is necessary to have a geographical as well as political circumstance in which institutions, the values, the way of living, the world view of the nation are established.

We would rather negotiate a small country for whites than a large country for blacks.

Boshoff draws a parallel with Israel, arguing that the existence of a Jewish state is crucial to the security of Jews in the Diaspora. 'I feel it is possible for Afrikaners to survive in the new South Africa on condition that we have got a stronghold, a state where Afrikaners are in charge of the political and different structures. The condition is that there is a motherland.' That 'motherland' would exist in Orania.

Orania was founded in 1968 when the government's Department of Water Affairs began building dams and developing canal systems from the Orange River into adjacent farming areas. When families of the white workers finished the project in January 1989, they left behind 90 prefabricated houses, a primary school, a church, post office and other facilities. Most of the town structures were falling apart when Boshoff and his foundation bought the town at an auction. They told the 400 coloureds who lived outside the town to pack up and go. They now live in the nearby towns of Hopetown, Petrusburg and Kimberley. 'This is the first Afrikaner town in the world. We bought the land, not the people,' said Orania's caretaker, Thys Fick.

Boshoff and his Foundation for Afrikaner Freedom (Afrikaner Volkswag) believe the area along the Orange River would first accommodate about 250,000 Afrikaners, and eventually two million. If Boshoff has his way, his new republic will eventually stretch from the southern border of the vast Kalahari desert, west of Kimberley, through to the western coastline, and incorporate several established towns. The earmarked area boasts three of the biggest dams in South Africa, fertile agricultural land, a coastline, a power grid, roads, a railway line and an airport in Upington. Although part of the potential homeland is desert, Boshoff believes it could be turned into a lush paradise and could eventually accommodate up to three million whites. Non-white inhabitants of the proposed Orandia currently outnumber whites by four to one. At least 300,000 would have to be moved to keep the area white. Boshoff insists that non-whites will not be removed forcibly, but would be encouraged to go and live where their labour would be required.

I asked Boshoff whether I could visit the Afrikaner homeland to see if it had lived up to white expectations. He would not mind me coming, he said, but he did not know how residents would receive me as a black person. I visited South Africa's prototype of a white homeland, which has no black servants. I found whites mixing cement, emptying rubbish bins, cleaning the streets, painting houses, saying they were proud of being the pioneers and vanguards of an Afrikaner homeland. Caretaker Thys Fick did not want to shake my hand. At first he did not look at me while talking but kept his eyes on David Ottaway, the *Washington Post* correspondent I had travelled with. Initially I did not ask any questions as he took us on a tour of Orania. When I eventually began putting questions, he answered them honestly.

'We are not going back in time. We are just fighting for what our ancestors left us, our culture, language and religion. We are not here because we hate blacks. We are not racists. It is a matter of self-preservation,' said Thys.

Thys and 360 other Afrikaners believe they have already fulfilled the dream of white hegemony in a pure white state as an alternative to the reform process. 'It might look racist,' he conceded. Indeed it does. No blacks are allowed to live or work in Orania, where even the most menial tasks are performed by whites. In a bizarre twist, the all-white town welcomed its first non-Afrikaner family in 1991 – all the way from the United States. Tim Vaughan, his wife and their children immigrated to Orania. Vaughan said they left the United States because they found life depressing. 'I could not stand seeing even homosexuals living together being allowed to adopt children.'

I found Orania to be a harsh, Calvinist motherland, far from the swimming pools and verdant verandas which most residents have left behind in white suburbia. The houses were flimsy and dilapidated, the roads cracked and buckled. The shortage of labour was a problem. Some paid white labourers sometimes refuse to do what they call 'kaffir' work and they resent living in houses formerly occupied by coloureds. It is doubtful whether Orania will ever be self-sufficient. Boshoff agrees, but he is banking on the homeland becoming part of a constellation of regional states to be bordered by the new South Africa.

Hendrik Verwoerd Jr, Boshoff's brother-in-law, also shares this vision. He is the leader of an exclusive Afrikaner settlement called Morgenzon, situated in the eastern Transvaal. As in Orania, I found whites serving tea to visitors. In Morgenzon, white women do all the washing, cooking and cleaning, things virtually unheard of in white South African suburbs. Whites ploughed their fields and ran their shops without black labour. At the nearby fabric and dry cleaning store, black customers and workers are barred.

Verwoerd and his organization, the Oranje Werkers (Workers), believe white dependence on black labour is partly responsible for the breakdown of apartheid. They warn that unless Afrikaners become more self-sufficient, they will be an impotent minority of three million dominated by the country's 30 million blacks. The Oranje Werkers moved into Morgenzon in 1985 to prove that whites can manage without blacks. 'We do not give them work, they find it is easier to move to other places, we go on to create new jobs for our own people,' said Verwoerd.

In the independent white state of Oranjeland, there will be no work for blacks, so there will be no excuse for them to wander outside their own territories. 'If you accept blacks as labourers, you must accept them as part of the community. We want to prove you can build a community free of black labour,' Verwoerd said. Unlike his father, who wanted to control most of South Africa, Hendrik Jr is willing to settle for a white homeland where whites can be left in peace. According to him, this means that blacks must be expelled by force, if necessary, from much of the Transvaal and Orange Free State, where Afrikaners traditionally settled. Then the blacks and anyone else who wishes to join them can make whatever arrangements they like in the rest of the country. 'If we have to resort to violence, it would be to drive out people that don't belong . . . then we would like to establish ourselves as good neighbours with them,' he said.

Like his father, Hendrik Jr is dedicated to the ideal of separate development. But, unlike his father, he believes that the survival of the Afrikaners can only be ensured if they have their own separate territory. 'We do not want to dominate blacks or anyone else,' said Hendrik Jr. 'We want a territory exclusively for the Afrikaners where we can lead our own way of life.' This idea goes beyond the theories of his father, Hendrik Verwoerd, who ruled South Africa from 1958 to 1966, and for whom apartheid meant white domination over most of the country except for some small black tribal homelands. Hendrik Verwoerd Sr dreamed of an all-white South Africa, with the black majority becoming citizens of nominally independent homelands while still providing labour for white industry. Through apartheid, his intention was not to deny black aspirations but merely to make sure that whatever aspirations blacks had would not interfere with the privileges of whites in white areas. Hendrik Jr believes that the government must accede to their demand for an Afrikaner homeland. If their demand is not met, he says, the Afrikaner nation 'will be forced to take drastic steps.'

Apart from political groupings such as the CP, AWB, and those who dream of establishing Afrikaner homelands, there are many fringe groups who are prepared to spill blood, and have already spilled blood to preserve apartheid. I spent another month following the court appearance of Barend Strydom, a member of the neo-Nazi Wit Wolwe (White Wolves), who was accused of the mass murder of blacks. In other courtrooms, the vicious deeds of the Israelites and the Order of Death shocked my senses as I sat listening to testimony recounting their massacres.

Barend Strydom lived up to the bloodthirsty stereotype of pro-apartheid right-wingers. While in the police force, he was once photographed holding the head of a black man in one hand and a knife in the other. His intention, he told a Supreme Court hearing, was to have the photograph blown up into a poster carrying the slogan 'ANC Pasop' (ANC be careful). 'If an ANC terrorist saw that, he would think twice.'

According to Strydom, 'Each black person threatens the continued existence of whites, even an 88-year-old woman. They are known to breed very fast. Scientists have shown that the oxygen is decreasing. This is the fault of blacks. They are threatening the life of the entire planet.'

Obsessed with the threat of blacks to the survival of the white race, he went on the rampage 'to show the world there were Boers on the southern tip of Africa who would fight for the maintenance of Christian Calvinism and fight communism.' In preparation for his own private massacre in the city of Pretoria, he made a pilgrimage to the Afrikaner shrine, the Voortrekker Monument. 'I prayed and asked God to do his will and not mine and, if he was not pleased, to deflect me from my path with some visible sign.' When there was no sign of God disagreeing with his intention, he went to a black squatter camp west of Johannesburg, where he shot two women, killing one of them. 'I wanted to use this as an exercise to see if I was physically capable of killing people,' he said. Seeing that he was capable, he went to prove it a week later at Strijdom Square in the centre of Pretoria. 'I wanted to make a point,' he said explaining the massacre. 'I did not want it to be seen as an idle threat of the type made by so many right-wingers who never carry them out.'

The place and time were carefully chosen. The place, J. G. Strijdom Square, was named after an apartheid ideologue who shared his surname and of whom he approved. The timing was also perfect, because it coincided with the nearby Appeal Court hearing of the Delmas Trial case, involving 19 anti-apartheid activists. He hoped he might be lucky enough to catch big anti-government people like Allan Boesak in his line of fire. His dress was also chosen with deliberation, a police camouflage uniform, 'to indicate aggression,' and a belt engraved with 'Wit Wolwe' because he thought it would win publicity for the right-wing organization.

Strydom was found guilty of eight counts of murder and 16 of attempted murder arising out of a random massacre of eight blacks in the centre of Pretoria in November 1988. He was sentenced to death. Pleading in mitigation of the sentence, he portrayed himself as a product of Christian National Education, driven to extremes by what he saw as a lack of vision on the part of an older generation. 'They [whites] seem to have given up the fight against communism. The country had nothing to offer a young man like myself.'

'I do not consider my actions as wrong, but as right. The shootings had not been murder, but an act of self-defence against blacks.' And the constant smile on his face as he murdered? 'The victims did not realize the seriousness of the situation. They smiled at me; since I am a friendly person, I would smile back at them and carry on,' he told the court hearing.

During the trial, it became evident that Strydom's father shared many of his beliefs about blacks. Asked by the prosecution whether he regarded blacks as people, Barend's father, Nick Strydom, thought carefully before answering: 'There is a good deal of debate about the issue. And it is the one I have given a good deal of thought. It is my opinion that blacks are in fact animals and not people. . . . I have read a lot of books about it. Whites are descendants of Israel, blacks are descendants of animals,' he said. Strydom's death sentence was commuted to life imprisonment in line with the Pretoria Minute agreement between the ANC and the government on 6 August 1990, granting leniency to all political prisoners.

'Animals that Look Like People'

Eugene Marais agreed to participate in an attack on a bus carrying black passengers as an act of revenge after a group of black youths in PAC t-shirts went on the rampage, killing one person and injuring eight others in attacks on whites on a Durban beachfront. Marais said he was not bothered because he saw the victims as a 'busload of animals'. 'All those people who are not Israelites have not been made by God, but by Satan. Blacks are animals of the field, animals that look like people,' he said.

Describing the shooting incident in Durban, one of the victims, Richard Zulu, said he had been returning from work on a packed bus when all of a sudden there were shots that came like lightning. 'When I stood up, I found myself losing power. People on the bus started screaming, "We are being shot by white men."' Zulu said the passengers had assumed they were being shot at by police.

'The man sitting next to me was dead. I stood up and found one of my arms was hanging from a piece of flesh.' He was rushed to hospital where his arm was amputated. He was also wounded in the left shoulder and the use of his left arm is impaired. 'I want to know how they feel about what happened. I can't even dress myself. My wife has to help me. They have destroyed my future and my ability to provide for my children,' he said. Marais and two friends who participated in the ambush were sentenced to hang for the murder of seven black passengers and for injuring 27 others.

A member of Covenant People, a sub-group of the Israelites, Marais and others believe blacks were born from the seed of Satan. They believe fervently that non-whites are animals; if questioned, they will present proof in the form of biblical texts or biological evidence. Many members of the Israelite community believe that blacks are in fact part of the animal kingdom, and that where the Bible speaks of wild animals, the reference was actually to black people. The Israelites believe whites are the true children of Israel and that Afrikaners are among the descendants of the Twelve Tribes. Those who are not Israelites are the work of Satan.

Little is known about the shadowy religious sect to which Marais belonged. According to documentary evidence presented in court, it was founded by a renegade priest who broke away from the Nederduits Gereformeerde Kerk (NGK, Dutch Reformed Church), an Afrikaner-dominated church which has been a staunch supporter of race discrimination. The shadowy group believes the word and blessing of God is directed only at the children of Israel. But, according to the Israelites, the chosen people of God are not the Jews, but white protestants. According to their doctrine, modern Jews are in no way the descendants of the tribes of Israel, but come from a line of Eurasian people, the Huns, who converted to Judaism. Marais told the Durban Supreme Court that the Israelites and Covenant People ate, drank and slept this church. They have an answer to every question, a Bible quotation to back every claim. They see blacks as a threat, and whites have to fight them.

A Soldier of the *Boerevolk*

Cornelius Lottering, a member of the right-wing white movement the Order of Death, wanted to make sure that he did not get cold feet when required to kill a political leader in a future race war. He picked on a black taxi driver because he was galled by a black driving 'white taxis' – a 'kaffir' transporting white girls. He made his victim drive to waste ground west of Johannesburg and stabbed him as 'part of my personal training in how to use a knife.' He bundled the man into the car boot, made him get out several times to show him how to work the car's alarm system, then drove to another place where he made the man kneel and practised stabbing his head.

'I decided to use my knife. I stabbed him in the back in an attempt to hit him in the kidney. He stood on his knees and I crouched in front of him. I decided to try again with my knife and stabbed him below the chin. The angle of attack was not 100 per cent right and I could not reach the brain,' Lottering told the court.

The taxi driver then ran away and Lottering shot at him with his 9 mm pistol. 'He fell, but to make sure, I walked up and pulled a trigger near his head. . . . Because blacks are my natural enemies and I am entitled, according to the Bible, to destroy my enemies, the act did not perturb me at all. . . . I do not doubt for one second that my political actions were for the survival of my nation.'

In a manifesto read out in court, Lottering raved about whites being the biological descendants of God and blacks the descendants of the devil. 'Only the purest white blood of Europe came to South Africa with Jan van Riebeeck and in years afterwards,' he said. He was also convinced that God had a special plan for South Africa and that the *Boerevolk* (Afrikaner people) were God's chosen people. 'My battle is against the heathen forces which threaten my *volk*'s existence as a Christian nation. . . . As a soldier of the *Boerevolk* I am compelled to act against elements which endanger our safety.'

Sitting on a Powder Keg?

Just how serious the right-wing threat is, is a matter of conjecture. Judging by the support that de Klerk has gained since he assumed the presidency, the majority of Afrikaners are ready to accept his proposal of power sharing with the black majority. Rightists who feel cornered by blacks encroaching on their farms and cities have repeatedly warned they will resort to violence to protect their inheritance. Not only do they boast of support within the military and the police force, but government legislation allows white South Africans to own up to 27 guns each. Whites can buy guns over the counter while blacks must go through a bureaucratic process with a 90 per cent chance of their application being turned down. In June 1990, there were three million registered firearms, nearly all in a white community of less than five million. There are millions more illegal firearms.

Police have already admitted it is impossible to control the massive quantities of explosives circulating in South Africa's mining and blasting industries. The bombs which ripped through buildings, houses and city streets were made with commercial explosives. Such explosives can be obtained easily by white counter-reformist groups. With 30,000 tons of explosives manufactured in South Africa every month, police and mine officials face an uphill battle in trying to stop thefts from manufacturers, transport companies and mines. Clandestine terror groups of right-wing fanatics would be extremely difficult to track down and could cause damage and major disruptions. If they withdraw their participation during the transition process, one in every four whites will have no say in a new constitution. If this happens, right-wing violence could become commonplace.

Boycotts and *Broedertwis*: the Weakness of the Right

One strategy that proved its effectiveness in defusing right-wing intimidation was the consumer boycott. Black community leaders successfully retaliated against right-wing vigilante patrols by boycotting white businesses. As the conservative reaction to de Klerk's reforms spread to the hinterland communities, blacks responded by with-drawing their spending power.

In the town of Welkom, for example, before hardline whites began their pro-apartheid antics, they may have paused to consider the economically devastating experience of Boksburg, where the application of rigid apartheid by the CP-controlled municipality precipitated a stinging consumer boycott of white businesses by coloured and black communities. Many shops closed and have never managed to reopen. Hardliners might also remember the disastrous effects of the same boycott in the mining town of Carletonville in 1988–9. The effectiveness of the consumer boycott was also demonstrated in the conservative town of Louis Trichardt after the incident mentioned earlier in this chapter, in which nearly 200 Sunday school children – some of them no more than four years old – were terrorized by some 40 khaki-clad white rightists, who insisted that a public park in the town was a 'whites only' preserve a few weeks after the de Klerk government abolished the Separate Amenities Act.

Internal problems within right-wing groups dampened their menacing power. Although support for conservative politics ran deep in white society, the right wing has never been able to present a united front in its campaign for Afrikaner freedom and separateness. Their major weakness is *broedertwis* (brotherly discord), a lack of cohesion and unity. Vying factions who support different goals have not been able to speak with one voice. The CP, which demands a much larger state, envisages a homeland where blacks would be admitted as 'foreign labourers', while in Boshoff's Orandia they would be forbidden any such foothold in the white state. They even differ on where the homeland should be situated. With six models of Afrikaner homelands already in existence, there was little chance that right-wing parties would form a united front to confront de Klerk. Many right-wing parties like the Boerestaat Party, led by Robert van Tonder, maintained they would not enter negotiations involving the ANC, but that they would submit representations to the government outlining their argument for restoration of the Boer republics of Transvaal, Natal and the Orange Free State.

Van Tonder compared Afrikaners with ethnic groups in the Soviet Union striving for independence from Moscow. 'There should be 15 separate states in South Africa. As Israel is to the Jews, the Transvaal, Orange Free State and Natal are to the Afrikaner. They are our territory. We have fought for them. They are our territory; we were the first to settle on them; we trekked for them; we say, give it back.'

In the meantime, however, what united the various right-wing factions was their common hatred of de Klerk and his reforms. In the eyes of the right wing, de Klerk had become one of the most hated political leaders South Africa has ever had. De Klerk appeared not to be bothered by the right-wing threat. 'The extremists exploit the atmosphere of uncertainty created by my reforms to whip up emotions. But I have the confidence also in my people that they will not be misled by the unreasonableness and hatred of this small group of extremists. The new South Africa is in the process of being born, and nobody can stop it.'

But the decisions facing de Klerk may become tougher, especially on potentially divisive issues such as power sharing and land redistribution. De Klerk has shown a willingness to keep order among restive unruly whites, as he did in Ventersdorp. But Ventersdorp remains an isolated incident rather than a model of future government conduct.

Mandela offered his advice to de Klerk on how to smother the power of the right. 'We are saying to Mr de Klerk: "Stop thinking of whites only when you are examining the problems of South Africa. Think in terms of all the people. . . . [I]f you extended the vote to every South African, you would be in a strong position and the right could never touch you."'

At the same time, Mandela reached out to reassure the white right that attempts had to be made to accommodate them, regardless of how repugnant the ANC found their beliefs and actions. Mandela says the extreme right forms part of South Africa's present and future. 'We do not want them to remain in the future South Africa as a Renamo [Mozambican rebels] force. Let us try to reach these people now and assure them that they have nothing to fear from majority rule; nothing to fear if the ANC becomes the future government of this country; nothing to fear from black people and from equality.'

But Mandela has blamed de Klerk for 'his timidity towards the entire [white] right wing'. 'He does not want to go down in history as the man who split the Afrikaner. He must give that up. If he does not take bold action and join the democratic forces he is going to put across this image of a man who has no backbone, who is chicken-hearted,' he said.

Yes or No?

Throughout 1990 and 1991, I concluded that the majority of whites had accepted the inevitability of transformative change, despite the increased right-wing backlash. However, a few days after the second anniversary of de Klerk's February 1990 landmark speech, we found ourselves hanging between the old and new South Africas. All of a sudden, another doomsday scenario had been drafted. The scenario went like this: Apartheid constitution passed. State of Emergency imposed as Nelson Mandela and F. W. de Klerk go underground to begin an armed struggle. Mandatory sanctions imposed against apartheid South Africa. Warships heads for South African harbours along Indian and Atlantic oceans as economic blockade by superpowers begins. Pro-apartheid President Andries Treurnicht says South Africa's hurriedly trained army ready to repel military intervention by superpowers. Treurnicht promises huge reward for information leading to the arrest of Mandela and de Klerk. International air links with South Africa broken.

As a non-voter in the country of my birth, I found myself on the sidelines once again as whites fought over whether to negotiate a power-sharing deal with blacks. In a whites-only referendum called by President de Klerk in March 1992, blacks were expected to play the role of passive bystanders. Since 1948, each time whites had voted they had chosen to strengthen apartheid. They blessed race classification, they supported notorious laws such as the Group Areas Act and its uprooting of blacks. They voted for detention without trial. They closed their eyes to torture and supported militarization and the destabilization of neighbouring countries. To many whites, wrong became right, democracy was called communism, fascism became freedom, colour not character defined people.

To be fair, this election promised to be startlingly different from others in the past. In order to negotiate successfully with the ANC and other groups, de Klerk first had to confront the divisions within white society to demonstrate that he had the authority to speak on behalf of the white tribes of South Africa. When the referendum was first announced, we were all reminded of the bad old days when whites determined their future by deciding on the best method to control black people. South African whites now found themselves at a political crossroads. They had to come to terms with the realities of majority rule or turn their backs on democracy. To many blacks, the referendum was irresponsible, a disguised white veto of the democratic process. But many understood it as a necessary evil we had to go through in order to lay claim to that democracy.

The question that was put before the white community was as follows: 'Do you support continuation of the Reform Process which the State President began on 2 February 1990, and which is aimed at a new Constitution through negotiations?' The choice facing South Africa's white minority was not between a return to the good old, bad old days of apartheid, or the disaster which the conservatives predicted from the reform process. The real choice was between the certainty of national catastrophe if de Klerk and his policies were rejected, and the hope of a somewhat peaceful and orderly transition to majority rule.

No doubt to some whites this change was unacceptable. As blacks advanced towards sharing the same privileges that gave whites the best jobs, the best schools, and a better standard of living, whites found themselves having to compete with blacks on many levels as never before. Many whites seemed sullen about the changes and pessimistic about the future. A survey by the Human Sciences Research Council confirmed a meagre 15 per cent believed life for them would be better in the post-apartheid South Africa.

A few days before the referendum was held, I travelled around the country to find out how white pro-apartheid conservatives and anti-apartheid liberals thought about the make-or-break referendum.

Treurnicht and his right-wing allies campaigned for a 'No' vote in the referendum, saying they wanted to perfect apartheid, not abandon it. Their mission was to reverse the tide of integration and protect South Africa's whites from the so-called tyranny of black majority rule. 'I am not a racist. There is a difference between racism and nationalism,' the Conservative Party leader Andries Treurnicht said, trying to sell his message to whites at a rally.

I consider a poor, uneducated white farmer to be one of my own. I prefer him to an educated black man who is not one of mine. I think that is the most natural thing in the world. . . . It is not a matter of blacks being inferior to whites. It is a matter of being different. And we are different. To be conscious of one's own race is not necessarily racism. I am an Afrikaner, a white South African. If that is prejudice, then I cannot help it.

One of his followers told me: 'I have blacks working for me. A black woman brought up all of my four children. But I will vote "No" because I think blacks are not ready for democracy.' For Koosie Kotze and his family, the choice was clear: 'Reforms are bound to end in chaos. De Klerk is trying to do something unnatural. He wants to sell our birthright to a black-dominated government. I agree with nothing this man has done. I do not hate blacks. If there is someone I would love to see destroyed, it is de Klerk,' he said.

Kotze and other Treurnicht followers believed a non-racial government would unquestionably result in an ANC government. They said an ANC government would lead to a civil war, economic collapse, emigration, black dictatorship, nationalization of major industries, a communist-inspired economy which could result in the redistribution of wealth and repossession of land previously owned by whites. They agreed that a CP government could also end up in a return to apartheid rule, civil war, mandatory sanctions, and the renewal of armed struggle by the ANC and others. As Kotze said,

It is better to live in such country you know will protect white privileges than a despot ANC dictatorship. I am not racist. I want to see them [blacks] live in their own areas and environment they would develop on their own. I understand that things need to change. The CP knows what to do. De Klerk is just giving away everything. The CP is right when it says blacks must work in the white areas. But they must not have political rights. Blacks must have their own homelands where they can start practising democracy. It can be done. Apartheid can be brought back the way it began – by simply passing the legislation.

On the other side, father and son Alwyn and Derrick Lubbe were going to vote 'Yes' in South Africa's referendum, but for different reasons. Alwyn, a 63-year-old civil servant, felt that a victory for de Klerk would strengthen his hand during the negotiations. His left-leaning son, Derrick, wanted to defeat pro-apartheid rightists seeking a 'No' vote.

Alwyn echoed the uncertainty that permeates the white minority, five-million strong, as it contemplates a future under black rule. 'We have to vote "Yes" to strengthen de Klerk's hand, even though I cannot say I know for sure what he will do with it.' Derrick and his wife Betsy, both members of the ANC, preferred to choose de Klerk as the lesser of two evils, rather than Treurnicht who wants to reimpose racial segregation.

'Treurnicht is not a leader as far as I'm concerned,' Derrick said. 'A "No" vote would bring the CP to power and there would be a civil war soon afterwards.' For Derrick, his father and their families, the consequences of a 'No' vote led to the abyss: de Klerk would step down and call a general election which Treurnicht would probably win. Then the ANC and other black groups would resume their armed struggle, Western governments would reimpose sanctions, skilled whites would emigrate and a race war would ensue. 'Unless we give de Klerk a chance, the door that has been opened will be closed for good and another door to Hell will be opened,' Alwyn said.

'The only way for South Africa to get anywhere is through negotiations. To stop them now would be to step back goodness knows how many years. What about the millions of blacks who have tasted a little bit of freedom since their parties were unbanned? What does the CP propose to do with them?' Derrick asked.

Alwyn, his son and their families thought the wording of the question favoured de Klerk because it was vague enough to win approval from all but the most committed racists. Though de Klerk's policies were seen by Alwyn as too vague, and by his son as 'rubbish', they were going to vote 'Yes' because they felt that we, the blacks, should not be powerless any longer. 'I am a South African like you, aren't I?' Alwyn asked me. 'I do not think it is fair for me to enjoy privileges that you cannot enjoy.'

For example, Alwyn had no problem with blacks living next door 'as long as standards are maintained' – a euphemism for cleanliness, sobriety and orderliness. But Alwyn feared de Klerk wanted a blank cheque to close a power-sharing deal that could amount to black domination. 'What the government is doing is the right thing,' Alwyn said. But, 'like many Afrikaners, I have this fear I am going to lose my Afrikaans language, culture and history.'

I spoke to many people like the Lubbes, who told me they would vote 'Yes' to convert their fears into hopes. They made it clear they would be voting to break away from constitutionalized racism, to abandon the link between skin colour and political and economic privilege. They said they would vote to end decades of ethnic and tribal politics. They would demand a future where issues concerned people, not racial differences. People like the Lubbes said they would demand a future where the state kept its hands off the media and the judicial system while protecting basic human rights. As Betsy Lubbe said, 'The referendum gives me a chance to participate in my own future. I intend to cross my own Rubicon, with trepidation but without wavering.'

From talking to the 'Noes' and 'Yeses', I felt that de Klerk had not prepared white voters adequately for the pending changes. Instead, he had left them confused, frightened, and anxious about the future. But for some like Derrick Lubbe, there could be no turning back. As he faced the prospect of the last whites-only election, he reflected on the challenge facing whites: 'I have lived all my life with feelings of insecurity, always wondering how long white domination would last, and how it would end. It is with a sense of relief that we now have a referendum where I can finally bury my fears. It would be a tragedy if the whites lacked the courage to go forward.'

On 17 March 1992 the Lubbes and two million other white voters dumped con-stitutionalized apartheid. They voted 'Yes' against 875,000 'No' votes – delivering a stunning one million majority in favour of a negotiated future with the black majority. 'The message of this referendum is that this is the new South African nation,' a jubilant de Klerk said in a victory speech from the steps of Tuynhuis, the State President's residence in Cape Town. Around him stood Democratic Party leader Zach de Beer and a crowd of well-wishers chanting 'Happy Birthday' to the President, who had just turned 56.

Today will be written up in history as one of the most fundamental turning points in the history of South Africa. Today we have closed the book on apartheid. Today is in a sense the real birthday of the real new South African nation. Today a deed was done which carries a powerful message of reconciliation, a powerful reaching out for justice.

The massive positive result sends out a powerful message to all South Africans . . . that those who have the power in terms of this present, imperfect constitution really mean it when they say they want to share power. We want it to be fair and equitable. This referendum, more than the 2nd of February 1990, has changed and will change the face of South Africa.

An astonishing feature of the referendum was the extraordinary interest it generated among the voters. Over 2.8 million of the country's 3.29 million registered white voters went to the polls, recording a massive 85 per cent turnout. In Johannesburg the percentage of white voters was 84 and the 'Yes' vote 78 per cent; in Durban the poll was 86.6 per cent and the 'Yes' vote 84.8 per cent; and in Cape Town the poll was 88.3 per cent and the 'Yes' vote 84.7 per cent of the total.

The breadth of support for de Klerk, from rural Afrikaner communities to urban English-speakers, surprised even the most sanguine party officials. Only hours before the poll, National Party organizers were predicting, at best, a 55 per cent 'Yes' majority, well below the eventual 68.7 per cent victory they received. Only in one region did whites vote 'No': the Northern Transvaal, where border farmers fought for years against ANC guerrilla infiltration, and drought and poverty had radicalized whites.

Treurnicht was a picture of defeat and despondency. Sullen, tired and resentful, he said his loss was only the beginning of the struggle for survival. 'The "Yes" vote will now pay its bill. They have voted for power sharing. They will now find out what it means to lose power and to have no power of your own to protect your own freedom.' Despite this outcome, Treurnicht and his followers still posed a danger. The 30 per cent of whites who cast their vote for the CP and its extremist allies still represented a potentially dangerous destabilizing factor. With the last constitutional opportunity to prevent political change now closed, there were fears that some of them could turn to violence. But de Klerk had been equipped with a mandate to deal with such a possibility, whereas before the referendum he did not know how many whites supported the apartheid zealots. My hope was that the results of the referendum would give black South Africans confidence, and help to end violence once and for all in the townships.

De Klerk's stunning win threw right-wing parties into disarray and it was only a matter of time before many disintegrated. The Herstigte Nasionale Party was not a political force. The AWB was more bluster than threat. Other right-wing organizations that had the Boerestaat as their main objective were too small to be a factor. This left the CP as the standard-bearer of the old Afrikaner nationalism. But it continued to haemorrhage. The inevitability of the negotiation process was getting to the right wing and many of its leaders were considering deserting Cloud-cuckoo-land in favour of the hard realities of the new situation.

The right-wing hoo-hah that gathered momentum before the March referendum, rekindling long-dormant Verwoerdian nightmares, rapidly dissipated into nothingness. The splintering and backbiting that characterized rightist politics was more evident than ever. The months following the 17 March referendum saw a growing desperation within the CP to extricate itself from its stalemate. There were hardliners who simply refused to acknowledge the realities of South Africa.

Some older members of the CP, led by Treurnicht, were content to remain locked in the past, indulging in old-fashioned apartheid. Others were inclined, without great conviction, to take the road to negotiations and fight for a smaller Afrikaner state. It seemed that it would take time for the CP to join CODESA, and that, even then, it was unlikely to get there in one piece.

The first cracks of a split widened with the expulsion of the party's stormy petrel, Koos van der Merwe. He had previously written a report which stated that the CP should take part in multi-party negotiations to determine the shape of a future constitution. He argued that at the negotiations it could present proposals for regional governments in one or some of which white voters might be a majority. He said a smaller state in which there was white predominance was an 'attainable goal'. Van der Merwe believed unity must be achieved to defeat the ANC in the forthcoming one person, one vote election. 'We need to get the highest degree of unity if we hope to defeat the ANC . . . . And I would want to work in the direction of an anti-ANC coalition,' he declared.

The second to be fired was Koos Botha, who had confessed to bombing a school associated with the ANC but suddenly became an advocate of negotiations.

The third split was the formation of the Afrikaner Volksunie (AVU or Afrikaner National Union) by five rebel parliamentarians led by Andries Beyers. The AVU said it intended building a future alliance and association between Zulus, Afrikaners and other peoples and parties who value their self-determination in a new dispensation which would make provision for joint decision-making on agreed matters. The new group was minuscule, but it had great influence. What was required, however, was not a handful of individuals, but leadership that could carry the right-wing constituencies. So early on and without an election to go by, it was difficult to judge whether the breakaway represented a significant constituency or not.

Beyers spoke out against the CP:

The trouble with the CP is that there are too many racists in the party, and there was no longer even a semblance of unity, especially because of the differences on policy. In the first place the CP refused to accept our proposal to move away from racism, and concentrate on the bargaining (through negotiation) of our rights on an ethnic basis. But the CP still wants to be a racists' organization and we differ there. In the second instance, we say we must have a realistic and fair plan for the future. We must keep our ideal of self-determination (as an eventuality) and to succeed with that we had to accept a drastically reduced fatherland. And within this fatherland, there must be no discrimination based on race, but we must be able to maintain a majority for the Afrikaner and, according to scientific research, that is possible. We want to use regionalism as a means to, in the end, our ideal of self-determination in a portion of the country. The majority of Afrikaners have accepted that the old country is gone. People are starting to accept that if we want self-determination, we will have to accept a smaller portion of the land.

Beyers and his colleagues envisage the AVU as a potentially powerful new movement towards a reconciliation of 'moderate' Afrikaners. If they succeed, all that will remain of old-style politics will be a shrinking assortment of die-hard fanatics on the far right.

The CP, Beyers's AVU and other right-wingers were floundering over the question of a *volkstaat* (Afrikaner homeland). The hard-line group led by the elderly CP leadership of Treurnicht and Ferdie Hartzenberg thought it could still assert Afrikaner hegemony over most of South Africa. There were others like the AWB which were not prepared to abandon the ideological bedrock on which the Boer republics – Transvaal, Natal and Orange Free State – were established: that there should be no equality between white and black, with citizenship rights consequently restricted to whites. Blacks living in these republics would have no votes and would be encouraged to leave. The CP's proposal was for a *volkstaat* based ·on the 39 parliamentary constituencies which the CP won in the 1989 election – most in the Transvaal, some in the Free State and a couple in the Cape. Any other region was free to apply to join the *volkstaat*. To avoid confusion, an Afrikaner should only be classified as a white Afrikaans-speaking person. The obvious drawback to this *volkstaat* was that it would not be in one piece.

Beyers and four of his colleagues came up with a different plan. They suggested that South Africa be divided into ten regions. In the north, a state with Pretoria as its capital was to be controlled by whites. In the south, an Afrikaans-speaking state would be established for white and coloured Afrikaans-speakers. The other eight states would accommodate various ethnic groups as well as a black multi-ethnic state. Beyers and his group were prepared to settle for a smaller Afrikaner state, thus sacrificing Afrikaner claims to vast tracts of land in return for recognition of the right of Afrikaners to their own fatherland. The new right acknowledged that if their demand for a separate Afrikaner territory was accepted it should be free of race discrimination. To get to their goals, they had accepted that they would have to negotiate with black nationalist organizations, primarily the ANC.

Soon after the right-wing defeat in the referendum poll, Carel Boshoff, the founder of Orania, approached CODESA's management committee to open negotiations on the principle of an Afrikaner homeland.

'We believe in negotiations and wish to further our ideas at CODESA. We want limited participation because we do not believe we have anything to say about a future constitution. We stand for secession and we believe we have a viable proposal,' Boshoff said.

The trouble with all these suggestions was that all right-wing parties refused to accept the reality that whites will no longer rule on their own. Any attempt to carve up the country to satisfy right-wing demands would be like setting off dynamite.

The CP was in danger of being sidelined while the future was being decided. It must join the negotiation process to avoid this. But Treurnicht refused to give up. Indeed, 'Dr No' may not have impressed Afrikaner yuppies or residents of affluent suburbia generally; he knew, however, how to play on the fears, resentments and hopes of rural Afrikaners and their wage-earning (and some salaried) compatriots in the towns and cities.

He regarded de Klerk as an appeaser, who in his eagerness to please the world and to gratify the ANC had turned his back on his own people. He often gave examples, pointing out that to begin with de Klerk was opposed to the idea of a transitional government. Later he was in favour of it. During the run-up to the 1989 election that brought him to power, de Klerk was opposed to majority rule; since then, Treurnicht pointed out, de Klerk had said he accepted the principle of majority rule and was prepared to serve under Mandela. He cited statistics for crimes of violence, specifically mentioning murders of elderly whites and policemen, to show that South Africa had become a much more violent society since de Klerk took over.

Mr de Klerk must take note that Afrikaner and English-speaking patriots will not allow themselves to be governed by a NP/ANC/SACP regime and that there must be a general election in 1994 in terms of the present constitution. The bottom-line policy of the party is the right to an own government, to an own territory, an own budget, control over own defence force and our own police force. The CP is irrevocably committed to the freedom of its own people in their own fatherland. The CP believes in economic interdependence and political independence, a system similar to the European Community where trade and aid are interchangeable.

It was clear that right-wing divisions would continue until the right's more sensible members either come to dominate their parties or leave them to form an alliance. These people would be the ones who realized that the country's future was going to be negotiated, and that only those taking part could affect the ultimate compact. They might not get what they wanted, but they would decide to give it a try rather than sulk on the sidelines. The CP and other pro-apartheid zealots were faced with a choice between the reality of negoatiations and the fantasy of a return to apartheid.

But is the Afrikaner state viable in South Africa, where whites constitute less than 15 per cent of the total population and Afrikaans-speaking whites less than 10 per cent?

Whites, let alone Afrikaners, do not constitute a majority in any of the nine development regions demarcated in 1980. It is clear that, even if they get their way, Afrikaners will be a minority in their own state and thus not in control of their own destiny; or they will have to deny equal rights to blacks and thus deprive their proposed state of moral justification, inviting resistance and conflict.

No one denied the threat the white right continued to pose. Indeed the belief that those who supported the CP, or even the fringe or far-right parties, would simply drift into obscurity and end up as marginalized anachronisms in a new non-racial society was unrealistic. But it was hard to see how the CP itself would not be marginalized. The reality was that even with the support of half the white population, the right wing would represent less than 10 per cent of a non-racial electorate. Without adapting or joining the negotiation process, or even forming a *volksfront* (national front) to fight for a common destiny of realizing the self-determination of the Afrikaner nation, loose ends of right-wing groups would be as irrelevant to the mainstream of political power in South Africa as those whites who continued to vote for Ian Smith in Zimbabwe. But they would remain a potential threat. 'They want to plunge this country into a racist, bloody civil war. Our task is to prevent that and ensure that elections take place,' Mandela said.

10
PREPARING TO GOVERN

> The ANC has never been a political party. It was formed as a parliament of the African people. Right from the start the ANC has been a coalition, if you will, of people of various political affiliations. Some support free enterprise, others socialism, some are conservative, others are liberals. We are united solely by our determination to oppose racial oppression. That is the only thing that unites us. There is no question of ideology as far as the odyssey of the ANC is concerned, because any question approaching ideology would split the organization from top to bottom.

> *Nelson Mandela, June 1990*

Waving the stump of his right arm in an *Amandla!* (power) salute, Albie Sachs walked to the front of the hall to claim his position as a member of the ANC's policy-making National Executive Committee (NEC) at the watershed congress in July 1991. Sachs, whose mutilation by a bomb planted in his car by agents of the South African government in Maputo in 1987 has not altered his gentle and soft-spoken character, is one of the few whites in the ANC's 91-member NEC. His life is a testimony that whites, too, have made terrible sacrifices in the struggle against apartheid. But Sachs is also a reminder to the ANC that few committed whites have joined the movement – which has admitted that since its unbanning it has failed to make major inroads into the white community, and that lack of white support is one of the organization's main shortcomings and could endanger its future strength.

At the congress, Sachs was joined on the podium by Chris Hani, who was the head of Umkhonto we Sizwe at the time. Since his return from exile, Hani had never minced words about the government. Before addressing meetings, he was known to use strong language to excite the crowd: 'We are meeting at a time when that illegitimate government is convening again its toilet parliament,' he once said. To most whites he was a hardliner and someone to be feared. For this he had gained popularity with the grassroots, which is where his power-base lay. His swashbuckling and unorthodox political style appealed to the younger breed in the ANC. Hani was a fascinating man, a controversial figure, and to some a frightening leader.

Lost in the theatre of militancy surrounding Hani was the suave and subdued diplomat of the ANC, Thabo Mbeki, head of the Department of International Affairs. While Hani was viewed as a hawk, Mbeki is a self-confessed dove. Mbeki has the right contacts in the right places in influential world capitals. His early contacts with liberal

South African captains of industry at the height of P. W. Botha's iron-fisted rule and his strong intellectual background make him a major asset.

Beside Sachs, Hani, and Mbeki there was Walter Sisulu, who was elected as Nelson Mandela's deputy. The elderly politician was a compromise candidate after delegates felt the election of either Mbeki or Hani could have been divisive and split the organization. Both in their late forties, Mbeki and Hani represented, respectively, the moderate and radical wings of the ANC. There was also Peter Mokaba, who leads a constituency which is potentially the most volatile and uncompromising part of the ANC family, the Youth League.

Some of the leaders were an enigma even to the movement. One such notable leader was Harry Gwala, a committed Stalinist and fiery hard-line Marxist who applauded the Soviet coup attempt that toppled Gorbachev in 1991. Unlike other leaders who talked peace and tried to educate their supporters about the nitty-gritties of constitutional negotiations, Gwala preached war, offered no compromise, and encouraged the seizure of power by the masses. Such leaders caused one of the biggest dilemmas for the ANC, for as its agreement with the government on the modalities of constitutional change grew closer, so the gap between it and leaders like Gwala widened.

It was Cyril Ramaphosa who stole the show. His election as secretary-general was a recognition that trade unions have played a major role in the struggle against apartheid. It also epitomized the need for a strong, businesslike negotiation team that would draw on his skills as the chief negotiator of the National Union of Mineworkers. As evidence of his popularity, he polled 1,156 of 2,000 votes cast. In his late thirties at that time, Ramaphosa represented the new generation of ANC leaders moving up to replace the older generation who had spent years in jail or in exile. His election put him in the running for the ANC leadership after Mandela. Until then, the obvious contenders had been Mbeki and Hani.

Also part of the new wave were many young men and women who, like Ramaphosa, had been blooded in the struggle against apartheid during the presidency of P. W. Botha. They were a new generation of activist leaders such as Popo Molefe, Terror Lekota, Moses Mayekiso, Sydney Mufamadi and others, who resisted apartheid from within while the prominent leaders of the 1960s were in prison or exile. Some continued to occupy leadership positions in the trade union movement. Some were influential within the Communist Party, while others represented the dynamism of civic organizations. They met their baptism of fire during the mass anti-apartheid struggles of the 1980s and their visible presence within the NEC greatly strengthened the ANC's ability to mobilize on the streets.

After the election roll call had been completed, the podium was full of people as diverse as the ANC hoped to attract in a future election, to form what Mandela calls a 'parliament of the people'. On the stage were a priest, a Zulu prince, women's leaders, lawyers, guerrillas, workers, teachers, poets, militarists, doves, hawks and others. There were seven whites, seven Indians and three coloureds, who reflected a 34 per cent non-African membership in the ANC's policy-making body. In addition, all of South Africa's major black tribes were represented, including a member of the Zulu royal family. The composition of the new NEC gave substance to the ANC's commitment to non-racialism, and the process of selecting executive members by secret ballot was highly praised as a model for future elections. 'We established for all of our members, from all over the country, that it is through the vote, tolerance and free speech that our problems will be solved,' Sachs said. Mandela echoed him: 'There are not many movements or organizations which can claim to measure up to these democratic standards. The very process that brings us together is an outstanding example of participatory democracy which augurs well for the future.'

This newly inducted leadership faced the huge task of preparing the ANC to govern. They had to confront demands from all corners. They would have to satisfy diverse critics from both the black and white communities. For the ANC to govern efficiently in the future, whites wanted it to focus on a particular set of issues: its relationship with the SACP; the role of free enterprise in a future South Africa; Congress involvement in political violence and the intolerance of some of its supporters; and the lifting of sanctions and other curbs the organization wanted the international community to maintain until a new government was established.

Blacks indicated that they would be happy if the ANC could put its house in order after three decades in exile and legitimize its claim to represent their interests and grievances. These were people who were sympathetic to the inevitable problems which faced an organization that had been exiled for 30 years, had its leaders imprisoned for decades, had struggled to maintain its disparate membership despite harsh repression and violence, and was now making the adjustment to a complex and rapidly changing political environment.

Alfred Nzo, who had served as the ANC's secretary-general for many years in exile, had the difficult task of assessing the organization's struggle to adapt to new demands as an above-ground movement and government-in-waiting. Nzo, himself a target of rebuke for organizational inefficiency, produced a fairly bracing assessment of the organization. In a frank, soul-searching and highly critical report on the ANC's performance one year after it had been unbanned, he said the movement was being blamed for the spiralling violence in the country and he cited the alliance with the Communist Party as one of the main reasons for the ANC's poor support amongst whites, coloureds and Indians. He also added that the organization was riven with factionalism, cliquism and ignorance, which hindered its effectiveness.

His report revealed concern within the organization about its inability to transform popular support into signed-up members. A constant refrain throughout the report was the need to adhere to the principles of democracy and accountability. Nzo said there was a sense of complacency, as though the organization's ascent to power was assured, whereas in fact it had been outsmarted on many issues by de Klerk's National Party, which had 'succeeded in creating an image of being winners.' He warned that complacency about the ANC's undisputed position as the leading anti-apartheid force could jeopardize its chances of coming to power.

> There is little doubt as to the capacity of the movement to command a degree of massive support. But it would be blatantly naïve of us to become complacent and act as if under no circumstances whatsoever can the ANC be threatened or even be removed from the leadership pedestal it now occupies.

The report said the ANC should not only increase its numerical strength, but raise its political profile so that people would feel it was addressing their needs and presenting viable alternatives to the present order.

> The ANC lacks enterprise, creativity and initiative to maximize support for its policies on major issues, even though these policies could be trusted. We appear very happy to remain pigeon-holed within the confines of populist rhetoric and clichés.

Slamming the ANC for a lack of self-criticism, Nzo urged the movement to 'objectively and realistically prepare our forces for the sharp and complex battles confronting us.' In particular, Nzo criticized the lack of imagination in the ANC's mass action campaigns. He said the organization tended to do the same old things over and over again until people became bored and attendance at mass rallies and marches sharply declined. 'On the one hand the quality of work done beforehand is poor. On the other hand the same forms of activity are repeated for the same demands. There seems to be little creativity or variety on campaigns,' Nzo said.

Mapping the Maze: From Liberation Movement to Political Party

At the time of the report, the movement was still divided on crucial aspects of its strategy and tactics. Hardliners clashed with pragmatists. The movement found itself wavering between its past as a revolutionary liberation movement and its future as a more conventional ruling political party. The unbanning did nothing to forge the long-awaited unity between various factions within the movement. Instead it created new divides. As apartheid eased, it was clear to most of us that the movement had split into moderates or pragmatists versus radicals or hardliners. Furthermore, it was divided into three camps: former exiles, an old guard who had spent decades in South African jails, and young activists who had borne the brunt of apartheid repression in the 1980s.

The first year after its unbanning was excruciatingly difficult for the ANC. Long-time activists, having campaigned over decades for the ANC, admitted it was a long way from being a disciplined, accountable, excellent organization. Tokyo Sexwale, head of the PWV, the ANC's biggest region, said bad administration was threatening to make the ANC ineffective and inefficient. He said officials often failed to report back on time or at all. Meetings were poorly attended and long-winded people bored audiences. The problem, Sexwale said, was that the ANC was still grappling with the change from the 'exciting politics of pure activism to new challenges of legality. We must recognize that there is a change, and change our methods.'

To many people it appeared that the ANC had been unprepared for the realities of open politics when its leadership arrived back in South Africa after decades in exile. Most ANC leaders admitted to me privately that the movement had not been able to cope satisfactorily with the politics of negotiation rather than the politics of protest. Months after arriving back in South Africa after years in exile, they were still clinging to liberation movement status, closely identified with the needs of the rank and file. The honeymoon of exile politics and internal militancy was soon over. The movement was struggling against township violence, lack of funds and its own poor attempts to re-establish itself as a legal party after 30 years in the political wilderness. Having once believed that a political transition would be brought about by the armed struggle it had waged for three decades, the ANC now found itself abruptly shifting its tactics and organizational structure.

To begin with, the movement was divided on many issues. Whether or not to lift international sanctions, for example, generated a heated debate, prompting senior members of the organization to plead for 'a more nuanced' approach towards sanctions. This view was roundly rejected by the vast majority of hardliners, who fought for the maintenance of sanctions even as many countries abandoned them. Another hotly debated issue as the ANC mapped its way towards governing South Africa was its decision to suspend the armed struggle in line with compromises reached during preliminary talks to remove the obstacles to negotiations. The suspension came under heavy fire from hardliners, most of them former members of the movement's military wing, who argued that the leadership had unilaterally abandoned its strongest weapon without gaining comparable concessions from the government. To appease hardliners, the ANC promised not to budge on the continued recruitment of cadres and to continue its strategy of mass demonstrations to press political demands. The movement also threatened to resume the armed struggle if negotiations failed.

Raymond Suttner, head of the ANC's Department of Political Education, admitted the suspension of the armed struggle had been difficult to handle. The wave of political violence compounded fears among rank-and-file ANC supporters that the leadership had made a grave error, leaving the organization defenceless by effectively immobilizing its military wing.

The decision to suspend armed action has been difficult for many of our supporters to accept. Radical critics have spoken of betrayal and the ANC stands accused of making unilateral concessions without corresponding concessions on the part of the apartheid regime. The ANC's main strength is political. . . . The armed struggle had been conceived as a political weapon in a situation where open, legal political action was virtually impossible. The reopening of the legal terrain has meant that the possibilities and need for action in this area have become much greater than before. If a compromise is necessary . . . we compromise. The political terrain is where we are strong. While we have engaged the regime militarily, this is not our most powerful area.

In other words, the ANC had to keep on talking. But this did not mean it would continue with this process no matter what was done to its members and to South Africans as a whole. The leadership strategy was to pursue the same goals it pursued through armed struggle – the transfer of power to the people and the fundamental transformation of South Africa – through negotiations. But this approach never gained wide acceptance among its militant supporters. In their view, the ANC had conceded a lot more than de Klerk in the pre-negotiation process.

Mandela worked hard to maintain a balance between moderates and radicals. He displayed strong leadership when tackling criticisms by hardliners while at the same time underscoring his views.

We welcome the frank criticism. We promise to look into all these criticisms honestly and objectively and there are certain issues where we will have to make radical adjustments. But our organization has in the past dealt with a variety of weaknesses and mistakes on the part of our membership as well as factions and cliques, men and women who used the platforms of the organization for unprincipled discussions, who played to the gallery, whose aim is to prove how revolutionary they are – who have no idea whatsoever of working in a mass movement, who are totally incapable of putting forward constructive ideas and who are quick to pull down what others have built.

That kind of criticism could only be made by those who do not understand the nature of negotiations and the practical problems that face us on the ground. There would have been no negotiations today – no future prospect for negotiations – if there were no confidential meetings between members of the ANC and the government. Confidential discussions and not secret meetings we propose to continue having with the government. We are not prepared to neglect our duties as the leadership because of views which, although we respect those who uttered them, are totally unreasonable.

The other problem the ANC faced was that, although it was now free to engage in political activity, the machinery of campaigning was still in the apartheid government's hands. Through the South African Broadcasting Corporation and government-leaning newspapers, the government was able to use almost all official channels of communication in the country to get its message across. The ANC found itself having to shout from the outside, and having to be on the offensive all the time. Many practical problems rapidly emerged. The government, playing the dual role of negotiator and referee, was able to dictate change at its own pace while seeming to outmanoeuvre the ANC. The ANC thus found itself having to play by the government's rules while at the same time addressing its constituency and its friends abroad. Hampered by the lack of money and effective organizational structures, the ANC had to follow while de Klerk led, dictating the timetable and procedure for the release of political prisoners and the return of exiles, for example. With the ANC appearing to have very little say in these matters, it came increasingly under pressure from its supporters, who regarded themselves as political pawns.

Another problem was that after its unbanning the ANC was slow to utilize the abundant leadership and intellectual talent at its disposal. Senior leadership was confined to former exiles and prisoners, most of whom were old and infirm. Experienced and capable leaders of the UDF and COSATU were at first not absorbed into the leadership structures, prompting rumours of a cabal. Neither did the organization make full use of black and white liberal academics and experienced researchers who had remained in South Africa while the ANC was in exile. This deprived the ANC of valuable energy and expertise in building a more effective organization. Even leaders from its own structures complained that the ANC leadership was autocratic and incompetent. 'I had hoped that when the ANC was unbanned, there would be a democratic process of rebuilding it. Instead the leaders have turned into autocrats,' Archie Gumede, former co-president of the UDF, told me. On the other hand, because of its diverse membership, the ANC constantly had to balance various constituencies, ideological differences and generation gaps. It was impossible not to be amused by conflicting signals coming out of the movement on particular issues, such as when Mandela said there was no alternative to negotiations while his wife was declaring that 'we might have to shoot our way to freedom.'

The failure to recruit a million members within two years was seen as a huge embarrassment given its claim to being the major black opposition group. Many of its own supporters found it hard not to rage against the organization and, in particular, its leadership. Even Mandela had come crashing down to earth – no longer a redeemer in the eyes of many, but a flawed, essentially human politician. Despite the criticisms, Mandela made some progress in broadening the anti-apartheid front. He persuaded four of the ten tribal homeland leaders to side with the ANC during negotiations. But there were important segments of the coloured and Indian populations which did not pledge allegiance to Mandela, preferring to side with de Klerk instead. This was a blow to the ANC, which had at one time enjoyed the sympathy of the majority of the 306 coloured and Indian members of parliament.

Ambiguous economic and political positions further drove the movement into a corner as South Africans and the international community demanded clarity on issues such as nationalization. Some ANC decisions had sent contradictory messages about how it would run a post-apartheid economy. The movement, which called for international trade sanctions against South Africa, asked German car maker BMW to supply it with 16 luxury vehicles free of charge. The request was denied. Other companies responded in a similar fashion to the ANC's request for funds for the repatriation of over 20,000 exiles. They urged the movement to tone down its rhetoric on nationalization and abandon its leftist economic policies. Some businessmen said there could be sympathy for funding the return of exiles and providing jobs for qualified people, but not for funding the ANC's infrastructure, indicating that the preparedness of business to fund the organization depended on whether it was viewed as a partner in a future based on broad free enterprise policies.

Most of the organization's shortcomings and weaknesses in handling economic issues could be found in its own statements and publications. Apart from its changing position on nationalization, the ANC came under harsh criticism for threatening to renege on loan commitments made by the de Klerk administration. The issue caused a storm, followed by denials that this would ever be future ANC policy. After a flurry of contradictory statements by various officials, the ANC officially said it reserved the right to evaluate loans given to 'the apartheid government'. The threat was indeed ill-considered because it undermined confidence in the ANC as a future government at a time when South Africa was desperately seeking a path to peaceful change and political stability. Furthermore, it created doubts in the minds of potential foreign investors about the security of their investments in the country should the ANC come to power.

The ANC also stood accused of detaining and torturing dissidents within its ranks in prison camps during its days in exile. Most of the dissidents, many of whom have returned to South Africa, have left the ANC. They speak of their 'comrades now lying in shallow graves in Africa' and have demanded an impartial investigation into their treatment by the ANC's security establishment. The ANC admitted that some of the charges of torture and executions were true and appointed a commission to investigate the allegations. The commission found that some security men had treated their detainees abominably, subjecting them to inhuman conditions and torture to extract confessions. The commission's report spelt out in horrifying detail how the movement's security department became a law unto itself. Noting that the abuses violated the high moral standards which the ANC had set for itself, Mandela declared that 'as a leadership, we accept ultimate responsibility for not adequately monitoring and therefore eradicating such abuses.' But Mandela's prolonged delay in naming those who were involved left a stigma on the organization which could be used by its opponents to discredit the ANC in the run-up to elections.

Thus, instead of emerging as a 'well-oiled and efficient' machine ready to assume the reins of political power, the ANC was a halting, fumbling, disjointed movement of varied peoples and attitudes, battling to maintain composure during its re-emergence as both liberation movement and political party. Mandela admitted that

> the ANC machinery is not as well-oiled and efficient as it should be. Corrective measures are being taken. . . . We have been engaging in discussions with the government and trying to organize campaigns of mass action, trying to merge different styles of leadership and methods and incorporating our various components into a united force. It would be foolish to suggest that we have managed this process. Indeed it would have been a miracle if we did.

With all these problems haunting the ANC, the de Klerk government found it embarrassingly easy to remain ahead of the ANC on tactical issues. The ANC had no leverage except extra-parliamentary pressures such as mass action, boycotts, and ultimatums. Sometimes, ANC opponents such as the PAC and AZAPO opposed these extra-parliamentary measures, leaving the movement to go it alone.

By far the strongest obstacle to the ANC's growth and re-establishment was the spread of township political violence. It hampered the movement's ability to prepare its membership for the negotiation process. It clouded all of the ANC's work, becoming the primary topic of all discussions. Political violence became the central issue in conferences, meetings and other gatherings. Working groups were forced to consider the impact of the killings on future ANC policies. As Cyril Ramaphosa told me, 'We found ourselves doing nothing else but going from place to place visiting victims of violence. When not visiting victims of the carnage, we were in boardrooms discussing how to end it.' In some ways, this was not surprising. The ANC leadership entered the 'talks about talks' at Groote Schuur and Pretoria at a time when most of their supporters had a very weak grasp of their implications for the movement's strategy. To compound this, the ANC grassroots watched in despair as their leaders suspended the armed struggle in exchange for very little. Thus, when the violence erupted, the movement did not seem to have the means to stop it, nor the arms to defend its people.

The failure of Nelson Mandela to defuse or stop the internecine strife in Natal disappointed many. His movement was also accused of being one of the sources of township political violence. There was widespread criticism of the ANC's initial reluctance to meet Chief Buthelezi in a bid to stem the violence, and of the organization's call for boycotts and stay-aways to press for speedy reforms. Mandela's task of preaching peace in the townships was made even more difficult by leaders within his movement who scorned such initiatives. People like Harry Gwala believed that the non-violence Mandela, Mbeki and others preached was misguided. Gwala had little time for peace accords or peace forums. He believed in the law of Moses – an eye for an eye and a tooth for a tooth.

> At times of crisis opinions differ sharply. Some people fear an insurrectionist and they deal in academic discussions of the lives of the people who are suffering. I am a black person. I enjoy no privilege and struggling is not an option, but something I have to do to survive.

For Gwala, peace accords and forums only served to appease people's consciences. 'How many people have been killed since the Mandela–Buthelezi celebrated bearhugs – thousands! If people think the struggle will be won through negotiations and peace accords alone, they are naïve.'

As the violence spread, more and more ANC regional members descended into Natal, to learn how Gwala and his men repelled attacks. This was hardly surprising to Gwala, who maintained that if people were attacked, they had no alternative but to hit back to impose peace. In his view, hitting back served as a deterrent.

> Make no mistake, we kill Inkatha warlords. Why be apologetic about it, when they come to attack us, we offer them no Bibles. We believe in a just war. The difference between us and Inkatha is that we do not kill women and children. We hit hard on those who target us.

The war, as Gwala saw it, was not between the ANC and Inkatha, not between the government and the ANC, but between those who wanted to preserve apartheid (and that included Inkatha) and those who wanted to enter a twentieth-century democracy. 'Until there is democracy,' he said, 'there will be no peace, because until then the security forces who are Inkatha's masters will persist with their agenda of engineering violence.'

Contrary to what Gwala maintains, ANC supporters were not always innocent victims of the aggression of others. Many within their ranks have not been models of political tolerance. This deterred uncommitted supporters from joining the ANC, for fear of being killed. The ANC lost further prestige when it was seen in cosy meetings with government officials, including police officers, while ANC supporters viewed the police as siding with their opponents. In this atmosphere of fear, Inkatha proved tough competition for the effective loyalty of the black majority. It stood to gain where the ANC lost.

As violence persisted, ANC support continued to decline, raising the possibility that the ANC could even fail to gain a majority in post-apartheid elections. Since violence prevented it from organizing as a political party, it had little choice but to persist with the rhetoric and tactics of the liberation struggle. Pressured by its grassroots supporters, the ANC formed self-defence units it said would be used to repel Inkatha, police and vigilante attacks. In addition to self-defence units, the movement launched pro-democracy protests, strikes, marches, boycotts and other forms of non-violent defiance. 'Until people are able to organize effective disciplined structures to protect their neighbourhoods, communities and housing, we have got no way of adequately halting this onslaught of violence,' said Ronnie Kasrils, one of the ANC's militant leaders. This was by way of acknowledging the desperate pleas of their grassroots members. 'If we do not defend our members while we are talking, there will be no one left to enjoy the democracy we are building,' said ANC leader Sydney Mufamadi. Mandela called on his supporters to ignore warnings that such units were a recipe for civil war.

Township residents believed defence units were vital for the ANC's survival because the police and the government were waging a war against the ANC in collaboration with armed bands linked to Chief Buthelezi's Inkatha. 'The motive is to weaken the ANC and inflate the strength of Buthelezi and Inkatha. The state wants to force the ANC into agreements that are beneficial to the state. We have been too slow to get these defence units going. It left us a bit naked and off balance. The ANC's constituency had begun to question it as not being capable of protecting its people,' Mandela said.

Although defence units saved numerous lives, they sometimes lacked community control. There was a revival of people's courts, often labelled kangaroo courts, where people were sentenced to death by necklacing – an atrocity in which a petrol-soaked tyre was placed around the victim's neck. Abundant evidence existed to show that members of the units committed crimes ranging from murder to rape, armed robbery and fraud. Moreover, weapons obtained for community defence were used to settle political differences within ANC ranks.

In a frank exchange, Chris Hani admitted that some defence units were causing problems within communities they were expected to serve and protect. 'Members of these units are seen to be ANC bully-boys. The ANC will lose membership if it does not address this problem. Community and political organizations must be seen to be punishing people who act contrary to the objectives of the democratic movement.' Mandela concurred and proposed the suspension or expulsion of ANC members who behaved unacceptably under the guise of providing defence.

Comrades and *Tsotsis*: The ANC and the Militant Youth

During my days as a young man, the perception among my peers was that our parents had failed to challenge the system of apartheid, either by force or through other means. A year after the ANC had been unbanned, many of my friends, who had joined the movement as students during the Soweto uprisings, became impatient even with Mandela. The ANC realized that having such a young and volatile constituency was fraught with problems. Raised on the romance and rhetoric of the armed struggle, many South African youths were increasingly impatient with those who advocated negotiations and non-violence as the best strategy for dismantling apartheid. 'It is not easy for us to sit and negotiate. Many of the youngsters are not really interested in negotiations. They are very angry about the suffering they have gone through under apartheid,' veteran ANC activist Walter Sisulu admitted. If the ANC's negotiations do not produce dramatic results, these youths, often called 'comrades' in the townships, could lead the country into a new cycle of violence.

Despite militant messages from the grassroots, the ANC's old guard led by Tambo and Mandela stayed firmly in control throughout this uncertain period. But the old men of the movement knew that they must beware the 'Young Lions', who could successfully flex their muscles in future. For example, it was clear that if constitutional negotiations with de Klerk on the transition to non-racial democracy did not yield fruit, the Mandela generation would get its marching orders from the rank and file, especially the Young Lions. South Africa has a young population typical of Africa and the rest of the Third World. In 1990, 60 per cent of South Africa's 28 million blacks were under the age of 24.

Leading songs and litanies of defiance, stabbing the air with fists in the black power salute, *toyi-toyiing* (dancing aggressively) in the streets, chanting in unison the names of their political leaders and emboldened by youthful idealism, South Africa's black youth are a ready-made army. They are the country's wild card in the poker game of apartheid reform, a youthful vanguard, prepared to fight and die for the freedom that escaped their grandparents and their great-grandparents. In the dark days of apartheid, they were at the forefront of the struggle, calling and enforcing work strikes or demanding the resignations of municipal councillors and black policemen, regarded as collaborators of apartheid. They called and enforced consumer boycotts against white-owned shops and led defiance campaigns against apartheid structures. Most of the people killed in township uprisings were between 11 and 24 years of age. Most people detained without trial or tried for anti-apartheid activities came from this generation. I have watched them spearhead revolts in townships across the country. In one township I visited in the Orange Free State, they urged and then helped all the homeless to occupy unused municipal land and create their own town of corrugated iron and mud. A mushrooming squatter community soon emerged. They have led and will continue to lead mass action campaigns. They are a major support of the township civic associations, street committees and many anti-apartheid structures.

Even after de Klerk unbanned the ANC and promised to dismantle apartheid entirely, hundreds of youths still left the country for military training with the still-exiled Umkhonto we Sizwe. Many have described them as the 'lost generation'. But they are very much with us, rebellious and often ill-disciplined. They are a generation that does not realize it is ill-prepared for the job market or for further education. For example, the average pass rate for white matriculants (university entrance examination) was more than 90 per cent, for Indians it was 85–90 per cent, and for coloureds 70–75 per cent. The average among Africans is less than 20 per cent. Although the ANC has denied that it ever championed the slogan 'liberation before education', its adoption took a terrible toll on young lives, impeding their future progress and employment prospects.

Criminologists say that disillusionment among the country's black youth has turned into hatred, with lack of respect for people and property. They also blame deteriorating urban living standards, economic depression, and the impact of the apartheid years on township life. Raised on inferior education in a township environment where over-crowding and violence form part of everyday life, the highly politicized youth are a source of both great strength and great weakness to the ANC. Those who remain in the classroom often wield so much power that fearful teachers and headmasters follow their instructions. They have forced them to change the names of the schools, often renamed after black nationalist leaders such as Nelson Mandela.

Some of the youths are over-zealous; often they use intimidation to get others to follow. Mandela tried to explain the roots of this problem:

> The banning of our movement in the 1960s, the banning of subsequent student movements removed a moderating influence. If the government allowed us to have the ideal conditions whereby we can talk to our youth, persuade them on the question of discipline both in regard to school and in regard to their general behaviour, I have no doubt they would have accepted that.
>
> Our whole system of education is not under our control. It was the responsibility of the government to create the conditions whereby we can make an appeal to the youth to discipline themselves, go back to school and concentrate on their studies.

Lacking control and discipline, these youths could pose a serious threat to the stability of a future non-racial democracy led by the ANC or any other government. Because of years of school boycotts which resulted in many dropping out, they are the group that will suffer unemployment, a fact that will increase their militancy. Given their already high expectations, it is going to be very difficult for the new government to meet their aspirations for jobs and housing. On the other hand, they form the bulk of the people attending political rallies and meetings, and they would probably form the bulk of the voters for a non-racial parliament.

Some of these militant youths are simply thugs whose actions have embarrassed anti-apartheid organizations. The *comtsotsis* ('comrade ruffians'), as they are called in town-ship slang, formed gangs which contributed to the rise of violence in the townships, posing a serious problem for the ANC. They terrorized the townships in the name of anti-apartheid groups or falsely claimed that their actions were being authorized by anti-apartheid forces, although most were not affiliated to the ANC or to other political organizations. They were and are still part of South Africa's underclass. In responding to the ANC's call to make South Africa ungovernable, they resorted to crimes such as looting shops belonging to suspected government agents or suspected spies, robbery and murder. They burned people, they forced people to eat their own ears. They raped girls, stopped people from reporting complaints to the police, operated people's courts, forced shebeen owners to give them free liquor, forced shop owners to give them free food, impounded people's cars and collected protection fees from households.

The *comtsotsis* found a vacant space for the expression of their gang culture in the anti-apartheid struggle, which further disorganized the ANC. In effect, they became the shock troops of the struggle. At the height of the 1984–6 uprisings, civic and union leaders capable of imposing discipline were in detention, and the *comtsotsis* had the townships to themselves. Even after the ANC was unbanned, and its leaders released from detention or from long jail terms, the *comtsotsis* resisted discipline and hijacked the anti-apartheid struggle for their own ends. There was an inherent contradiction between the discipline that Mandela appealed for and required for the political struggle and *comtsotsi* unruly behaviour. Instead of mobilizing new members and consolidating its ranks, the ANC has been diverted into putting out the fires of sectarian strife and gang warfare. Regional leaders, already overworked and stretched to the limit, were forced to throw the bulk of their time and energy into quelling internecine strife.

Comrades and Allies: The ANC and the SACP

Adding to the trials and tribulations of the ANC, many South Africans, especially the black middle class and most whites, saw the organization's relationship with the South African Communist Party as an albatross around its neck. The ANC has tried and failed to convince white mainstream South Africans that it is not a communist organi-zation, although communists serve in the ANC's top policy-making bodies. Leadership is shared and dual membership of the party and the congress is encouraged. The conference dismissed Alfred Nzo's warning that the ANC's relationship with the Communist Party was damaging its image and making it difficult for the movement to make inroads in the white, Indian and coloured communities. The white media disparagingly referred to the ANC–SACP alliance as horse and rider – the rider being the SACP.

Many South African and other potential donors have questioned the ANC's peculiar relationship with the SACP. Within the movement, some members are concerned about the negative effect of the SACP on the movement's ability to raise funds. In the past the SACP's strong relations with the Soviet Union and Eastern Bloc countries was a guarantee of a steady cash flow. But with the collapse of the Soviet Union this source has virtually dried up. In the past some countries were reluctant to give the ANC financial help because of the SACP presence within its ranks; they continue to be tight-fisted for the same reason today.

The ANC's alliance with communists made it difficult for it to recruit among whites, who have been brought up to fear and loathe communism. Polls demonstrate that while the ANC still commands over 60 per cent of the potential urban African vote – with an additional 12 per cent who would probably vote for the ANC if it came to the crunch – the organization has failed to gain substantial support from other population groups. Polls record no significant white support for the ANC, a situation ascribed to the visibility of the SACP within the ANC's ranks.

The election of several staunch communists to the ANC's top policy-making body has raised concern about the implications for future ANC policy choices and the future of South Africa should the ANC come to power. But this does not worry the ANC. 'The continuation of the alliance might well present a problem,' said the ANC's director of publicity and information, Pallo Jordan. 'But do not forget that to 75 per cent of the population, it is not a problem at all. We are not going to cut our cloth to suit the political tastes of others; we are not going to cut loose an old and reliable friend for the sake of new friendships – which are not even secure,' Jordan said. He argued that the government and its allies would like to see the ANC as a middle-class organization. 'But we have a powerful working-class support base and we will not lose sight of the fact. Alliances arise out of perceived commonalities of interests. But they exist among groups with independent objectives. When the commonalities diminish, then the parties will part company,' he said.

Mandela has referred to the matter aggressively, calling the SACP a 'firm and dependable ally in the common struggle . . . a separate organ that does not seek to dominate the ANC.' But the ANC leader is flexible as far as the alliance is concerned:

> There is no doubt in my mind that most of the concern is quite genuine because people believe in free enterprise, and Marxist economic models have not been able to ensure free enterprise. We are saying that people should be able to accept not only the democratic process, but the democratic result. . . . We are also guided by our own experience. In the mid-1940s, people like myself moved a resolution in an ANC conference to expel communists. We were attacked and humiliated by people like Dr Xuma and Professor Mathews – anti-communists who said: 'The ANC is the parliament of the African people: do not come here and seek to change our traditions.' And the West itself has not hesitated to form a common alliance with the Soviet Union when they have a common objective.

While defending his communist allies, Mandela has made it clear that the ANC does not share the vision of the SACP. 'The SACP has declared that their cooperation with us is only up to the point of the overthrow of the apartheid state. After that they take their own line, which we will not follow. We do not follow socialism. We have got our own programme,' he said. Chris Hani, who was elected leader of the SACP shortly before he was assassinated, tried to downplay the alliance, saying in effect that nobody really minded whether they were voting for a communist or not. Noted communist Mac Maharaj said that when he was acting on ANC causes he acted solely as a member of the ANC and ignored his SACP connection. Even Joe Slovo has tried to clarify the confusion about NEC members who appear to wear two hats simultaneously: 'I believe the SACP has a role to play within the ANC as it exists at present in shaping its policies and actions. But this does not mean that I will get up at ANC meetings and say, "No, the SACP does not agree with that." I was elected to the NEC because of my contributions to the ANC struggle, and that is how I operate on the NEC.'

Despite their close alliance, it is important to understand how the two organizations differ. In its vision of a future post-apartheid South Africa, the SACP has defined a two-stage programme of liberation. For the first phase, the national liberation struggle, it has adopted economic and other policies closely identifiable with those of the ANC. Particularly significant here is the adoption of a mixed economic programme with limited nationalization and a multi-class alliance. It is only in the second phase, that which succeeds the transfer of power, that the SACP would pursue its own specific and socialist goals. Slovo, the former SACP general secretary and now its chairman, emphasizes that the SACP would not be pursuing the Stalinist objectives its opponents impute to it. 'In the wake of the lessons of Eastern Europe, we have moved away from our previous approach. We believe in multi-party democracy. We do not believe any more that we are the vanguard of the working class,' he said.

On economic issues, the SACP view is somewhat murkier, neither in favour of adopting the free market nor wholeheartedly behind central planning. 'We accept as a party the need for injections of capital, both domestic and foreign. We understand that we need to provide security and confidence to potential investors and the SACP would guarantee these things,' Slovo said. Ultimately, though, the SACP believes that a new brand of socialism will triumph in South Africa.

I have complete confidence that ultimately South Africa will arrive at a socialist system. Existing socialism in Eastern Europe failed because it was separated from democracy. We believe that democratic socialism is the only rational future for human kind. And we will continue to propagate it and to work for conditions in which it can be realized in a future South Africa.

In an attempt to pre-empt further criticism of its relationship with the SACP, the ANC has reverted to describing itself as a broadly based liberation movement 'committed to the transfer of power to the people as a whole.' But there are still those who believe that unless it succeeds in reaching out to whites, the National Party is likely to emerge as the most multiracial party in South Africa with a coloured, African and Indian membership which outnumbers its white supporters. There are many who are inclined to support the ANC, but they want to be clear that by supporting the ANC, they are not also endorsing the policies and practices of the SACP. Even before parties could publish their election manifestos, potential voters were already claiming the right to know for whom they would be voting, and what policies they could expect.

Comrade Nomzamo: The Fall of Winnie Mandela

Finally, on a more personal front, the ANC has had to watch the career of its president's wife come crashing down since she was convicted of kidnapping and assault in 1990. The alarming disclosure that she was involved in beatings inflicted on young activists, one of whom was found dead, provided ready ammunition for the detractors and enemies of the ANC. A month before the actual trial began, the ANC criticized it for being a political trial that was a continuation of 30 years of harassment of Mrs Mandela and a conspiracy by 'elements opposed to the peace process'. Alfred Nzo, then secretary-general of the ANC, said the trial was a violation of the spirit of agreements negotiated between the government and the ANC. He called for the suspension of the trial, and lashed out at 'trial by media'.

Despite demands that the trial be divorced from the movement, the ANC allowed large unruly demonstrations, some by its official organs, to take place outside the court. Then one of the key prosecution witnesses was kidnapped and smuggled out of the country by ANC sympathizers, causing other witnesses to refuse to testify in fear of their lives. To some, the ANC failed to put its weight clearly and publicly behind the due process of law as the appropriate channel for the pursuit of justice. As a result its image was tarnished.

The temporary refusal of witnesses to testify, and the disappearance of others, showed that law and order had failed under the pressure of the ANC, and many suspected it could fail again should the ANC become the first majority government. But the trial also subjected de Klerk's motives to scrutiny, after it emerged that the state failed to protect key witnesses in custody, lost track of the four missing defendants and waited 21 months before charging Mrs Mandela.

Mandela, who loyally defended his wife against all criticism, believed she was a victim of persecution for her long fight against white domination. It was true to say that Mrs Mandela had been shaped largely by the cruelties of apartheid, including courageously borne spells in detention. The trial came at a time when Mandela was trying to force concessions out of the government, which seemed increasingly confident of retaining power in coalition with other ANC opponents.

The way the ANC handled the trial damaged its reputation. The first blow was when she failed to win the leadership of the ANC's Women's League. As Mrs Mandela pondered her appeal, universities, cities and other bodies across the world also pondered how to dissociate themselves from her. Some said they would rename buildings or other structures they had used to honour her in the past.

The court found that Mrs Mandela was present at the beatings that ended in the death of 14-year-old activist Stompie Seipei. During the trial prosecution witnesses, who finally agreed to testify after being threatened with imprisonment, described how she not only looked on as Stompie and other young men were being beaten with empty bottles and thrown from above shoulder height, but had even hummed a tune and yelled at them that they were 'not fit to be alive', and personally assaulted them with her fists.

Months after the court ordeal had passed, Stompie's ghost refused to disappear as fresh allegations surfaced. Two convicted fellow-accused, Xoliswa Falati and John Morgan, made statements alleging they committed perjury during the trial to protect her. They said she participated in assaulting Stompie and ordered that his body be removed from her house and dumped elsewhere. Other reports which surfaced at this time linked her to the death of Dr Abu-Baker Asvat, a doctor who allegedly examined Stompie. Her diminished stature reflected heavily on Nelson, and he came under increasing pressure to act decisively against her.

Informed circles claim that pressure within the ANC forced him to announce his separation from his wife of 34 years. His voice broke once as he informed the press: 'I part from my wife with no recriminations. . . . I am sorry. I embrace her with all the love and affection I have nursed for her inside and outside prison from the moment I first met her. I shall personally never regret the life Comrade Nomzamo and I tried to share together. Circumstances beyond our control, however, dictated that it should be otherwise.'

Beleaguered by all the charges, devastated by her separation from her husband, Winnie Mandela quit her post as the head of the ANC's social welfare department, but insisted that the move was not provoked by the 'false allegations' against her. 'Nothing can make me waver in my commitment to my organization, to my husband, and to the oppressed and impoverished people of South Africa. I have taken this step because I consider it to be in the best interest of the ANC, whose cause and policies I will support to the end of my life,' she said.

Since 1984, I had followed and reported on Mrs Mandela's banishment and harassment. I admired her courage and resistance. I will never forget the day I followed her from Brandfort to Johannesburg when she ignored a government banning order prohibiting her from entering Soweto. She defied the government and fought to return to Soweto. I was one of the few journalists who reported on police attempts to remove her forcibly from her Soweto house.

Her resignation from the social welfare post did not solve the organization's dilemma of having in its senior ranks – the NEC – a member whose standing was constantly being questioned. At first the ANC said it would not ask her to resign from the elected position, despite the fact that the image of the organization was at risk. Even when allegations of abuse of power within the ANC's Women's League surfaced, the ANC did nothing to discipline her, either because they did not want to embarrass her husband, or because her suspension would impact negatively on the organization. But the pressure on her to quit became obvious and overwhelming, affecting her children and grandchildren and making the situation unbearable for her. Although her standing has been damaged by all the allegations linking her to murders, assaults, misuse of ANC funds and extra-marital affairs, in the ranks of the liberation movement she remains a formidable figure, both hardened by the struggle and oppression, and made arrogant by leadership and success.

Having endured such trials and tribulations, the ANC now appears to have a more coherent, democratic and reinvigorated leadership with a widely supported mandate to negotiate and deliver a democratic constitution. The new ANC leadership was elected not on emotional or charismatic grounds, but for their negotiation skills and practical approach. A new integrated leadership comprised of the likes of Ramaphosa, Mbeki, Mahomed Valli Moosa and Hani emerged, incorporating a number of the younger former UDF leaders to complement older leaders such as Mandela, Sisulu and others.

The ANC has always been an amorphous organization, more of a coalition than a conventional party. Its reluctance to define itself as a political party has left many grey areas. But ANC leaders, including Mandela, say that by remaining a movement it can better retain its diverse constituencies and sweep into power on a tide of populist sentiment. A liberation movement is also involved in the contest for power. Its very existence, a refusal to recognize the legitimacy of the existing constitutional system, enables it to utilize various strategies, which can range from tactical participation in the existing system to insurrection and the armed seizure of power.

But despite all the problems the ANC has had, and may continue to have, it has now placed the country more firmly on the road to a political settlement. The reshaping process has been traumatic, but it has helped the movement to clarify its goals and timetables. Now the ANC knows what it wants. It wants a future South Africa to be a unitary state, and not a federal system of government as argued by the National Party, Inkatha and many others. It wants the administration and management of education and the development of education policy to be governed by a single and non-racial education department. It wants racially based local governments to be deracialized and brought under a single municipality with a single tax base. It wants all South Africans to have a right to decent housing and to essential services such as water, sanitation, refuse removal and electricity.

The ANC says its government would back a mixed economy, where the size of the public sector would be increased in certain areas through nationalization, purchasing a shareholding in companies, establishing new public corporations and going into joint ventures with the private sector. It would introduce, 'as a matter of priority', measures to ensure that landless people gain access to land on fair terms, and a legal process to resolve competing land claims. The ANC also knows that the flip side of political empowerment is economic empowerment, and economic empowerment begins with education. Normalization of learning would be one of the top priorities of an ANC-dominated government. As for how the organization will deal with the danger of not being able to meet the rising expectations held by its supporters, Mandela has offered these words of caution: 'A great number of our membership now understand the resource constraints that an ANC government will face and that there will, therefore, be no quick fix to decades of apartheid destruction.' Other ANC leaders have warned against 'quick-fix solutions to centuries of deprivation, and decades of corruption and mismanagement of our economy'.

The ANC acknowledges that it offers no easy solutions beyond its commitment to end apartheid, but having entered the final phase of the liberation struggle, the transition has begun from the politics of protest and resistance to the politics of negotiation and, beyond that, of electioneering and administration. The ANC's chief concern now is how to get the best deal out of the talks. Political conflict may now be more about the outcome of negotiation, and less about the process itself. Mandela has spoken about the need to prepare to participate in elections – something the ANC has never done in its 80-year existence – and to prepare policy positions 'for when we become the governing party.' He made it clear it was going to be tough negotiating a new constitution. 'We are dealing with a group of politicians who do not want to negotiate themselves out of power.'

Despite being battered by violence against its members, coping with bureaucratic hurdles and trying to manage its difficult relationships with communists, militant youths and township thugs, the ANC is now stronger and more united. The organization has an assertiveness and self-confidence which have been missing since its return to the country in early 1990. It has managed to build more than 900 branches and bought a 20-storey headquarters in central Johannesburg. It has released a democratic constitution calling for one person, one vote; for a senate and national assembly; for a president who would be elected by popular vote or by parliament; and for a Bill of Rights to safeguard individual freedoms. It now accepts that negotiating its way to power is the only realistic option. Although its huge, unruly army of supporters are in a hurry to see it assume the reins of power, Ramaphosa, the man who may one day succeed Mandela, has proudly declared: 'The ANC under the leadership of Comrade Nelson Mandela is ready to govern.' Mandela concurs: 'About the ANC there is no doubt whatsoever that they are ready to govern. This is the organization that is best equipped to pull the country out of the present situation.'

11
ON
THE BRINK

> Just as the Nazis in Germany killed people because they
> were Jews, in South Africa de Klerk, the National Party and
> Inkatha are killing people because they are black.
>
> *Nelson Mandela, July 1992*

Boipatong township, south of Johannesburg, will not only be remembered as the place
where the youngest and oldest victims – an unborn child in the mother's womb, a
nine-month-old boy and an 80-year-old woman – were recorded among the 49 people
massacred by assassins, but also as a place where the country's State President was
hounded, insulted and forced to flee for his life while police protecting him added three
more deaths to the toll already inflicted by the rampaging mob. On a sunny day in June
1992, de Klerk travelled to the township to express his condolences to the families of
the victims of one the country's worst massacres. It was the first time he or any other
white leader had made such a gesture. ANC and PAC regional leaders were on hand to
fan the flames when de Klerk arrived in the township.

Furious residents were clearly angry and determined to drive him out of the township. The placards said it all: 'How many more deaths?', 'To hell with de Klerk', 'De
Klerk Get Out', 'Go Away Murderer', 'De Klerk Wanted for Apartheid Crimes', 'De
Klerk, Kill Apartheid, Not Us'. For the first time de Klerk came face to face with black
rage at the slaughter many South Africans believed was orchestrated by his government's security forces. Their anger was understandable but damaging for prospects of a
negotiated settlement. The ANC issued a statement, denouncing his visit as 'a cynical
public relations exercise'. 'We demand action, not de Klerk's crocodile tears,' it said.

The next day a battered ANC mass base hailed Mandela and his entourage as heroes
when they visited the township. But it was clear that Mandela's followers were fed up
with the continuing slaughter of relatives and friends. Once again the placards, this time
directed at Mandela, had a clear message: 'CODESA, a white elephant, let us fight',
'Mandela, we want arms now', 'Mandela give us permission to kill our enemies'.
Sensing anger and frustration, Mandela cautioned them: 'As we brace ourselves for
what lies ahead, we must call for discipline among our ranks. Do not allow yourselves
to be provoked into unplanned violence.' As Mandela toured the squatter settlement
where marauding killers had slaughtered residents, he was followed by a huge crowd of
supporters, stamping their feet in unison, cursing de Klerk, the man they had two years
earlier hailed as 'Comrade F. W.'. They repeatedly asked Mandela to give them guns
and permission to kill their enemies.

Mandela, fighting back tears, listened attentively as resident after resident told tales of death and destruction by people they said were accompanied by white members of the security forces. But it was the story of Simon Moloi, who lost his wife, eight months pregnant, at the hands of the assassins that caused Mandela to lose his composure:

Comrade President Mandela. My name is Simon Moloi. My ordeal started five minutes after I and my wife went to bed at about 10 p.m. We heard gunshots followed by screams from my neighbour. She was joined by her two children who screamed even more loudly. I went to the door to see what could be going on. I saw two men chopping my neighbour with axes. Two white men with automatic rifles were standing behind them. The attackers shouted in Zulu: 'Let us kill these dogs.' I and my wife decided to run and hide in a swamp. I never had a chance to get dressed, so I fled with my underpants. My wife was sick because she was in her last weeks of pregnancy. We had to go through a barbed wire fence to reach the swamp. I tried to lift the fence so that my wife could creep under it, but because of her pregnancy, she could not.

The attackers were hot on our heels. My wife pleaded with me not to leave her behind. With bullets ricocheting in the ground past me, I had no choice but run away, hoping they were looking for me and would not hurt a pregnant woman. I spent a night in the cold swamp. In the morning, I crawled out of the swamp and went to a friend's house who lived not far from the swamp. He gave me clothes and accompanied me back home but my wife was not there. I followed the same route I took with her the previous night. I found her still lying under the fence but covered with a blanket. I lifted the blanket and saw it was her. She had been shot and hacked. That is how I lost my pregnant wife.

Most people in Mandela's group looked numb after Moloi had completed his sad story. I have seen the wholesale slaughter of defenceless people. I have met and spoken to many orphans, widows and widowers. I have listened to and written down many shocking, barbarous and unthinkable stories of death and destruction. The killings were no longer just tragic and outrageous, they filled one with horror, anger and indignation. But after listening to Moloi describe how he lost his wife, I was convinced South Africa had to be saved from the abyss. While more and more people yearned for peace, South Africa was at war with itself.

'I have gone around and been briefed. After listening to the briefings, I am convinced we are no longer dealing with human beings but animals. We will not forget what Mr de Klerk, the National Party and the Inkatha Freedom Party have done to our people. I have never seen such cruelty,' said a visibly shaken Mandela.

His supporters still wanted to drive their point home: 'You behave like lambs when we are being killed,' they chanted loudly. This time they had driven their point home. Mandela took the microphone to say: 'I have heard you. The negotiation process is completely in tatters. We are back in Sharpeville days. After the murder of our people I have instructed Secretary-General Cyril Ramaphosa that he and his delegations will have no further discussions with the regime. I have called a full meeting of the National Executive Committee to review our role and participation in CODESA,' he said to the applause of his followers.

When the ANC leadership took the organization into CODESA, it was after militant supporters were convinced that their aims could be achieved through negotiations. The massacres that followed pushed that consensus close to the edge. 'We are now convinced that this president's method of bringing about a solution to this country is war. . . . The duty of a mass organization is to listen to the masses. We must take account of their feelings,' Mandela said.

Mandela had no alternative but to announce that he and his ANC were suspending bilateral talks with the government. More than two years after Mandela's release, the ANC seemed as far away as ever from their main objective: the establishment of a non-racial, democratic South Africa.

Boipatong and the Credibility of Negotiations

From the very first minute on 2 May 1990, when we South Africans and our friends across the world welcomed that historic occasion when the ANC met the government at Groote Schuur to discuss obstacles impeding full-scale negotiations, it was clear that the main problem was going to be whether these principal players would succeed in building trust between them and among their supporters to carry them through the transition. We had largely pinned our hopes for a peaceful future on the Mandela–de Klerk axis. They had in turn to support each other to steer our country away from anarchy. But two years of negotiations and almost 8,000 deaths later, the spectre of death and destruction hung over South Africa as never before.

As head of state, de Klerk's duty was to protect life and limb. For millions of blacks, his inability to stamp out the violence which previous National Party governments suppressed so effectively was evidence of collusion. The slaughter of their supporters posed a moral dilemma for black leaders participating in CODESA, the democratic forum which was supposed to usher in a new order in South Africa. Friends and neighbours began to urge the ANC to abandon the talks and mobilize its armed wing to curb the violence. Calls for a seizure rather than a transfer of power dominated the language of grassroots activists. The Boipatong slaughter sparked anger, not only against the suspected perpetrators, but also against leaders of the ANC who were perceived as having been too soft in their negotiating stance at CODESA.

Why was it that the Boipatong massacre caused such a crisis when people were being randomly killed every day and there had been 48 other massacres since Mandela was freed, none of which were accompanied by the same outcry locally and internationally? Most importantly, the Boipatong massacre was set against the background of the breakdown of constitutional talks at CODESA II, which had met in May 1992, and therefore took on a greater significance. Secondly, since the beginning of the year both Mandela and de Klerk had been experiencing constituency problems. De Klerk had to endure the daily wrath of the white right. Mandela's constituency was boiling with rage, after a long build-up of black resentment at the rampant vigilante attacks in the townships, the growing perception that the police were involved, and the failure of the negotiations to rectify any of this.

Prior to the massacre, there had also been a hardening of attitudes on both sides and an escalation in the verbal hostility between Mandela and de Klerk. Many South Africans believed the government's referendum triumph had created a dangerous sense of arrogance, foot-dragging, over-confidence and complacency in the National Party. After winning the referendum, de Klerk was making major advances in building support in the coloured and Indian communities. The exact opposite held for Mandela. Every major outbreak of violence meant a loss of support for his ANC. Internally, the ANC was faced with a restive membership and even some leadership disputes over the wisdom of placing too much faith in negotiations. For the ANC, Boipatong was the final straw. As Mandela said, 'I can no longer explain to our people why we continue to talk to a government which is murdering our people.'

A few days after the massacre, constitutional negotiations crumbled when the ANC and nine of its allies pulled out of CODESA after a two-day emergency meeting, presenting the government with a list of 14 demands it said must be met before talks could begin again. The ANC wanted an end to security force covert operations, including hit-squad activity; the disarming of special forces; prosecution of security force personnel involved in township incidents; the closing of migrant worker hostels; the release of political prisoners; the repeal of repressive legislation; an international inquiry into Boipatong; and international monitoring of the violence. Some of these demands looked similar to the ones the ANC had submitted to the government in April 1991.

De Klerk had to fly back from a scheduled visit to Spain to chair a crisis cabinet meeting. They thrashed out a strategy which rested on two pillars: maintaining international support and sending strong signals that the government was committed to negotiations. For de Klerk to accede to all ANC demands would have amounted to admitting that his government had been conducting a duplicitous strategy of negotiations on the one hand and calculated mass murder on the other. Pressures on de Klerk not to give in too much to ANC demands came simply from his own political need not to be seen to be kowtowing to the ANC. The other factor that prevented de Klerk from compromising was fear of alienating members of the security forces, who still regarded the ANC as 'enemy number one', and other future political allies such as Inkatha. In the end, the government offered a two-day summit to deal with the impasse and made the minor concession of allowing international observers.

CODESA II: Settling for Less?

This was not the only stumbling block. Both the government and the ANC were convinced the other party had lost the will to negotiate in good faith. The deadlock at CODESA II on 15 May over the government's insistence on a minority veto in the final constitution made matters worse. CODESA II broke down at the time when the parties were making substantial progress in working groups. The ANC wanted the creation of a democratically elected constituent assembly to draft and adopt a non-racial constitution. The National Party agreed that a proportionally represented National Assembly and Senate should be set up. Here the gap was narrowing, although the government wanted strong regional powers. The ANC wanted the establishment of an interim government of national unity, to be appointed by CODESA. De Klerk accepted that white minority rule must end and wanted a transitional constitution to set up an interim government, including an elected executive council. Here the gap was also narrowing because both parties agreed on the need for multi-party interim rule leading to full democracy.

On the other hand it was clear that the negotiators had made spectacular progress by tackling the easier things first. When they came to the more fundamental divisions between the ANC and the National Party, both sides refused to budge. The ANC placed the responsibility for breaking the deadlock squarely on the government. The camaraderie and optimism that had marked this 19-party process, anchored by the government and the ANC, evaporated into thin air. The breakdown was rooted in CODESA's failure to broach South Africa's central constitutional question, roughly posed as the choice between a democratic or a negotiated power-sharing constitution. Delegates woke up to the realization that CODESA's guiding document, the Declaration of Intent, was obscure when it came to committing the parties to a democratic outcome. For the ANC the declaration meant the possibility of a constituent assembly with proportional representation. For them, negotiations served only to construct the modalities by which democratic transition would take place, the interim government being the ultimate goal.

It looked as if every one had forgotten that since the government began reforming apartheid, it had been hammering the fact that it was looking for a 'power-sharing agreement'. This meant it was aiming for an equitable political compromise between two more or less equally balanced power blocs. It emphasized strong regional powers and at one stage argued for a 'constitutional state' to protect individual and group rights. It wanted an interim constitution, leading to fears that the government was looking at ways of indefinitely entrenching the interim constitution which had been drawn up by CODESA, a body seen by many as unrepresentative. The fear became greater when the government suggested that a 70 or 75 per cent majority would be needed to amend the constitution.

'The National Party wants a system where people can vote, but the result is fixed beforehand,' was Mandela's trenchant comment.

All parties, they say, would have veto power. So if an ANC majority in government wanted to change the apartheid policies on education or housing, they would be able to do so only with the consent of the white minority. In Russia, Hungary, and Eastern Europe generally they have democracy. In Namibia and Zambia they have democracy. Why do we have to settle for something less?

Boipatong further underscored the likelihood that an attempt to resume negotiations on the basis assumed at CODESA II would fail. CODESA did not falter over a dispute about voting percentages; it faltered because too many people saw it as dragging on interminably and doing little to address black expectations. The ANC was seen by its constituency as lacking aggression and meekly giving in to the government. Disenchantment with the snail-like pace of CODESA threatened to wipe out grassroots support for ANC negotiators, sharply reminding them to pay greater attention to their supporters' demands. The extent to which black frustration and anger limits the ANC's room for negotiation cannot be ignored. Leaders of the ANC and their allies had to show their followers they were tough negotiators.

Resolution 765: South Africa Returns to the World

As the Boipatong massacre continued to reverberate across the world, Mandela thought one of the ways to convince his followers that the ANC had not lost control of the crisis-ridden climate was to contact the United Nations and ask it to convene a special hearing of the UN Security Council 'to find ways and means to normalize the deteriorating situation in South Africa and try to resume the negotiations which had broken down.' The UN responded by giving all of the 19 CODESA underwriters, including those who were not party to the deadlocked convention, an opportunity to state their case before the world body. Unaware that they were pursuing negotiations through another lofty forum, leaders of most South African political parties took South Africa's problems to the UN in New York. The proceedings were televised live at home and seemed to offer the best hope since CODESA floundered.

Mandela told the UN Security Council that the violence which had forced the ANC to suspend constitutional talks could be traced to the South African government and its 'surrogate', Inkatha, which it trained, armed and funded.

It is more than clear to us that the violence is both organized and orchestrated and is especially directed at the democratic movement whose activists, members and supporters make up the overwhelming majority of its victims. . . . It constitutes a cold-blooded strategy for state terrorism intended to create conditions under which the forces responsible for the introduction and entrenchment of the system of apartheid would have the possibility of imposing a government on a weakened democratic movement at the negotiations. The regime has the law enforcement personnel and the legal authority to stop the violence and to act against the perpetrators. As the government authority it has the obligation to protect the lives and the property of all the people. It has failed dismally to do this.

On behalf of the South African government, Foreign Minister Pik Botha said it was beyond his comprehension that anyone could accuse the government of fomenting violence when its consequences were disastrous.

It hurts me to be accused of fomenting violence between ethnic groups when we have at last removed ourselves from apartheid. We have every intention of making the National Party a majority party. That can only be done if we succeed in gaining a substantial number of votes from every section of the population. I urge this council to accept, once and for all, that my party is not a white party any longer. We offer a political home for every South African subscribing to the party's principles.

Holding up a ceremonial stick, Inkatha leader Mangosuthu Buthelezi defended the carrying of traditional weapons by Zulus, and said the real problem in South Africa was 'the culture of violence'. 'The thing we have to deal with in South Africa is the culture of violence because you can use a woman's shoe to kill people,' he said.

After the debate, both the government and the ANC claimed victory when in fact both of them received a sharp whack from the world body. Among other things, the UN resolved to send Cyrus Vance as its Special Envoy to South Africa to give all the parties a hearing. Resolution 765 also gave notice to all South Africans that negotiation was the only game in town. The resolution tactfully avoided any apportionment of blame, emphasizing the urgency to resume talks. By passing such a neutral resolution, the UN sent an important signal to all parties that it intended playing a constructive role without becoming anyone's battering ram. The resolution heralded South Africa's return to the world and the world's return to South Africa.

Fresh from doomed peace missions in Yugoslavia, Vance arrived in South Africa to hear divergent views about our problems and possible solutions to them. It looked as if the UN did not want to intervene, but was encouraging the parties to find a solution themselves. It seemed to be rather less than totally disenchanted with de Klerk, though the evident inability of members of the security forces to stop violence raised questions. When Vance arrived the government wanted to portray his arrival as confirmation of the UN's call for the ANC to resume negotiations without further ado. The ANC wanted Vance to pay attention to the continuing butchery in the townships. Vance quickly appraised the complexity of factors behind the violence. As a political broker, he soon realized that the various contenders had opposing views about who or what was behind the unfortunate events.

At the end of Vance's mission in South Africa, UN Secretary-General Boutros Boutros-Ghali sent at least 30 UN peace observers and urged the Commonwealth, EC and OAU to supplement them. The observers worked closely with structures of the National Peace Accord and the Goldstone Commission to monitor township violence. Boutros-Ghali urged the Goldstone Commission to probe the activities of the South African Defence Force, South African Police, KwaZulu Police, Umkhonto we Sizwe and the PAC's military wing, the Azanian People's Liberation Army to help stop the violence.

Following Vance's mission to South Africa, peace observers became a regular feature of the country's political landscape. Not only were numbers of foreign observers increased, but the ambit of their involvement widened. The UN observers, joined by those from the Commonwealth, the OAU and the EC, helped wherever they could to limit the intensity of the violence. For many years we had not foreseen any role for bodies such as the UN, the EC or the OAU in our settlement process. For years the South African government resisted what it termed unwarranted interference by outsiders in our domestic affairs. Even visits by heads of state, the government had made plain, should be undertaken without prejudice to the position of the government on the question of non-interference in our internal affairs.

To white South Africans, the idea of external intervention, especially by the United Nations, seemed strange, and possibly suspect. But if the country was to arrest the social and economic degeneration that gathered pace by the day until the fate of Yugoslavia seemed like a warning, the international community would have to herd Mandela, de Klerk and the others in the direction of statesmanship. The failure of the second plenary session of CODESA and the tragic events at Boipatong changed the attitudes of the government and its white supporters towards the international community. The futility of resisting repeated offers for help, often genuine and well-meaning, at last dawned on de Klerk and his colleagues. Nerves frayed and tempers ran high, and both the government and the ANC looked looked for ways to return to the negotiating table, and hoped the international community could help.

Mass Action: The ANC Goes Back to the People

After Vance's departure, the ANC and its allies continued to to take the battle for democracy to the streets by resuming and intensifying their mass action campaign. Elements within the ANC had been lamenting a growing gap between the negotiators and the rank and file. What better way to cement relationships between the leadership and their supporters than by taking politics 'back to the people'? It would also be a good way to mobilize and consolidate voter support for a future election. Having tried the whole gamut of strategies to force the government from power, the ANC leadership found itself trapped between the militancy of its followers and the obstinacy of government.

Many saw the campaign as the first real test of the ANC's ability to use its popular support to advantage through coordinated protest marches, strikes, consumer boycotts and work stoppages. For Mandela and his followers, negotiations had to be accompanied by mass action to have political clout. They often pointed out that despite apartheid reforms they still could not vote. 'We have reached the position where we are now because of mass action,' Mandela said.

The launch of this campaign proved to be one of the most emotive and divisive issues in South African politics. To some it was the final door to liberation, to others the grimmest manifestation of lawlessness and intolerance. The debate over the wisdom of mass action was best summed up by two opposing newspapers. The *New Nation*, which often reflects ANC views, said: 'It is asking too much, that having abandoned the armed struggle to help facilitate the process of negotiations, the ANC must now be expected to give up its sole legal and legitimate means of organizing.' The government-supporting *Citizen* said: 'Mass protests, marches, stay-aways and boycotts, which President F. W. de Klerk says can lead to violence and are therefore unacceptable, are not simple expressions of mass feeling. They are organized to disrupt life as well as to demonstrate the ANC strength so that blacks are convinced of the ANC's invincibility.'

Indeed, mass action stretched tensions between the government and ANC to breaking point. For de Klerk, mass action complicated negotiations because his white electorate would see any concessions to the ANC as a sign of weakness. The de Klerk government suspected the ANC had decided long before the breakdown at CODESA and Boipatong that it no longer wanted multi-party negotiations. It insisted that radical elements within the ANC, especially communists and unionists, had pushed for mass action to be resumed, rather than continuing with negotiations. It was also argued that mass action would harm the economy, but Mandela countered this view by saying: 'Our economy has been so mismanaged it can hardly be hurt by mass action.'

But everyone knew that nobody was prepared to invest in South Africa until there was stability – not just a political settlement, but an employer-friendly workforce and a reduction of political violence. However, Mandela was right.

Mass action is not responsible for the decline in the state of the economy and for the suffering of the people. We know that apartheid and its policies of economic mismanagement and high-scale corruption are responsible. That is why we have to rid ourselves of this illegitimate minority government.

Mandela also declared that mass action was now to be pursued relentlessly.

Mass action will continue right up until the installation of a democratic government. We are committed to negotiations, but if we are unable to get the cooperation we deserve and expect, then we have to use our power. If the government is not prepared to cooperate, they must be prepared for turmoil. That is the lesson of history in this country. From now on, negotiations will be coupled with mass action.

Claiming to draw their inspiration from the 'people's power' revolutions in Eastern Europe, the organizers of the campaign drew up a four-phased plan: mobilization, starting with a one-day strike on 16 June 1992, the anniversary of student uprisings in 1976; a national offensive (involving mass demonstrations, occupations of government buildings such as courts and police stations, and petitions) to run for the whole of July; a national strike to start in August; and, finally, 'exit gate' – when the marches, sit-ins and factory occupations, combined with the jamming of government telecommunication systems, would eventually sweep the government from power. Mock trials were also held, with de Klerk and Chief Buthelezi heading the list of the 'accused'. In most of the trials, Chief Buthelezi and de Klerk were either sentenced to 'death' or 'to life imprisonment'.

Just as the government used the whites-only referendum in March to test its support, so was the two-day strike on 3 and 4 August 1992 a black referendum. The successful stay-away by millions of workers gave the ANC its mandate to continue as the chief representative of black interests.

After the strike de Klerk moved a few inches to accede to some of the ANC demands. He promised to phase out hostels, replacing them with family accommodation. But he said this could not be done without asking hostel dwellers. Consultation led to a deadlock, since many of them were Inkatha supporters and would not want to cooperate with the ANC. When the ANC called for the installation of fences around them, de Klerk insisted hostel dwellers must not feel caged. When the ANC asked that hostels be guarded and those occupying the hostels illegally be expelled, de Klerk again insisted that hostel dwellers must be consulted.

De Klerk also disbanded special forces such as the notorious Koevoet and Battalion 32, and promised to prosecute any security force personnel involved in the violence. A tough nut to crack for de Klerk was a demand that he stop repression in the apartheid-created homelands, as some of the nominally independent homelands still claimed he had no jurisdiction over them.

Another crunch was the demand that the government ban the carrying of dangerous weapons in public. It had already banned the carrying of cultural weapons in public places which had been declared unrest areas. Inkatha supporters had flouted the ban and ANC supporters also often carried sticks, machetes and other dangerous weapons.

The release of political prisoners was one of the sticking points. Two years after an agreement to release all political prisoners, the ANC insisted there were still 400 more behind bars while the government said that, as far as it was concerned, all political prisoners had been freed. It added, however, that the matter was open for debate.

Bisho: The Bloodbath, the Blunder and the Blame

Brushing aside government concessions, the ANC pressed ahead with a series of civil disobedience campaigns such as work stoppages, sit-ins, strikes, demonstrations and marches against government-controlled structures, including homelands. On 7 September 1992, an ANC march aimed at deposing Ciskei military dictator Brigadier Oupa Gqozo ended in a bloodbath when Ciskei soldiers opened fire, killing up to 28 and wounding nearly 200, virtually torpedoing South Africa's peace process when everyone had hopes that negotiators would soon begin talking again.

The soldiers opened fire after a section of the crowd broke through a razor wire barricade, determined to occupy the homeland capital of Bisho. The troops poured two bursts of automatic fire into the marchers. The first fusillade lasted for two minutes, then there was a pause, followed by another one-minute burst of shooting. At the end bodies lay scattered in pools of blood along the line of razor wire erected to contain the marchers.

The breakaway group was led by Ronnie Kasrils, a stalwart of ANC protests. Kasrils said march organizers had given instructions for another column of marchers to go through the stadium, leave the stadium, and to go through the gap into town. 'The plan was to move as fast as possible into the centre of Bisho where we would stage a peaceful occupation,' he said. Leading the march, Kasrils leaped over the fence and saw the deployment of troops to the north of the stadium. He attempted to move away from the troops, hoping to clear their flank. 'As we pulled through, soldiers began shooting. Lying under the volley, it seemed like it lasted half an hour.' Kasrils said the demonstrators were taken by surprise, thinking that with the eyes of the world upon them, Gqozo's troops would not dare open fire.

De Klerk said the massacre resulted from the ANC's failure to observe march conditions agreed with Ciskei authorities. 'I did not start mass action, the ANC did. It is a fallacy, an unsubstantiated lie, that my government was involved,' he said. Mandela differed with him. 'The creation of a climate for free political activity, including in the homelands, is an important condition for us to return to the negotiating table. An enormous responsibility rests with the South African government to create that climate,' he said. Gqozo said he had been devastated and shattered by what had happened. He accused ANC demonstrators of opening fire first, killing a soldier. He said his troops had acted with restraint.

Two judges investigating the massacre came to somewhat different conclusions. While Judge Goldstone said the shooting was morally and legally indefensible and deserved the strongest censure, Ciskei Chief Justice B de V Pickard said the ANC leadership must take the blame. The two divergent findings helped South Africa's political leaders to read the reports selectively, exonerating themselves and blaming their adversaries. Both the Ciskei and the ANC were to blame. The judges agree on that, although they appeared to disagree on the exact allocation of blame.

Once again the crackle of gunfire had thrown into question the entire future of the subcontinent, leaving the nation desperately trying to gauge the consequences of the massacre. The reasons why the ANC marched on Bisho were understandable and well-known. In the face of the collapse of the negotiations, the movement had to do something to show its supporters that it still held the initiative. While the government had at its disposal the full power of the state, ranging from the armed forces to the media, the ANC only had the power of numbers, the power to mobilize crowds.

The organization had also been under great pressure from its members in the homelands to do something about tough conditions there. The government felt it had to defend its potential election allies if it was to survive a vote. It believed that with the help of some homeland allies, it could win an election. At stake also was the government's notion of a federal state, with strong regions counterbalancing central government power. Without the homelands and homeland leaders, its federal option would be short-lived. Many still believe that the confrontation had little to do with the drive for free political activity, but everything to do with winning votes. It was clear that the fundamental problem bedevilling our transition from apartheid to democracy was that our major political players were electioneering and negotiating simultaneously, incompatible activities in a volatile situation like ours.

The Bilateral Route: Meyer and Ramaphosa Reach a Summit

With recriminations flying from both camps in the midst of death, destruction and the continuing mobilization for mass action, the focus shifted to bilateral talks between the new government chief negotiator Roelf Meyer, who took over from the ailing Gerrit Viljoen, and the ANC's Ramaphosa. The two men worked long hours to settle their differences. In an apparent backdown on constitutional issues which had tied up negotiations at CODESA II, the government offered revised formulations on three issues, which it hoped would be more acceptable to the ANC. The government suggested a senate in which parties would be represented proportionally – its earlier proposal had been that all parties receiving a certain number of votes should receive equal representation. It proposed that if a transitional constitution had not been replaced within three years, a general election would be held. The government indicated that it would be prepared to accept a 70 per cent 'special majority' to approve all aspects of a new constitution except the Bill of Rights, for which a 75 per cent majority would be needed. This appeared to match the ANC's compromise position offered at CODESA II immediately before the deadlock in Working Group 2. In effect, this was a belated acceptance of the ANC's compromise proposals tabled at CODESA II, where the government insisted on a 75 per cent majority to approve all aspects of the constitution concerning regional government. The government was now also prepared to accept a democratically elected senate, based on 'electoral regions' delimited for that purpose. It said delegates to the senate would be allocated proportionately according to the support their parties received in each region – a departure from the government's previous insistence that each region be granted equal representation in the senate. 'We believe we have presented a basis to resolve the impasse. If the ANC denies this opportunity, it will be unreasonable,' the government said. But the ANC pressed ahead with mass action.

A positive aspect to emerge from the horrors of Boipatong and Bisho was that the key players in the South African negotiation process were compelled to rethink strategies and options. While mass action was useful in mobilizing a constituency and as a tool to break the CODESA logjam, it was not going to bring the South African government to its knees. Amid violence, tension, and countrywide gloom, Meyer and Ramaphosa's bilateral 19-day talks gave birth to a summit on 26 September 1992. The 'Record of Understanding' endorsed by the summit ended the acrimonious and damaging mood which had prevailed since the collapse of CODESA II. The Record of

Understanding dealt with five basic issues: interim or transitional arrangements, hostels, dangerous weapons, release of prisoners, and the ANC strategy of mass action.

New agreements reached on the interim government were that it should be drafted by a constitution-making body in a fixed time, have an adequate deadlock-breaking mechanism, and be elected within a set time. Although the government insisted it had already released those political prisoners falling within guidelines negotiated with the ANC, it nonetheless agreed to the phased release of remaining prisoners, identified by the ANC, who had committed their offences with a political motive before 8 October 1990. The government held that all those who had committed similar offences, but had not been charged and sentenced, should be indemnified. This was tantamount to a general amnesty. The ANC did not agree, and the matter was left for future bilateral discussions.

On a constitution-making body, it was agreed that there will be a democratically elected constituent assembly which will serve as an interim parliament. It will draft and adopt a new constitution, sitting as a single chamber and taking decisions by a special majority. It will only be bound by those principles which have been agreed beforehand. It will operate for a fixed time and will be elected within an agreed time frame, and it will have deadlock-breaking mechanisms. Overseeing the constitutional assembly or interim parliament will be an interim government of national unity, operating in terms of an interim constitution. The constitution will provide for national and regional government and a Bill of Rights.

Exchanging Prisoners

The ANC seemed to have got more out of the summit than the government. Most of the agreements were responses to demands made by the ANC when it broke off talks twice, in April 1991 and after the Boipatong massacre in June 1992. In agreeing to release all remaining ANC prisoners, the government included controversial cases such as Robert McBride, whose car-bomb killed three young women outside a bar on Durban's beachfront, and two ANC guerrillas, Mthetheleli Mncube and Mzondeleli Nondula, who between them killed seven people in landmine blasts at Messina, a town on the border between Zimbabwe and South Africa. Also released was Barend Strydom, a neo-Nazi fascist who killed eight blacks he said were threatening the survival of the white nation just by breathing (see Chapter 7).

The release of prisoners who had received the death penalty for what some called crimes of conscience, and others terrorism, caused a lot of debate. High-profile prisoners like Strydom, McBride, Nondula and Mncube were controversial. People said the government was being opportunistic and politically expedient, that this was a serious assault on the legal system that would create more problems that it solved. It was difficult to comprehend how the government was going to get the talks back on track if it did not respond dramatically.

The release of Strydom was difficult for the black community to accept. A host of reasons, such as the fact that Strydom was a freelance bigoted psychopath who killed innocent blacks, were advanced. If his release was unjustifiable, it was nevertheless inevitable that, in the negotiation process ahead of us, unpalatable compromises would have to be swallowed. Controversy over various prisoners will rage for years. De Klerk faced a stark choice: he could refuse to release any more political prisoners, and plunge the country deeper into the political morass; he could release only those identified by the ANC and invite the venom of the right; or he could go all the way and release the Strydoms with the McBrides, risking condemnation from his constituency to get talks going, and so nudge the country towards a negotiated settlement. He chose the third course. But the more extreme the case, the more it brought home the price that has to be paid for reconciliation – a cleansing process we had go through if South Africa was to begin life anew, with the slate wiped clean. If, indeed, evil choices sometimes achieved good ends, we hoped that greater good for a greater number of people would flow from this decision. But there were also bungles when the government and the ANC could not even handle the selection of other political prisoners for release. A few common criminals and murderers were released by mistake.

For months, the government had resisted meeting ANC demands. But point by point they were forced to relent at the peace summit. The government once spoke of transitional arrangements; now it accepted an interim government of national unity. The government was forced to concede the election of a constituent assembly which will write South Africa's new constitution and also act as an interim parliament. The only thing the government won was that the principles of a new constitution should be decided in advance.

Of the few remaining concessions the ANC still had to wrest from the government involved a dispute over the protection of minority rights. Another issue was the granting of indemnity for anyone who had defended apartheid, which the ANC opposed. The summit reflected the emerging realization that constitutional negotiations could not succeed until the problem of violence had been addressed. It also reflected the lesson learnt at the breakdown of CODESA II, that multilateral talks could not hope to succeed unless the two main players – the ANC and the government – agreed on the fundamentals. The ANC and the government agreed that lasting peace would only be achieved once an interim government and constitutional-making body were in place.

After the success of the bilateral talks which led to the 26 September summit and the signing of the Record of Understanding, the ANC and its allies restricted talks on transitional matters to such bilateral discussions with the government. A forum like CODESA would only be convened for ceremonial purposes to rubber-stamp agreements reached at the bilateral level. Disenchantment with multi-party forums had been repeatedly expressed by the ANC, largely because they accorded equal status to all parties irrespective of their political standing among the people. Fringe parties, as a result, shared the same status as the ANC and the National Party. But the move drew flak from Chief Buthelezi and other homeland leaders.

Two Steps Forward, One Step Back

It was typical of what had become the cynical dynamic of South African politics that when Mandela and de Klerk took two steps forward by finding a formula to bring the ANC back into the negotiation process, the furious reaction of Chief Buthelezi drove negotiations one step backwards a day later.

In front of well over 10,000 Zulu warriors, Chief Buthelezi declared that any attempt by the government to disarm them would be defied, that fencing outside their hostels would be destroyed 'with bare hands', and that any constituent assembly would be rejected emphatically. To crown it all, he said Inkatha and KwaZulu were pulling out of CODESA.

> If this bilateral agreement is set to be the scene for the future negotiation process, count me out. President de Klerk signed an agreement with the ANC while knowing full well that I would oppose it vehemently – and in doing so, Mr de Klerk

has made a fundamental mistake that could lead to his isolation. I am appalled and disgusted and so is the IFP and the KwaZulu government at the content of this agreement.

The government, Buthelezi said, was 'making Zulus the sacrificial lamb that must be slaughtered and sacrificed on the altar of political expediency in order to placate the ANC–SACP alliance.' He had, he said, found the words of Sir Winston Churchill on appeasement to be particularly apt: 'Some people try to please the crocodile in the hope that it will eat them last.' He accused the ANC of continuing to run, organize and arm South African citizens in their private army in defiance of the law, while these actions earned them 'no more than a slap on the wrist from the government'.

'I warn against the danger of South Africa indulging in what would amount to ethnic cleansing. The ANC's action against hostels is motivated by anti-Zulu racism. The focus on traditional weapons is totally disproportionate, when considering the destruction and devastation caused by the ANC's military wing,' he said.

Admittedly, Buthelezi had good grounds for concern about Umkhonto activities. A strong case could be made for stricter control over the organization and, particularly, the arms it had cached all over the country. Inkatha said more than 300 of its leaders had been assassinated, mainly by the ANC's military wing. The assassins had operated with military precision, usually armed with sophisticated weapons.

To both the government and the ANC, it is now your turn to hear our demands. Both the IFP and KwaZulu charge that without the immediate disbandment of the ANC's ruthless army, Umkhonto we Sizwe, and the demobilization of its military personnel, negotiations cannot go ahead. . . . Umkhonto has got to go. There can be no negotiations at a national level while the ANC army remains intact.

I often asked Chief Buthelezi about accusations that the KwaZulu Police were virtually an army for the Zulu homeland, and that this was underlined by his own position as the KwaZulu Minister of Police. The Chief said:

That is rubbish. People who want to propagandize for the ANC can do so, but the fact is our police are trained to maintain law and order. If there are any members who transgress any law, they would be severely dealt with. I have never and would never give them orders to kill people. There is never any hullabaloo or hue and cry when our people are killed, even in droves every day. I have compromised the position of the Zulu people as far as I can go, before I too [like de Klerk] will be a sell-out to the ANC. Any demands beyond this constitutes a direct attack against the Zulu nation.

Chief Buthelezi had often insisted that it was he who discovered de Klerk as a man to be trusted long before Mandela called him a man of integrity. Now the chief no longer looked on de Klerk as a man who could be trusted. Their relationship weakened after Mandela's release catapulted de Klerk to the international scene and opened many doors that had for years been closed to the South African governnment and its leaders. De Klerk soon realized that if he wanted the process of political transition to move forward he had to cultivate a working relationship with Mandela, in the same way as he had developed such a relationship with Chief Buthelezi. Given the fact that the ANC and Inkatha were not often on speaking terms, de Klerk's task was indeed going to be difficult. History has shown that it is not always easy to befriend equally two deadly enemies and remain untainted by the animosity they generate.

This was confirmed when the relationship between Chief Buthelezi and de Klerk soured as negotiations gained momentum. The first point of friction was when de Klerk could not help Buthelezi fight the exclusion of the Zulu king from CODESA. Then, whereas the government and Inkatha had held convergent views for years, a growing chasm appeared between them in CODESA's working groups and committees.

Before the 26 September summit, the government, like Chief Buthelezi and his Inkatha, was adamant that there would be no interim government or constituent assembly during the process of political transition and that CODESA would draw up the constitution. At CODESA and during the ANC–government bilateral talks, Inkatha was left alone as the government inclined towards the ANC, agreeing that there will be an interim government and an elected constituent assembly consisting of a single chamber.

Then the ANC also lobbied tirelessly against cultural weapons and hostels. Initially, de Klerk was adamant that Inkatha members were entitled to carry traditional weapons when attending cultural gatherings. Again under ANC pressure, the President shifted his ground and banned these weapons in unrest areas. Chief Buthelezi accepted the initial ban. The ANC then put de Klerk under more intense pressure to ban cultural weapons entirely. De Klerk banned their carrying without a permit.

De Klerk then adopted a similar approach on the fate of hostels. After initially visiting Soweto hostels, he promised that, as a matter of priority, they would be upgraded. No progress was made in this regard. Again, under pressure from the ANC, a new priority of fencing off rather than upgrading the hostels thus came to the fore. On the other hand, Chief Buthelezi felt his own lobbying for the disbanding of Umkhonto we Sizwe had been brushed aside or totally ignored by the government, the ANC and the international community.

It seemed that de Klerk had reached a stage where he could no longer afford to please both Mandela and Buthelezi. Perhaps he had discovered that it would be more beneficial in the transition process to ignore Buthelezi and his party and placate Mandela and his ANC. Or maybe de Klerk had realized that after putting together a considerable international support network, Buthelezi's fortunes and his usefulness were rapidly dwindling.

As one tries to understand Chief Buthelezi's position, one wonders how the ANC would have felt if a government–Inkatha summit had resolved to disband Umkhonto we Sizwe without any input or cooperation from the ANC. This was something like what happened to Chief Buthelezi on the cultural weapons and hostels issues, let alone what they had agreed about mechanisms of transition to democracy.

The Inkatha leader maintained that the policy 'of rendering the Zulu people impotent' before major changes occur was not a new one. The British had had the same in mind as a prelude to the unification policy. Buthelezi saw a clear trend in which Zulus were being targeted 'including the systematic assassination of hundreds of middle-level leaders of Inkatha and traditional chiefs.' The Zulu ethnic minority, said Buthelezi, is the only major social formation in South Africa that is not armed. White minorities as well as the ANC have piled up immense hidden arsenals. He distinguished the kind of modern weapons they have from cultural ones, which 'are a sign and a token of militancy of this ethnic group to defend its cultural and ethnic identity. They are a tool of self–identification and a reminder of their ethnic roots and history. Their primary purpose is not to cause injury to others.'

Buthelezi and Natal Talk of Secession

Buthelezi's furious response to the de Klerk–Mandela rapprochement followed hints that he was considering leading his homeland of kwaZulu to secession. His denunciation of the agreements placed a question mark over the Record of Understanding's likely efficacy in curbing violence at a time when constitutional negotiations appeared to be back on track. In his view, joint decision-making by the government and the ANC on issues affecting the Zulu people was simply unacceptable. 'The ANC will not succeed in destroying KwaZulu. There will always be a KwaZulu,' Buthelezi warned.

The danger for the country was that Chief Buthelezi's unwillingness to cooperate shifted him closer to the right-wing Afrikaner nationalist camp, creating a serious problem for de Klerk and the ANC. It heightened the risk of an all-out war in Natal between Inkatha and ANC supporters. Buthelezi spoke quietly and sadly about a blood-torn country – a land he loves dearly.

I have never been this depressed. We are already engaged in a low-intensity civil war. My supporters – despite what the media say, they are not only Zulus – are now angry. The South African government and the ANC are making deals behind our backs. . . . If this happens, Zulus will not listen. I see at the very least massive civil disobedience in Natal, and at the most civil war. I shudder when I say this because it is something you do not say lightly.

Fearing violence, Buthelezi argues that a new constitution should be drawn up not by an elected body or national convention, but by a committee of experts. He maintains that no revolutionary movement has ever drawn up a constitution which enables opposition parties to win an election and form new a government.

A constitution is the result of a process of development and negotiations, and its characteristics are likely to resemble the characteristics of such a process. The ANC–government agreement short-circuits this process and has buried the ideal of pluralism. Only pluralism, as territorial, social, economic and cultural pluralism, is our guarantee for democracy and freedom in South Africa. The alternative could be totalitarianism.

The constitution, Buthelezi believes, should organize only the limited powers of the South African federal government. It should respect the general powers of the member states, and of the individuals in universities, families, churches, trade unions and so on.

Buthelezi also opposed the idea of a constituent assembly to draft a new constitution. He argues that

A constituent assembly, vested with the power of the electoral suffrage, will not feel bound to follow any principle. As any other body, it will claim the greatest amount of power possible, and will draft a constitution which will bring under its scope and will organize the greatest amount of powers possible.

The IFP stands for a federal system characterized by residual powers in the member states and regionalization within each state. We believe in pluralism, personal and local autonomy, and a limited role of government.

Inkatha wants to ensure representation of the people and their interest, not representation of their affiliation to vague concepts used to aggregate people at a national level. We believe and demand single individual constituencies in which anybody can run for office without the control or approval of national parties and organizations. We want to ensure that political representatives are elected through the electoral process, rather than witnessing elections which for all practical purposes elect political parties which in turn allocate their votes to the individuals they have previously chosen.

Two months after withdrawing from the CODESA talks, on 1 December 1992, Chief Buthelezi unilaterally proposed to merge his KwaZulu homeland with the white-run Natal province in a future largely autonomous federal state. He said he would in future seek a regional referendum to endorse the plan, which had already been approved by his Inkatha-dominated KwaZulu government. 'I feel that the adoption of the constitution of the state of KwaZulu/Natal reflects an immediate and clear mandate from the people of my region, who will have the opportunity to exercise their sovereignty through a democratic referendum,' he said. Buthelezi slammed government–ANC bilateral talks, saying they were meant to clinch deals behind the backs of other political parties.

> With the degeneration of the negotiation process into bilateral negotiations between the government and the ANC to the exclusion of significant portions of the population, it becomes imperative to go back to the people to test their wants and aspirations to find the lead to restructure the process of transformation of the country. . . . If anyone looking to the future of South Africa expects Inkatha to vanish, they [had] better go and and reread their Zulu history. . . . I serve [notice] that Inkatha is a national political force and the KwaZulu government [of the homeland of KwaZulu] is an historic reality which can only be ignored at the peril of the negotiation process.

Some South Africans interpreted this announcement as notice of a secessionist option if things did not go his way in the future. But for the government and the ANC, the content of Chief Buthelezi's proposals, the process it proposes for realizing them, as well as their express final objective, rode roughshod over the negotiation process.

Now or Never: Towards Our First Election

The negotiations crisis focused on de Klerk's inability to lead South Africa out of its latest impasse. Gone were the brilliant political strokes with which de Klerk enthralled the world and unsettled opposition at home. Gone too was the element of boldness that had characterized his ascent to the presidency. Violence continued to escalate, crime was rampant, the security forces were implicated up to their necks in orchestrating the violence, details of corruption in government-controlled homelands were emerging, and the negotiation process was on wobbly legs. De Klerk the reformer, like Mikhail Gorbachev and others who reformed their countries, was now under attack from all quarters. There were whispers of a split within the party and even a possible *putsch* against him.

In the three years since the ANC was unbanned and de Klerk boldly proclaimed his vision of a new South Africa, the country had become more polarized, racially and politically, than when Mandela wrote his now famous letter from prison. The economy was disappearing into a black hole. Anarchy was increasingly engulfing the townships. Fear was the order of the day in the suburbs and the black ghettos. South Africa was full of massacres waiting to happen, waiting to throw the talks off balance and lead to further delays and chaos. Events at Bisho and Boipatong brought the country to a divide between negotiation and confrontation, between settlement and revolution, between peace and civil war. Amid the anger and bloodshed which threatened to engulf South Africa was an inescapable truth: at the heart of the crisis facing South Africa was a deep lack of trust between de Klerk, Mandela and Buthelezi. It was also an inescapable truth that the de Klerk administration could no longer govern South Africa without the consent of the ANC, Inkatha or other parties. It was also clear that neither Inkatha, the ANC or the right wing could overthrow de Klerk in the foreseeable future. Thus, once again, a stark reality faced all South African political parties and their followers: either negotiate a settlement or face a long war of attrition in which there will be no winners but only a descent into anarchy.

The endless cycle of violence increased the need for a speedy political settlement and, at the same time, imperilled the chances of a successful settlement. Mandela and the other leaders agreed about such a need. 'Violence is a serious obstacle that can only be addressed when a democratic government is elected. The . . . current government . . . have no legitimacy, lack credibility and are massively corrupt. A democratic government will have the advantage of legitimacy and have the confidence of the political majority,' Mandela said.

Like him and other leaders, we were appalled at what had befallen our beloved country. We were all aware that only a political settlement could deliver our desired goal: to cast our votes for the first time, to choose what we could at last call a representative government, and thus to remove one of the root causes of the carnage. On the other hand, we were also aware that continued violence made an election increasingly difficult to organize. With every new killing or massacre, the prospects of free and fair elections diminished. Those of us who live in the townships knew that an election held in the midst of mindless violence could only be won by whoever controlled the most neighbourhoods in every disputed ghetto. Our first election seemed destined to be fought on the streets, and after dark. That was hardly likely to prove a hopeful prelude to the new democratic dawn we had all been yearning for.

12
SHARING
POWER

We politicians have all had our say. It is now time for the people to have their say. For the past three years we politicians have spoken to each other, at each other and past each other. We have been in bilaterals and multilaterals. Out there beyond the walls of the World Trade Centre there is growing impatience with our speechifying. And the most direct way to have their say, of course, is through an election. Let the people elect their representatives to draw a constitution they will call their own.

Joe Slovo, in the multi-party negotiating forum, April 1993

The beginning of 1993 found South Africa poised between hope and ruin. The talks had stalled, violence continued unabated, and people grew disillusioned about the future. The official resumption of the talks in March, after a ten-month hiatus, followed a series of bilateral discussions between the government and the ANC, and later the government and Inkatha. Almost all the parties, at various times, were drawn into one-to-one meetings aimed at relaunching the talks which had broken down at CODESA II in May 1992. Inkatha needed to be persuaded to return to the negotiating table after pulling out in protest against the government–ANC 'Record of Understanding' of 26 September 1992. The bilateral talks also had the aim of making the negotiation process as inclusive as possible and resolving the stand-off between all the parties previously involved and those expected to join, such as the PAC, the CP, the Afrikaner Volksunie and traditional leaders from the four provinces. For the ANC and the government, the one-to-one talks brought new agreements on the nature of power-sharing arrangements after elections for a constituent assembly. Significant compromises were made on both sides.

The ANC's National Working Committee, often referred to as South Africa's future cabinet, accepted a document drafted by Joe Slovo arguing that any future government could not run the risk of alienating the bureaucracy and armed forces empowered by the present state. Slovo argued that there could be no total victory for either side – the government or the ANC – in negotiations. His premise was that major compromises were necessary because the ANC was 'not dealing with a defeated enemy'. He suggested an offer of amnesty to all those who were engaged in enforcing apartheid, and job guarantees and assured pension benefits to generals and civil servants to ensure their cooperation with the country's first democratically elected government. 'We are not

31 *Chief Mangosuthu Buthelezi leading a march of Inkatha Freedom Party supporters to protest against what he called the 'ethnic cleansing' of Zulus by ANC supporters.*

32 *President F. W. de Klerk, Nelson Mandela and Chief Mangosuthu Buthelezi on 14 September 1991, when they signed the National Peace Accord they hoped would help end political killings.*

33 *The late Chris Hani and Joe Slovo, the man he succeeded as general secretary of the South African Communist Party. Hani was gunned down outside his Dawn Park, Boksburg home on 10 April 1993. He was the most popular ANC leader after Nelson Mandela, and was tipped by many to succeed Mandela as president.*

34 *ANC secretary-general and chief negotiator, Cyril Ramaphosa, and his government counterpart, Minister of Constitutional Development Roelf Meyer, conferring in a corridor at the World Trade Centre. The two men worked hard for a convergence of ideas between their rival parties.*

engaged in armistice talks. I wish we were. But the truth is neither side won the war. The National Party could not rule any longer, and we could not seize power by force. So that means both sides have to compromise. That is reality,' Slovo said in a report prepared for discussion by the ANC's policy-making National Executive Committee and later ratified by the shadow cabinet.

The shift from earlier demands for a complete transfer of power to the concept of shared power was profound. The ANC had accepted that it would share power with the white minority for a limited period after the country's first non-racial elections. It was an alliance that no one had expected, between former Marxist revolutionaries and white supremacists. Now the two opposing ideologies were striving to keep the transition to democracy on track. In a statement distributed to all its 14 regions, the ANC said:

> In the interest of reconstruction and peace and the need to minimize the potential threat to democratic advance from divisive forces in the period immediately following the adoption of a new constitution, we declare our support for an interim government of national unity which would exist up to the point of the adoption of a new constitution.... The balance of forces, and the interests of the whole country may still require of us to consider the establishment of a government of national unity so that parties that have lost an election will not be able to paralyse the functioning of government.

The Coalition Option: Compromise or Capitulation?

Under the government–ANC plan, supported by most parties except the IFP and the CP, an elected constituent assembly would draft and finally enact the first democratic constitution. From the constituent assembly an interim government of national unity would emerge that would propose legislation and supervise the making of the new constitution. The bicameral interim legislature would serve for five years and, to assure whites that they would not be shoved to the political margins, the government of national unity would remain in power throughout this period. There would be a single president with executive powers, but on certain specified issues decisions would be taken by a two-thirds majority in the cabinet. The US model of democracy would exercise a strong influence, and the lower house would be elected by proportional representation. The upper house would reflect an explicit attempt to give whites a disproportionately large voice. Only in 1999, after the enactment of the new constitution, would elections be held to return the first democratic government on the basis of majority rule.

The interim government would be a coalition comprising party representatives in proportion to votes cast for the assembly. Thus, for instance, de Klerk could serve in the same cabinet as Mandela if the ANC emerged victorious. De Klerk's party had failed to sell its 'troika' idea that leaders of the top parties in the first election be equal partners in a revolving presidency, giving minority parties the same power as majority parties. The National Party also failed in its bid to vest power in an executive committee comprising party leaders, leaving the president to perform ceremonial jobs. Another de Klerk concession sidelined his demand for upfront guarantees of power sharing in a final constitution. The way he saw it, 'We are talking about the need in a government of national unity to be governed on the basis of consensus between the main role players when considering fundamental issues. With regard to matters of average importance, one can always have an agreement as to how differences between them can be settled.'

In a major concession to Inkatha, the ANC agreed that an unelected negotiating council would draw up an interim constitution and that the principles embodied in that constitution on federalism and other matters would be binding on the elected constituent assembly. The ANC also conceded that there would be strong, meaningful regional governments as long as this did not emasculate the powers of the central government and seek to maintain racial and ethnic divisions. The concession meant that Inkatha had wrung from the ANC its long-standing demand that the framework of the constitution and its guiding principles would be established by the unelected multi-party negotiators rather than by an elected constituent assembly, where the ANC and the government would dominate smaller groups.

The main sticking point was that the government and the ANC interpreted their agreement on an interim government of national unity differently. For the government it was tantamount to sharing power. For the ANC it was no more than an interim measure to unify the country and create stability. As Ramaphosa told reporters, 'The objective is to unite our country, bring about stability and ensure that we embark on a reconstruction programme.' To many smaller parties, the agreement on power sharing came as a relief. As DP leader Zach de Beer pointed out during a parliamentary debate,

> Neither the NP nor the ANC can govern South Africa alone. . . . Anyone in his or her senses would rather trust a partnership or coalition between the National Party and the ANC than trust either organization by itself, for the presence as a partner of the ANC would greatly restrain the natural racial arrogance of the National Party whereas the presence of the National Party would be an effective antidote to the totalitarian tendencies of the ANC.

The idea that outright majority rule would be put on hold to ensure stability caused great consternation among ANC followers. The ANC's militant supporters accused its leadership of forsaking the movement's liberation struggle and being too naïve. There was even growing concern among senior ANC leaders that negotiators were becoming increasingly detached from the rest of the leadership and even more so from grassroots supporters. Ordinary members became angry over what they perceived as 'secret deals' struck behind closed doors between their movement and the government negotiating teams.

Facing criticism from its constituency for agreeing to share power with de Klerk, the ANC emphasized that the proposed interim government of national unity would not compromise the principle of majority rule. The ANC said it had defeated the government's power-sharing proposals to give minority parties a veto over the party obtaining the majority of votes in the first democratic general elections. It maintained that its proposal for a government of national unity 'does not seek to share power but to harness it for the purpose of rebuilding and reconstructing' our society, and that the composition of a government of national unity would reflect 'voter preferences and nothing else.'

Despite these assurances, the power-sharing deal was received with hostility among radical leaders in the more militant regions of the ANC such as Natal, where Harry Gwala's reaction was typical. As he told me in a telephone interview,

> We find the agreement unacceptable. It is a drastic departure from what we have always known the ANC to stand for. This is indeed a strange way of appeasement. We are already setting down the rule of surrender before we meet the enemy. If we go out to negotiations with such terms of surrender, where do we draw the line? The ANC plans to take ready-made state apparatus and control it with the National Party. For this to succeed, we must throw in retrenchment packages as sops which will appease the dragon [and] a general amnesty at some stage [as well].

Mandela's wife, Winnie, who continues to enjoy support among ANC youths and militants, said sharing power was undemocratic and would produce a backlash from disillusioned masses if their interests were abandoned in the rush for a future gravy train. At the funeral of anti-apartheid activist Helen Joseph in January 1993, she warned that

> The leadership ought to be aware that the masses fear being compromised. They fear that our organization is about to enter into big compromises with the state.... That needs to be explained thoroughly to the people.... We have been fighting all along. We [the ANC and the government] regard each other as enemies. It is crucial to take the masses along with us on the question of power sharing. And it is the masses who must give a mandate to the leadership about their interpretations of power sharing. Because if we do not do that we are likely to find ourselves an élite group leading the masses while we are not in touch with them. We do not know their aspirations.

Mrs Mandela accused the ANC leadership of getting into bed with the National Party for reasons of political expediency. In an essay released to journalists and published in all major newspapers in January 1993, she wrote:

> The quick-fix solutions sought by our leaders can only benefit a few and will backfire massively on the country as a whole. The disillusion that will follow when the masses awaken to the fact that they have not been included in the new freedom and in the new wealth enjoyed by their leaders will worsen implications than what we experienced in the 1970s and 1980s, and will plunge the country irrevocably into yet another vortex of mass violence and protest, this time not against the National Party but against the new government which the masses will have discovered to be representing the same class interest as the National Party it fought so bravely.

The concept of power sharing was also criticized by intellectuals within the ANC such as Pallo Jordan. Jordan said such an approach would mean the entrenchment of a civil service with no interest in the ANC's constituency and a perceived interest in undermining democratic rule. Attacking Slovo for being 'charmingly ignorant of the history of the twentieth century', Jordan argued that these measures 'would amount to capitulation to some of the core objectives pursued by the regime.'

Mandela and many of his colleagues have strongly defended the principles of a government of national unity while making it clear that they do not regard it as a form of power sharing. Speaking in Mamelodi in April 1993, Mandela drew two parallels with the history of African nationalism – one from the 'Uhuru' decade, the other much closer to home in time and space:

> In 1966 Kwame Nkrumah was deposed. He had got 98 per cent of the vote of the country in an election. It was one of the strongest governments in the world. But he was overthrown by a chap who hardly had the rank of a colonel, through a coup. In Angola, President José Eduardo dos Santos won the election, but Jonas Savimbi almost overran the whole country. We have to be very careful in our country, to make sure that we take all precautions to prevent a situation of that nature happening here. The only way to do so is to ensure that all political parties committed to democracy have a stake in government.

All in all, however, bilateral talks produced significant outcomes. The ANC's insistence on 5 per cent of the votes cast as the threshold for entry into the cabinet under a government of national unity, rather than the 10 per cent threshold preferred by the NP, was viewed as an impressive display of its desire to accommodate the smaller parties who would thus gain some say in the interim government of national unity. The organization's decision to accept something less than full majority rule in the interests of national reconciliation and consolidating democracy was an event of the same magnitude as de Klerk's seminal speech in February 1990. It formalized the historic compromise which Mandela outlined in his prison memorandum to the government, in which he set the goal of negotiations as reconciling the black demand for majority rule with the white demand for structural guarantees. It also marked the realization of de Klerk's promise that negotiations would lead to the end of white domination. From the negotiations standpoint, the future of the country seemed promising. However, the prospect of ruin would soon loom as close.

April is the Cruellest Month: The Assassination of Chris Hani

Everyone has vivid moments concerning the tragic death of a great person. The death of Chris Hani was one such incident, to be recounted to our children and replayed in the mind's eye for as long as we live. It was with his untimely death that we found ourselves once again poised between hope and ruin.

I first met Chris Hani at an international football match. Then one day I ventured into his home unannounced, accompanying a friend. On that day we discussed many things: my family, his family – and the complaints of my ANC-supporting friends that the movement was compromising too much in the democracy talks. During our discussion we discovered that our daughters' schools were situated next to each other. Hani asked me to arrange a barbecue at my house and invite a few friends so that he could explain the ANC's policies on the transition to democracy. I thought he was joking, because he was such a busy person. Whenever we met he kept reminding me that I had not fulfilled my promise.

I had the opportunity to talk to him again several months later, when he and his colleague Essop Pahad had lunch with me and Reuter Bureau chief Rodney Pinder. I was struck by the way he remembered everything we had discussed during our first meeting, including the names of my wife and daughters. Again he took me to task for not keeping my promise. Over lunch, he told us how he loved travelling to the remotest areas of South Africa to address villagers, the elderly and the young about the upcoming democracy. 'When I am with the villagers, I speak basic Xhosa. By so doing I make sure I am able to articulate their aspirations and my organization's policies in the language they understand best. I speak no English or Afrikaans.'

Much later I decided to take him up on his offer. I wrote him a letter suggesting a date for a meeting at my house when he could meet my friends. He called me and accused me of unnecessary formality in writing a letter instead of telephoning. He then set a date for the meeting. Our barbecue for Chris Hani was set for the weekend he was buried.

On the few occasions when I had met Hani face to face, I had found him to be an ardent advocate of peace, a man who oozed warmth, zest for life, tenderness and boundless optimism. Then a Polish immigrant put an end to Hani's life in a short, sharp burst of gunfire. The alleged assassin, Janusz Waluz, who was arrested soon after the shooting, turned out to have been a member of the neo-Nazi AWB since 1986. Police said the murder weapon found in Waluz's possession, a 9mm Z88 pistol fitted with a silencer, was part of a consignment of weapons stolen from an Air Force armoury in 1990. The man who stole the weapons, Piet Rudolph – leader of another right-wing organization, the Order of the Boerevolk – was freed under a 1991 amnesty agreement between the ANC and the government. Barend Strydom, the murderer of eight blacks in 1988 who was released from prison on parole under the same amnesty, boasted that Waluz was a member of his White Wolves movement. When police searched Waluz's house, they found a hit list which included Mandela, Foreign Affairs Minister Pik Botha, Joe Slovo, ANC negotiator Mac Maharaj and Judge Richard Goldstone. A few days after Waluz's arrest, five others were arrested on suspicion of complicity and conspiracy to carry out the assassination. Three were freed. The other two, Conservative Party parliamentarian Clive Derby-Lewis and his wife Gaye, have been charged with murder along with Janusz Waluz.

Hani's murder showed the power which white extremists have to cause havoc. Often dismissed as a small and inconsequential, hopelessly divided bunch of lunatics, with this assassination they demonstrated the destructive force conferred by their ready access to weaponry and training, and their freedom to move and act without hindrance from the police. Hani's death left a gaping hole in the leadership of the ANC. A generation younger than Mandela, his unique importance lay in his strong appeal to young township militants attracted partly by his communist beliefs and partly by his defiant style as chief of staff of Umkhonto we Sizwe. His killers knew that Hani was loved by ordinary people throughout the country. His popularity would have made him a key leader during the election campaign, when the ANC would have looked to him to discipline the radicalism of its younger supporters – a role he had already begun to assume. Shortly before his death, Hani castigated those who did not believe in nego- tiations. 'I feel we have achieved something in this country when those who oppressed us in the past are actually talking to us and showing readiness to negotiate for democratic elections,' he said at a rally in Daveyton township. In a short autobiography simply called *My Life* and distributed in pamphlet form at his funeral, Hani wrote:

> The racist regime has reluctantly recognised the legitimacy of our struggle by agreeing to sit down with us to discuss how to begin the negotiation process. In the current political situation, the decision by our organisation to suspend the armed action is correct and is an important contribution in maintaining the momentum of negotiations.

Despite his association with a communist ideology that was discredited and dying in so many other countries, Hani was the most popular ANC leader after Mandela. If there was anyone who could give young militants their marching orders, it was he. Mandela was listened to, but at times was not obeyed. It was not surprising that Mandela was jeered when, trying to put across a message of peace with de Klerk at Hani's memorial service, he chose to emphasize his own continuing working relationship with the NP leader. Mandela was booed and jeered when he said he had received messages of sympathy from de Klerk following Hani's death. 'I understand your anger. There is no party that has been more responsible for the pain [of apartheid] than the National Party. We do not want to think of the past. We want to think of the present and the future.' He was booed and jeered again when he said he was prepared to work with de Klerk to build a new South Africa.

By contrast, the PAC's Clarence Makwetu, whose organization claimed responsi- bility for the killing of scores of whites, was cheered when he shared the platform with Mandela. The PAC, which had joined the negotiations only in March, was more acceptable to the radical black youths in the crowd, who regarded the PAC's 'One settler one bullet' chant as particularly appropriate in the case of Waluz.

For the government, the death of Hani brought home all too clearly that having lost its legitimacy it no longer had the ability to govern the country alone, especially in times of crisis. Powerless to act, de Klerk found that his pleas for calm were scorned by the black community. He had no alternative but to hand responsibility for defusing the anger of the masses to Mandela, who for a few days became *de facto* president. Millions watched as Mandela appealed for calm in a state of the nation television address:

With all the authority at my command, to all our people: remain calm and honour the memory of Chris Hani by remaining a disciplined force for peace. Chris Hani is irreplaceable in the heart of our nation and people. To the youth of South Africa, we have a special message for you. You lost a hero. You have repeatedly shown that your freedom is greater than the most precious gift, life itself. But you are the leaders of tomorrow. Your country, your people, your organization [want you] to act with wisdom. A particular responsibility rests on your shoulders. We must not let the men who worship war and who lust after blood precipitate actions that will plunge our country into another Angola.

But the young militants seemed to be saying that no one should expect the terrible murder of Hani to be forgotten or passed over lightly. Disaffected, they went on the rampage through shopping districts in Port Elizabeth, Cape Town, Durban and Pietermaritzburg. Cars were torched, storefronts were smashed and widespread looting followed. Over 70 people died and material damage ran to millions of rands in the aftermath of Hani's death. Relative to the scale of demonstrations from over two million people who attended 85 rallies to mourn Hani's murder, the level of violence was low, yet the violent aftermath reflected the deep resentments and racial polarization brought about by decades of apartheid.

As the nation counted the cost of Hani's assassination, most people agreed that his most fitting memorial would be the rapid closing of the deal he defended: the election in 1994 of a non-racial government in which the various parties would have a share of power proportionate to the votes cast. In this way Hani's assassination galvanized the people of our nation in their search for a political settlement. Never before had so many South Africans from such diverse backgrounds shared a political emotion as intense as the horror they felt at this deed. Mandela and de Klerk invoked the memory of Hani as a powerful factor to support underlying agreement on how to move beyond the crisis sparked by the assassination. They agreed that continuing negotiations represented South Africa's only lifeline and its surest defence against the forces of anarchy. For the ANC, the roots of the crisis caused by Hani's death lay in the unrepresentative and therefore illegitimate nature of the government, and the answer lay in rapid progress towards a popularly elected government.

April 1993 was a dark and terrible month for South African politics. Clouds of gloom settled over us with the natural deaths of other political leaders following Hani's killing. Conservative Party leader Andries Treurnicht died three days after Hani had been laid to rest, a few weeks after his party reluctantly joined the negotiation process for fear of being sidelined. Two days after Treurnicht's death and five days after Hani's burial, the 'cruellest month' claimed Oliver Tambo, the former president of the ANC and its national chairman. Although Tambo's death had little impact on national politics, his passing depleted further the ANC's old guard, reminding us all of the mortality of those who survive him.

Committee, Council, Forum, Plenary: Negotiating as a Process

Although many of the thorny issues affecting the transition to democracy were partially resolved in bilateral talks, the consensus forged by the government and the ANC on power sharing and the structure of an interim government of national unity was to be tested in the multi-party talks.

Before the demise of CODESA II, there were two power blocs: the government had its allies, and the ANC had theirs. Inkatha sided with the government on many issues, as did the leaders of Bophuthatswana, Ciskei and QwaQwa; de Klerk could also count on the backing of a few political parties that had participated in apartheid-created structures for many years. The situation changed after 26 September 1992 with the signing of the Record of Understanding, which called for the fencing of Inkatha-dominated hostels and restrictions on the carrying of cultural weapons. The government–ANC agreement infuriated Chief Buthelezi, who caucused with Bophuthatswana's Lucas Mangope, Ciskei's Oupa Gqozo, the CP and the Afrikaner Volksunie to form a third power bloc, the Concerned South Africans Group (COSAG). They accused the ANC and the government of secret deals. The ANC could count on Transkei, KaNgwane, KwaNdebele, the SACP, COSATU, and the Transvaal and Natal Indian Congresses. The PAC, the Democratic Party, and the homeland governments of Venda and Gazankulu were freelancers, switching their support as the occasion demanded.

Despite a shift in power alignments, the 1993 talks were the most representative political consultations ever held in South Africa. They included the 19 parties that launched CODESA and seven others: the KwaZulu government, the CP, the PAC, the Afrikaner Volksunie and traditional leaders from the four provinces of Natal, Orange Free State, Transvaal and the Cape Province. Negotiators appointed seven technical committees of experts to research and submit proposals on issues crucial for the transition to democracy. Those issues were: constitutional matters, violence, fundamental human rights during transition, the transitional executive council, independent media commissions and an independent telecommunications authority, an independent electoral commission, and the amendment or repeal of discriminatory laws. Other constitutional matters were the form of state to be adopted, transitional regional government, the constituent assembly, and the future of nominal independent states. The seven technical committees, set up outside the negotiation process and consisting of nine members each, were appointed to produce reports on the above matters for consideration by participants so as to speed up a political settlement. The committee on constitutional matters was charged with the difficult job of presenting a report based on different perspectives of the future.

These issues were to pass through four bodies crucial to the negotiation process: the planning committee, the negotiation council, the negotiation forum and the plenary. The ten-member planning committee, consisting of the top negotiators, worked under the directive of the negotiation council on the planning and eventual submission of recommendations on procedural and substantive issues to be discussed by negotiators. The ten men – Cyril Ramaphosa (ANC chief negotiator), Roelf Meyer (government), Rowan Cronje (Bophutatswana), Joe Slovo (South African Communist Party), Colin Eglin (Democratic Party), Frank Mdlalose (Inkatha), Zamindlela Titus (Transkei), Benny Alexander (PAC), Pravin Gordhan (Natal Indian Congress), and Mick Webb (Ciskei) – met daily behind closed doors and were the kingpins of the process. They debated reports from the seven technical committees and prepared positions and agreements on pertinent issues.

The negotiation council, the engine room of the process, was a 104-member body. It was here that every major decision affecting the future was debated until agreement was reached. It was here that parties filibustered, here that they won or refused concessions on all the major constitutional or political issues, from the shape of the new constitution to the powers of the new president, or even the duties and functions of future regional governments. It was here that parties rose in unison to 'walk out in disgust' after losing support for their submissions, here that they accepted submissions from others after lengthy and often boring debates. Some debates were aired live on television and radio for the nation to see and hear where negotiations were leading. In the council, indeed, the future was determined.

The council reported to the negotiation forum, a body which formally ratified council decisions in public, with three delegates and two advisers from each participant in attendance. The forum broadened support for council decisions which would be taken to the plenary. The plenary was a ceremonial body to which each participant sent nine delegates, including its leader, to ratify agreements from time to time.

At the reconstituted talks, negotiators expected agreement on a wide range of issues. The NP wanted agreement on power sharing, regional governments with defined powers and functions as opposed to a unitary state, a free market system, and multi-party democracy. The ANC and its allies wanted multi-party democracy, a limited interim government of national unity, equal voting rights for all, a Bill of Rights and proportional representation. It wanted a strong central government with entrenched regional powers that would not be overridden unless regional governments exceeded their clearly defined powers. The ANC thus appeared to favour a form of limited federalism on the US model.

The PAC wanted a constituent assembly to draw up a new constitution, multi-party democracy, a Bill of Rights, proportional representation, and international intervention to ensure stability during the transition. The Democratic Party wanted democratic elections, proportional representation, regionalism and federalism. The COSAG group wanted self-determination and the protection of minority or ethnic rights. They wanted the new South Africa to be a federation of powerful regions, so that they could retain their individual identities and their powers.

Buthelezi, in particular, wanted strong regional governments and a weak centre. Common ground existed between the government and Inkatha. They shared many of the same views and objectives regarding South Africa's future constitutional arrangements. De Klerk was happy to accept an arrangement that left the functions, duties and powers of regions to an elected body to determine, subject to two provisos, that decisions relating to regions be approved by a special majority of regional representatives in the constituent assembly and that the need for autonomous regional governments be approved in principle by the negotiation forum. Inkatha, however, wanted all this agreed upon prior to elections. Some members of the COSAG group warned that they would withdraw from negotiations if they believed the principle of self-determination had been neglected or dismissed at the multi-party talks. As CP leader Ferdi Hartzenburg put it: 'If that door is closed, we shall not stay there and arrange our own funeral.'

Free and Fair: the Transitional Executive Council and the Elections

Along with multi-party negotiations, a new mini-government would soon prepare for elections – the Transitional Executive Council (TEC). The TEC would operate alongside the white-dominated cabinet but would have powers of intervention at all levels to nurse the country towards free and fair elections. It was to be another milestone on the way to establishing a new constitutional order. It would be responsible for making sure that each party was treated fairly during the run-up to elections. To do this, it would appoint a number of sub-councils, made up of representatives of various political organizations. The sub-councils would maintain law and order through joint control of the security forces, defence, foreign affairs, finance, local government, and the independent media and electoral commissions which were to be set up. The electoral commission was to see to it that the infrastructure for free and fair elections had been established. The media commission and an independent telecommunications authority would ensure that all parties have equal access to the electorate through the media. A commission on regionalism was to finalize a report on how South Africa, including the homelands, would be divided into regions. As elections for the interim government would take place on both national and regional lines, negotiators would have to agree on regional boundaries, powers and functions.

There was also the need to set up a specially trained independent peace-keeping force to hold the ring during the elections. Local and international monitors would be asked to help. The TEC would have wide-ranging powers and its sub-councils would take full control of the portfolios entrusted to them. For the ANC and other anti-government groups, the security sub-council seemed the most vital. It would establish joint control of the SADF, the SAP and National Intelligence. If this could not be achieved, phase one of the transition would lose its legitimacy.

Representation on the TEC was to be fairly evenly divided three ways, between the NP, the ANC and the other participants: with its creation, South Africa would have its first taste of power sharing. While the government and homeland authorities would continue to run South Africa until elections were held, their activities would be subject to scrutiny and intervention by the TEC. It would operate like a cabinet, meeting regularly to debate issues of importance in South Africa's transition to democracy. The ANC and the NP were careful to point out that the intended role of the TEC and its sub-councils was merely to level the playing field for elections, and that they would not represent an early form of interim government.

Not Yet, Benny: Lighter Moments

Real progress was made at these talks, so that it may surprise the uninitiated to learn that negotiations were nevertheless a slow and tedious exercise. I and many journalists had to endure many hours of nit-picking, bickering and senseless debate. Delegates argued about petty issues, such as whether one courier company was preferable to another when it came to delivering documentation to delegates on time. They fell out and failed to reach an agreement over the name of the forum. Thirteen wanted CODESA retained, nine wanted the South African Constitutional Forum, some wanted a combination of CODESA and various far from snappy acronyms. Many days and hours were spent squabbling over procedural issues such as what should come first on the agenda, and what should come last. The ANC and the government often expressed disappointment at the lack of progress. There were many causes: other parties felt they were being rushed to make decisions, or delegates had not received documentation from technical committees on time. Amid all the tedium and delay, the star turns shone out: Cyril Ramaphosa, chief negotiator for the ANC, and Roelf Meyer, the NP's representative, who did their best to convince their colleagues that time was of the essence.

There were lighter moments, too, including birthday, wedding and anniversary celebrations. There was the afternoon when Inkatha's Frank Mdlalose was chairing the proceedings and the ANC's Joe Slovo praised him for the way he had handled the day's events: 'If your conduct and your political acumen match one another the future is bright.' 'I do not know if that is a kiss of death,' Mdlalose responded. There were other such moments when individuals dropped their guard. After a government press con-ference Roelf Meyer turned to the PAC's Benny Alexander and announced, 'The PAC will now take over from the government,' then quickly added, 'But you cannot rule yet, Benny.'

It also came to light that participation in the talks could bring handsome rewards. A delegate was paid R32,000 a month for representing one of the four independent homelands. We were told that this was to compensate him and his law firm for the loss of income he would otherwise have received as an advocate. An adviser to one of the parties earned R1,000 a day. There were even foreigners who tried to push their way into the negotiations. One of them was Mario Ambrosini, an American citizen and constitutional lawyer who advised Inkatha in that capacity. Ambrosini was kicked out of the negotiations on many occasions for not being a South African. He attempted to get honorary citizenship in the nominally independent homeland of Ciskei to allow him to take part in the talks. Sometimes he managed to sneak in, looking rather miserable. Another American often included in Inkatha ranks was former Rutgers University law professor Albert Blaustein. Unlike Ambrosini, he never argued the point when the ruling was made that foreigners could not attend as negotiators or advisers. More embarrassing for Inkatha was the disclosure that one of its officials at the talks was a self-confessed gunrunner. Before Bruce Anderson was summarily deported from South Africa, he confessed to newspapers that he had channelled arms and ammunition to Inkatha.

Just as negotiators produced a declaration of intent at the first meeting of CODESA in December 1991, the climax of the negotiation process 18 months later was the setting of an election date and the approval of the following building blocks of our new constitution:

> The constitution of South Africa shall provide for the establishment of one sovereign state with a common South African citizenship and a democratic system of government committed to achieving equality between men and women and people of all races.

> South Africa will have a multi-party democracy based on proportional representation with strong central and regional government.

> The constitution shall be the supreme law of the land and shall be binding on the organs of government, shall prohibit racial, gender, and all forms of discrimination and promote racial and gender equality and national unity.

> There shall be representantive government embracing multi-party democracy, regular elections, universal adult suffrage, a common voter's roll and in general proportional representation.

> All shall enjoy universally accepted fundamental rights, freedoms and civil liberties protected by justiciable provisions in the constitution.

> The diversity of language and culture shall be acknowledged and protected, and conditions for their promotion shall be encouraged.

> Collective rights of self-determination in informing and joining and maintaining organs of civil society, including linguistic, cultural and religious associations, shall, on the basis of non-discrimination and free association, be recognised and protected.

> Provision shall be made for participation of minority political parties in the legislative process in a manner consistent with democracy.

Negotiators also unveiled a nine-region draft map for South Africa. The Commission on the Delimitation and Demarcation of Regions (CDDR) took 304 written and 80 oral submissions into account while drafting its recommendations. It indicated that there had not been enough local community involvement. The proposed regions are Northern Transvaal, Pretoria-Witwatersrand-Vereeniging (PWV), Eastern Transvaal, KwaZulu/Natal, Orange Free State, Eastern Cape, Western Cape, Northern Cape, North West.

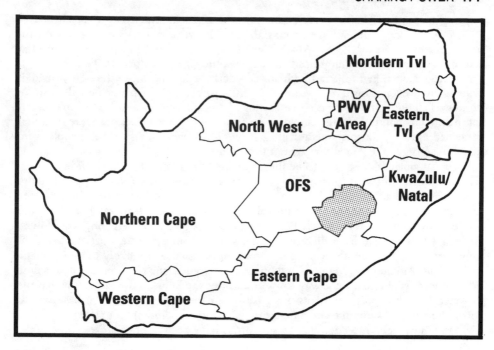

South Africa's future regions as proposed by the Commission on the Demarcation and Delimitation of Regions (CDDR).

While making progress in the modalities of transition to democracy and maps of the democratic society, the negotiators were often reminded that for three years they had been in the throes of this process as brokers representing us, the toiling masses black and white. It was ordinary South Africans – in townships, on farms, in city streets and in their homes everywhere – who suffered the agonies of unbridled violence, political uncertainity and deepening economic recession as three years of painful negotiations unfolded. Negotiators were aware that, until non-racial elections were held, the country would undoubtedly witness incidents of shocking violence orchestrated by elements opposed to a constitutional settlement. This led them to give the black and white massses something to look forward to: an election for the government of their choice. Alongside negotiating the nuts and bolts of the transition to democracy, they set a target date on which the people would go to the polls. That all-too provisional date – 27 April 1994 – was nevertheless a beacon of achievement planted by all those who have struggled, sacrificed, died and, in some cases, endured to see the end of apartheid.

There Is Also a Sarajevo Here

The announcement was greeted with a mixture of joyful relief and anxiety. As if on cue, a surge of violence swept the townships around Johannesburg shortly after the announcement. As I went to rescue my sister from the smouldering township violence in Katlehong and neighbouring Tokoza, the smell of roasting human flesh hung in the air. I witnessed a crowd of 20 with spears, axes and stones gathered around three burning bodies lying behind refuse bins. '*Sizitholie izinja, siyazitsisa!*' they chanted – 'We found the dogs and we are burning them!' The victims, two men and a woman, were Inkatha supporters. 'Viva ANC, Viva! Long Live ANC, Long Live!' Shots and screams indicated more killings nearby. There was no sign of the police. To get through the carnage I often had to plead with armed youths, many no more than 16 years old, who wanted everything I had – my car, my money, and even my petrol to make bombs. 'Tell the world there is also a Sarajevo here,' said one when I told him I was a journalist. The political tensions building up ahead of the April elections were such that it needed only a spark to ignite a conflagration. That weekend, over 120 people were killed in an orgy of violence throughout the country.

Political violence continues to be the single biggest obstacle to a smooth beginning. Each major step forward, virtually every political peak – the Groote Schuur Minute which launched the negotiations process in April 1991, the Pretoria Minute three months later, the signing of the National Peace Accord on 14 September 1991, the whites-only referendum in March 1992 – was accompanied by a staggering loss of lives. At least 10,000 people have died in political violence since the negotiations began in February 1990. The months leading to the 27 April election are likely to be traumatic and violent. Although, as Mandela and others have argued, the election of a democratic government would go a long way towards curbing the killings, the sad fact is that the violence has taken on a life of its own. Although much of the violence has political roots, the vengeance motive and an increase in crime are adding fuel to the fire.

Mandela has acknowledged that his supporters have been responsible for some of the killings.

> There are members of the ANC who are killing our people. We must face the truth. Our people are just as involved as other organizations that are committing this violence. And people who are doing that are no longer human beings, they are animals. It is no use when I speak the truth for you to say: 'No, no, no, no.' You want me to blame Inkatha only. I am not going to do that.
>
> It is true that the government is involved in the violence. It is members of the army, members of the police force, members of their intelligence service who are also behind this violence, because they want to cripple and weaken the ANC. But I am not going to criticize only the government and Inkatha. People who participate in this violence, for whatever reason – kill innocent people because others have killed innocent people – are not serving the cause of freedom. Those of you who have in your midst members of Inkatha, PAC or AZAPO, *do not use violence against them unless it is self-defence*. Let them do their political work in the community. They are entitled to do that. The ANC's strength is not violence. Our strength is the correctness of our position. You should be tolerant of those who have views that are different to yours. Because you will win by the correctness of the position that you take on all major national issues.

This frank admission, in a speech at a funeral in Mamelodi township east of Pretoria on 7 April 1993, was a striking reversal of Mandela's previous stance on the violence. In the past, he had consistently laid all the blame on Inkatha and the government, once accusing de Klerk of Nazi-style genocide against blacks. Now he was willing to risk alienating those in the ANC still resolutely committed to the violent pursuit of political goals. He was admitting that his people were not angels, that there were animals amongst them.

His speech reflected a new mood of self-examination within the ANC, which also acknowledged that it had lost control of some of the 'self-defence' units it had set up to protect black townships. The units, recruited mainly from young militants with little military training or discipline, were intended to protect their communities from attacks by Inkatha or the 'third force'. In the eyes of township residents, however, many of the unit members were little more than armed criminals. Mandela's new attitude was further proof that there could be no answer to the problem of violence until its complexities had been analysed and understood. Harry Gwala was another whose disgust at the violence was turning to anger, as he told me in an interview:

> Yes, I am angry. Every day I meet people badly wounded. I see acts of cruelty I cannot believe. I have seen bodies burnt into blocks of charcoal. When you see such wounds and misery you become extremely angry. You read about the atrocities of the Nazi camps, but I never thought I would see them in real life.

Violence has become pervasive, a dread which hangs over all races and lingers in every household as crime, political killings, police brutality and suicides fill morgues and hospitals.

Violence against whites has also increased dramatically. Led by the Azanian People's Liberation Army (APLA), the military wing of the PAC, a campaign of terror against white civilians has recently led to attacks on whites in their homes, neighbourhoods, and public places. These killings have shattered white illusions about their immunity from tragic suffering and death, and served as a warning to all that violence begets more violence. The PAC has come under heavy criticism from all sides, including its allies in the ANC, for dismissing the outcry over the killing of whites as 'hullabaloo', a word used by Benny Alexander, the PAC's general secretary:

> There is a lot of hullabaloo around the attack purely because white people have died. We are angry at the regime, the police and the media for their blatant racial approach to the killings. This is the type of racial attitude by the regime, the security forces and the media which leads many ordinary Africans to the conclusion that the violence will be treated more seriously if it is not confined only in the townships but spills over to the white areas.

Although many blacks sympathize with this view, the further escalation of violence on all sides threatens to delay the day when South Africa will enjoy a peaceful and stable democracy.

The country must also contend with those who wish to prevent or postpone elections at any cost. This was demonstrated when the right wing went on the offensive. Black-clad toughs of the AWB staged an audacious coup on 25 June 1993, seizing South Africa's surrogate parliament, the World Trade Centre, by force. Toting combat rifles and dressed in their neo-Nazi uniforms, they swaggered down the corridors of the conference centre where negotiations were taking place, shouting orders and spraying racist graffiti. AWB leader Eugene Terre'Blanche and his henchmen took over the central negotiating chamber and sang the national anthem as a sign of victory.

Taking it on the jaw: report from the danger zone

I had arrived early in the morning to cover a planned right-wing protest and to report on the talks. At the time, I did not feel threatened. White right-wingers had always accused black demonstrators of violent and disorderly behaviour, thus leading us to believe that their protests would be non-violent and orderly. Before going into the conference centre, I drove through hordes of armed protesters and spoke to farmers as they sipped morning coffee laced with brandy before the demonstration. All of them assured me it would be a peaceful stand to back their demand for a separate white state. But my presence raised eyebrows among some of the men, who read aloud the word

'Press' from my identifying armband. 'One black one, one bullet,' someone said.

I realized there was going to be trouble when they barged their way into the grounds of the conference centre, forcing the main gate. Men and women in AWB uniforms – some with their children – farmers in floppy hats and muscular young men with close-cropped hair walked along the road carrying banners, placards, the South African flag and cooler bags. Many of them were carrying firearms in holsters and hunting knives in sheaths. Some carried hunting rifles in quilted or leather bags. They evaded a line of policemen trying to stop their advance – but not trying as hard, it seemed to me, as they do when intercepting black protesters. An armoured car followed in their wake. Seconds later, it plunged through the glass-panelled entrance of the World Trade Centre and right-wingers swept around it into the building. Fearing death, negotiators fled to safety and took refuge under the protection of security forces in back rooms as more than 300 AWB members, some in the black uniforms of the Victory Commando, occupied the chambers. They tore up documents, sprayed graffiti – *Eie volk, eie land* (Own people, own land) – and occupied seats vacated by the negotiators. They helped themselves to drinks and took special pleasure in urinating against the chamber walls.

Any blacks within eyesight were harassed or assaulted, including myself. The first threat came when I was attempting to assess the damage caused by the armoured car's break-in. A young neo-Nazi said to me: 'Kaboutertjie, jy moet weg van hierdie plek gaan.' ('Little imp, you must leave this place.') When I asked why, I was told, 'Because you are in a danger zone.' I went to shut myself in the Reuter office, but then decided to head for the ANC offices to see Ramaphosa. I was told that he and other negotiators were holed up, guarded by soldiers. As I talked to white fellow journalists, a white man clad in a AWB khaki uniform hit me in the face and began punching and kicking me. 'This is one of the apes. What does this ape want here?' he shouted. White colleagues intervened to prevent a second AWB man from attacking. 'You are a disgrace to the white race,' said my assailant to Patti Waldmeir of the *Financial Times* and my colleague Judith Matloff when they intervened. 'You are a disgrace to the human race,' Waldmeir retorted.

These apostles of apartheid occupied the chamber for nearly two hours while their representatives handed over demands for an Afrikaner homeland and negotiated their departure from the complex. When they finally left, they marched away like a conquering army, beating drums. Surprisingly, armed policemen in riot gear stood passively by. If the invaders had been black, police would have opened fire at the slightest provocation and many, even hundreds, would have been killed. Instead of removing the AWB, police removed their caps and stood at attention during ostentatiously offered prayers and the singing of the white national anthem, *Die Stem*. They made no attempt to prevent vandalism or to stop right-wingers from slapping delegates, swearing at blacks and spitting at women. While all these things happened in front of their eyes, police took no action. There was no line-up of armoured cars, as there usually is when black protests are expected, no barbed wire, no fire hoses, no water cannons nor sneeze machines to keep the crowd at bay. Why were demonstrators allowed to enter the grounds bearing arms? Why was no attempt made to arrest anyone? The right-wingers simply did what they had come to do, then marched away with impunity.

In storming the centre, the stormtroopers of the far right flexed their muscles and demonstrated their capacity to create havoc. They proved that they can stop the fragile process of negotiations, even if only temporarily. Although most negotiators reject an Afrikaner homeland, the invasion clearly showed the build-up of armed right-wing resistance, a threat that may have to be accommodated. Even if it means giving them their own piece of land? It is doubtful that this would satisfy them, since they want to choose where their Afrikaner state would be situated. Their struggle is best understood as a bid to perpetuate apartheid in a disguised form.

And then there is Chief Buthelezi, who has predicted civil war would result from the proposed election of an all-race constituent assembly. He and the other members of COSAG represent a powerful bloc dedicated to derailing many government and ANC plans for the country's future structure. COSAG members, of course, have different visions of the future: theirs is a marriage of convenience that may or may not last. COSAG is strongly opposed to the 27 April election date, arguing that in the prevailing climate of violence the outcome of such an election is not to be trusted. It is also opposed to the idea of mandating a popularly elected constituent assembly to draw up a new constitution for the country. A number of independent polls predict that Inkatha cannot expect to get more than six per cent of the vote in a future election. The other members of COSAG are unlikely to fare much better. Banded together, however, their disruptive force far exceeds their numerical strength. Consequently, both de Klerk and Mandela will need the active support and cooperation of Buthelezi in order to make any agreement stick. As Buthelezi told an Inkatha rally at Currie's Fountain stadium, Durban: 'The ANC will never win a war against us. Nor will we win any war against them. Right now we are locked in a conflict which can only continue degenerating past politically motivated anger into the anger of criminals and all else.'

To complicate matters, while we view change as the birth of a new age of hope and prosperity, many white South Africans see the demise of apartheid as the end of their world. Driven to extreme nervousness at the prospect of a black-run government, many are preparing to flee the country, taking their money and skills with them. They claim that, for all its compromises and assurances, the ANC does not inspire confidence with its unclear policies, its threat of nationalization, and its plans to redistribute wealth and restore land to the black masses. Not prepared to watch their living standards decline, these whites would rather start afresh elsewhere. In an open letter to Mandela signed 'Packing for Paris' and published in *The Citizen* newspaper, one of them wrote:

> Let me tell you Mr Mandela that I and most of the middle of the road South Africans will not stay to watch you destroy this country. I will leave the country and make my life work somewhere else.... You say that you want white people to stay and make this country work. What assurances can you give me that my family will be safe in this country because you are unable to control your followers?
>
> If you come into power, will you abide by the promises that you make now, or is your rhetoric aimed at instilling a false sense of security into gullible people to gain votes? We need to know now before you close the borders to prevent us from leaving.
>
> As things stand now, I and many like me are already exploring overseas possibilities, before it is too late. Convince me to stay, Mr Mandela.'

To reinforce these sentiments, removals companies report a 57 per cent increase in inquiries. Some are even offering seminars on how to emigrate. Choice destinations include Australia and the United Kingdom, with the United States, Canada, Israel and the Netherlands following. Those looking to get out include successful businessmen, professionals, and technicians with superior skills and education. The ANC fears that many of these people are slowly impoverishing the country by sneaking their assets out of the back door. Although Mandela has appealed personally to whites not to leave the country, his repeated assurances seem to have fallen on deaf ears.

While whites are busy planning to emigrate, illegal immigrants are pouring into South Africa from neighbouring and more distant countries plagued by civil war, chronic instability, recession and drought – such as Angola, Mozambique, Zaïre, Malawi and Uganda. They are a burden to the country's already depressed economy and will make the redistributive attempts of the next government that much harder and more expensive. Some immigrants are legal professionals who are drawn to South Africa's higher standards of living, better salaries, and first world facilities. For example, a medical doctor in Ghana earns less than $90 a month, an amount he could get in two consultations in South Africa. Most illegal immigrants, however, are penniless refugees bent on survival. Already resentment against them is mounting in the black community as they compete with locals for jobs, housing, and other opportunities. The Department of Home Affairs said in a recent statement that a total of 82,000 people were repatriated last year. Of these, 61,000 were from Mozambique, 12,000 from Zimbabwe, 6,200 from Lesotho, and 3,000 from other African countries. The United Nations High Commissioner for Refugees estimated that as many as 300,000 Mozambican refugees were presently living in South Africa. Since reliable figures are hard to come by, this figure may well understate the total number of refugees in the country.

The April 1994 elections will probably take place in an atmosphere of violence, intimidation and intolerance, in which much dirty linen will be aired on all sides. Inkatha will be haunted by past disclosures that it was funded by the government. The government will be haunted by apartheid and will have a hard time convincing blacks that it has changed. The ANC will be haunted by allegations of human rights abuses in its camps while it was operating in exile. Long denied free political activity themselves, some black radicals have already declared their townships 'no-go' areas for white politicians who would like to begin campaigning for black votes. Ironically, the first victim was the Democratic Party, a party of white liberals which has worked to defeat apartheid. Black youths disrupted one of their first meetings in Cape Town, roughing up whites and tearing up banners. This intolerance also prevents black politicians entering some townships 'ruled' by their rivals, whether ANC or Inkatha. If the contending parties cannot agree to make free political activity a norm, then our elections will be rendered meaningless by violence. And if our first elections are not accepted as legitimate, our future as a country will be on the line.

Does South Africa Have a Future?

Building a new society is going to be more difficult than resisting and finally defeating apartheid. Even if elections are free and fair, they will not be a cure-all for the country's ills. A successful transition to democracy will depend also on such key determinants as a stable and prosperous economy. For millions of blacks, democracy without material gains would destroy the standing of a new government, producing a crisis of unfulfilled expectations. It is highly unlikely that a new government will be able to deliver at the speed and on the scale expected by the black majority. Things may get worse before they get better. Will South Africa be able to compete in a global economy?

My hope is that our country's economic situation will not become so desperate that our leaders will be afraid to take the courageous and often unpopular decisions that will be needed to get the economy back on track. The true proof of leadership will not be demonstrated by policies designed to avoid defeat in the next elections, but by the vision and political tenacity that will guide us into a secure future.

One question that will put the new government to the test is how South Africa, a nation with divergent cultures, histories and languages, will manage its diversity. Will some groups be prepared to be ruled by others? Will a Mandela-led government be regarded as a Xhosa government? Will the white far right start a civil war to attain their homeland soon after democratic elections? Will the divide-and-rule policies of apartheid inhibit the development of a new sense of national identity in the country?

Many such questions lurk in the minds of black and white South Africans. Will there be peace? Will crime abate? Will people be safe in their houses? Will all children receive an adequate education? Will some be taught at all? Will the country's infrastructure – roads, sewerage, phones, electricity, water supply – continue to function as they used to under apartheid, or they will go the way they have gone in other African countries where these facilities are not working or are a luxury? White South Africans are asking whether their assets will be nationalized by the new government. They are asking whether after the elections millions of homeless blacks will simply move into empty luxury homes in suburbs previously reserved for whites. Some are asking whether there will be time to emigrate before April 1994. These are some of the difficult questions we South Africans are asking ourselves as we look ahead to the years of reconstruction after the first all-race elections.

Naturally I am excited that for the first time in my life, like 22 million other black voters, I will be able to vote for a democratic government next April. I will walk to one of more than 10,000 polling stations and cast my vote. My vote will bring an end to the humiliation and injustices of apartheid which we have suffered for decades. It is my fervent hope that my vote will complete the dismantling of statutory apartheid and allow our country to take its place in the community of nations.

While I am excited that a new era is about to dawn, I must temper my excitement with a sense of realism, knowing all the while that we stand between hope and ruin. Ahead of the polls, the verbal onslaughts of the contending parties will almost certainly lead to mass action, strikes, intimidation and violence. Right-wingers, realizing that within a few months white minority rule will have run its final course, will try to sabotage the transition. South Africa's endemic racism may poison the election campaign and play into the hands of both left-wing and right-wing racists. The neo-Nazi AWB and several white pro-apartheid groups have threatened mayhem if they are not given the white homeland of their choosing. It would be naïve to dismiss their threats. The great majority of South Africans, meanwhile, are unaware that it will take decades of reconstruction to turn their lives around: to curb violence, alleviate poverty and find millions of jobs. For many of us, miserable township conditions will remain what they are; quite possibly, they will get worse. Almost 50 per cent of black workers are either unemployed or work in the informal sector. Yet our hopes are high. Our political settlement must lead to boom. We do not want to be just another African wastebasket state. We want to be different.

All these things indicate that the April 1994 election, instead of ushering in a new order, could well lead us into more chaos and carnage. Our three years of full-scale talks, which followed talks about talks and led to the setting of an election date, have led us on a bewildering and cruel journey. Our only consolation is that the mere opportunity to vote will signal the end of white rule and give black South Africans a chance to determine how they are governed, and by whom. As Joe Slovo put it, for three years the leaders have had their say and now it's our turn. Next April South Africa turns a corner. We enter the final lap of our marathon – or what Cyril Ramaphosa called 'the last mile' from decades of racial oligarchy to mass democracy.

Despite the enormous problems and challenges facing us, I am optimistic about the future.

Appendix
THE RISE
& FALL
OF APARTHEID

1652 Jan van Riebeeck arrives in Cape Town to set up a refreshment station for the Dutch East India Company.

1652–1795 Dutch colonial rule. South Africans are divided into whites, who are company officials and their descendants, free blacks, black slaves and the Khoisan, the indigenous African people occupying the Cape when the Dutch arrive.

The division lays the basis for privileges and benefits to be accorded to whites while non-whites remain subordinate. Whites begin to move east along the coast and to invade the interior, coming into conflict with the Bantu-speaking African peoples who occupy these regions. The pattern of conflict has been set in the first encounter with the Khoisan:

> Only last night it happened that fifty of these natives wanted to put up their huts close to the banks of the moat of our fortress, and when told in a friendly way by our men to go a little further away, they declared boldly that this was not our land but theirs and that they would place their huts wherever they chose. (Jan van Riebeeck, diary entry, 1655).

Van Riebeeck and his men begin to constrain the movement of blacks. They introduce compulsory labour and the prototype of the system of 'passes' confining the Khoisan to certain villages and regions.

1828 The British government, ruling the Cape from 1795 to 1802 and then from 1806 onwards, introduces a more liberal policy for blacks, but still deprives them of political rights. They are restricted to 'tribal' land; later, hut and poll taxes compel blacks to seek employment rather than depend on farming for a livelihood.

> We are to be lords over them, treat the natives as a subject people as long as they continue in a state of barbarism and communal tenure; be the lords over them, and let them be a subject race. (Cecil John Rhodes, 1888).

1840–99 Republics are established in the Transvaal and the Orange Free State, and briefly in Natal, by the Boers (as the Afrikaner farmers come to be known). The British extend their Southern African empire, especially after the discovery of huge deposits of diamonds (Kimberley, 1868) and gold (Witwatersrand, 1886). The Xhosa, the Zulu, the Sotho, the Tswana, the Pedi, the Venda, the Swazi and other African peoples lose their independence to the technological superiority of the invaders – though both the Boers and the British suffer defeats at the hands of black armies (in 1879 an invading British column is decimated by the Zulu King Cetewayo's generals at the Battle of Isandhlwana). Defeated, African people are crowded into 'reserves', losing their land to white farmers and governments. Forced labour measures, pass laws and taxes become ever more repressive, political rights remain virtually non-existent. South Africa's coloured population is by now quite large – but coloured people, too, are second-class citizens. Meanwhile the first Indians have arrived in South Africa in 1860 as indentured labourers to work on the sugar plantations in Natal. In time a substantial Indian population will develop – without gaining political rights.

1899–1902 The Anglo-Boer War, in which the Boer republics are defeated by Britain, raises hopes among black leaders of a new political deal when the war is over – but these hopes are soon dashed.

1906 A rebellion by the Hlubi, under Chief Bambata, is savagely crushed. It will be half a century before blacks again begin to consider the option of armed resistance.

1907 A law is passed in the Transvaal enforcing all male Asians to register and obtain a certificate (much the same as a pass). A young Indian lawyer, M. K. Gandhi, leads a campaign of *satyagraha* (passive resistance) which has a lasting impact on methods of struggle in South Africa.

1910 The Union of South Africa is formed from the former Boer republics and the British colonies. The new political dispensation enshrines the principle of racial discrimination. More segregationist laws are promulgated.

1911 Blacks are relegated to cheap labour status, and skilled work is reserved for whites, by the Native Labour Regulation Act and the Mines and Works Act. The Squatters Bill, forerunner of the Land Act, makes thousands of rural Africans homeless in their own land.

1912 Formation of the South African Native National Congress, later to be known as the African National Congress (ANC), as black South Africans begin to organize political resistance. Almost a century of struggle lies ahead. 'We do not hanker after social equality with the white man. All we claim is our just dues; we ask for our political recognition as loyal British subjects.' (Sol Plaatje, first general secretary, South African Native National Congress)

1913 The Land Act is passed. Even after later additions, it awards only 13 per cent of the land to blacks, while whites, though outnumbered more than five to one, have the rest. Pass laws, which inhibit the movements of blacks, are tightened.

1914–18 Black South Africans give their lives in the First World War and the ANC sends a delegation to the peace negotiations at Versailles – but once again fails to win political concessions.

1921 Formation of Communist Party of South Africa (CPSA). Bulhoek and Bondelswarts massacres illustrate government's brutal intolerance of any perceived threat to its authority.

1923 Segregation extended to the urban areas (Urban Areas Act).

1925 Indians are encouraged to go back to India, and stricter residential segregation of Indians is proposed in the Areas Reservation, Immigration and Registration Bill.

1925–6 Superior earnings and status of white workers guaranteed (Wage Act, Mines and Works Amendment Act).

1927 The Native Administration Act gives the government wide powers to manipulate the traditional tribal structures within which it attempts to channel African grievances and political aspirations.

1936 Small number of blacks (property owners) still on the voter's roll in the Cape Province are finally disenfranchised.

1936 Provisions of Land Act strengthened, forcing the few blacks who had managed to buy land before 1913 to move to the borders of reserves.

1939–45 Second World War creates huge demand for industrial labour and greatly accelerates black urbanization. Shanty towns spring up amidst appalling overcrowding.

1946 'Ghetto Act' forces Indians to live and trade in urban ghettos. Indian response takes the form of Gandhian passive resistance.

1947 The ANC and the Natal and Transvaal Indian Congresses unite to fight apartheid.

Hard-line Apartheid

1948 D. F. Malan becomes the newly elected National Party's first Prime Minister. His party adopts apartheid as its official policy: 'separation between the white races and the non-white racial groups, and the application of the policy of separation also in the case of the non-white racial groups'. Now the lives of Africans, coloureds and Indians are regulated from the cradle to the grave by statutory apartheid.

1949 The Mixed Marriages Act prohibits marriage between people of different race groups.

1949 The ANC adopts its Programme of Action to counter stringent apartheid laws. The organization resolves to embark on civil disobedience campaigns and strikes.

1950 The Population Registration Act is passed. It compartmentalizes South Africans into whites, coloureds, Indians, Africans and 'other race groups' in the case of people such as Syrians.

1950 The Group Areas Act decrees where and with whom people can live.

1950 The Immorality Act prohibits sex between people of different race groups.

1950 The Suppression of Communism Act is passed. The Communist Party of South Africa decides to dissolve, though it is reconstituted three years later as the South African Communist Party (SACP).

1950 First political strike called by the ANC on May Day.

1950 In November, police kill 14 black villagers demonstrating against apartheid in Witsieshoek, Orange Free State.

1952 Influx control measures constraining the movement of blacks are tightened by the ironically named Abolition of Passes and Consolidation of Documents Act.

1952 Defiance Campaign launched, with Mandela as volunteer-in-chief.

1953 National Party increases majority and tightens apartheid in General Election. As Minister of Native Affairs, Hendrik Verwoerd articulates the apartheid dream. His dream rapidly becomes the nightmare of most South Africans, invading every sphere of their lives.

1953 The Separate Amenities Act segregates facilities such as toilets, libraries, hotels, pubs, beaches, parks, hospitals, trains and buses. Facilities reserved for whites are always better than the ones reserved for blacks. The facilities are mostly maintained by blacks although they are not allowed to use them.

1953 The Bantu Authorities Act decrees the formation of separate, semi-autonomous authorities for blacks, bypassing and undermining their village councils for apartheid control purposes and preparing the way for government-rigged ethnic 'homelands'.

1953 The Bantu Education Act completes the segregation of education institutions. Blacks are to receive inferior, underfunded education to prepare them for menial jobs.

> When I have control of native education, I will reform it so that natives will be taught from childhood to realize that equality with Europeans is not for them. People who believe in equality are not desirable teachers for natives. . . .
>
> There is no place for him in the European community above the level of certain forms of labour . . . for that reason it is of no avail for him to receive a training which has as its aim absorption in the European community. . . . Within his own community, however, all doors are open. Until now he has been subjected to a school system which drew him away from his own community and misled him, by showing him the green pastures of European society in which he was not allowed to graze. (Hendrik Verwoerd).

1953 Formation of Coloured People's Organization (later the Coloured People's Congress).

1955 Formation of Federation of South African Women. Boycott of Bantu Education – South Africa's inferior education for blacks – is launched.

1955 Coloured people removed from the common voters' roll.

1955 About 60,000 blacks are removed at gunpoint from Johannesburg's Sophiatown and Western townships under the Group Areas Act. The white suburb of Triomf (Triumph) rises from the ruins.

1955 The South African Congress of Trade Unions (SACTU) is formed as an ally of the ANC in the workplace.

1955 The Congress of the People, organized by the ANC and its allies, adopts the Freedom Charter after gathering on open ground in Kliptown outside Soweto. The Freedom Charter sets the guidelines for a non-racial democracy in South Africa.

1955 About 20,000 women march on the Union Buildings in Pretoria to present a petition against racist laws.

1956 156 leaders of the ANC and other organizations, including Nelson Mandela, are arrested. The so-called 'Treason Trial' lasts four years, but they are all acquitted.

1958 Revolt against the imposition of apartheid puppet authorities in rural villages of Sekhukhuneland in the eastern Transvaal. Sixteen protesters are killed by the police.

1958 Upheavals right across Natal against pass laws, cattle culling and other apartheid measures aimed at blacks.

1959 The Bantustans are given self-governing status. Government plans creation of more ethnic 'black homelands' according to language and culture, and moots independence for these territories.

Meanwhile, blacks have fewer political rights than ever in South Africa itself. Their movements from the rural areas to the cities are curtailed. Millions of blacks are caught up in a cycle of poverty, unemployment, poor education and other socio-economic disabilities. Apartheid's hold on the upward mobility of blacks is unrelenting. Anti-apartheid movements urge the government to reconsider their racial policies; instead, it uses repressive methods such as the banning, detention and banishment of opposition leaders. Hundreds of leaders are jailed. Others flee the country. As a result of the government's intransigence, anti-apartheid movements resort to unconstitutional means in a bid to topple apartheid.

1960 (21 March) Sharpeville massacre: 69 blacks killed, most shot in the back, as police open fire on an unarmed crowd during a pass-law protest.

1960 ANC's Oliver Tambo leaves South Africa to establish the organization's mission in exile.

1960 ANC and PAC banned. State of Emergency declared.

1960 Government crushes a peasant revolt in Pondoland against the imposition of stooge chiefs and Bantu Education.

1961 Mandela, following a resolution taken at an 'All-in African Conference' in Pietermaritizburg, sends a letter to Verwoerd. He demands the calling of an all-race and sovereign National Convention to draw up a new non-racial and democratic constitution for South Africa.

> Conference noted that your government, after receiving a mandate from a section of the European population, decided to proclaim a republic on 31 May....It was the firm view of delegates that your government, which represents only a minority of the population in this country, is not entitled to take such a decision without first seeking the views and obtaining the express consent of the African people.... Conference feared that under this proposed republic your government, which is already notorious the world over for its obnoxious policies, would continue to make even more savage attacks on the rights and living conditions of the African people.... It was the earnest opinion of the conference that this dangerous situation could be averted only by the calling of a sovereign national convention representative of all South Africans, to draw up a new non-racial and democratic constitution. Such a convention would discuss our national problems in a sane and sober manner, and would work out solutions which sought to preserve and safeguard the interests of all sections of the population.

1961 South Africa declares a republic after a whites-only referendum. A nationwide strike organized by the ANC against the establishment of a whites-only republic is observed by millions.

1961 12-day detention law passed. House arrest added to existing repressive laws for banning and silencing opponents of the government.

Armed Struggle

1961 ANC's newly formed military wing, Umkhonto we Sizwe, begins its attacks on government installations. Umkhonto issues a leaflet justifying the resort to arms:

> That time comes in the life of any nation when there remain only two choices: submit or fight. The time has now come to South Africa. We shall not submit and we have no choice but to hit back by all means within our power in defence of our people, our future and our freedom.

1961 ANC leader Albert Luthuli wins Nobel Peace Prize for his non-violent resistance against apartheid.

1962 The United Nations urges member states to break ties with South Africa and moots arms embargo.

1962 Mandela, after evading arrest for more than 18 months, is arrested in Natal.

1962 The Congress of Democrats, a tiny white anti-apartheid party allied to the ANC, is banned.

1963 90-day detention law passed.

1963 Police raid on Rivonia farm outside Johannesburg nets eight ANC leaders, including Walter Sisulu. Maps and documents identifying targets for sabotage and the ANC's grand plan to topple white rule are seized.

1963 Looksmart Ngudle is tortured to death. It is estimated that up to 1,000 political prisoners will die in this way over the next 30 years.

1964 The Rivonia trial begins. Mandela, already serving a five-year sentence for incitement and leaving South Africa illegally, is brought to court to join his colleague Walter Sisulu and eight others. Life sentences are imposed on Mandela, Sisulu, Govan Mbeki, Denis Goldberg, Ahmed Kathrada, Andrew Mlangeni, Raymond Mhlaba and Elias Motsoaledi. In court Mandela speaks the words he will repeat on his release in February 1990:

> I have cherished the ideal of a democratic and free society in which all persons live together in harmony and with equal opportunities. It is an ideal which I hope to live for and achieve. But if needs be, it is an ideal for which I am prepared to die.

1966 Verwoerd assassinated in parliament by a messenger whose confused motives are personal rather than political. B. J. Vorster is elected Prime Minister.

1968 The Prohibition of Political Interference Act prevents different race groups from belonging to the same political party.

1969 First ANC consultative conference in exile is held in Morogoro, Tanzania.

1971 Homeland Citizenship Act decrees that every black South African must be a homeland citizen. By this time, ten ethnic homelands have been created.

1973 Wave of strikes in Natal leads to unionization across the country. Worker organizations concentrate on economic issues, but lay important new foundations for political resistance.

1973 Having created legislative assemblies in all the homelands, the government is ready to complete its window-dressing exercise by granting 'independence' to black South Africans in their 'own areas'. One small detail remains. Many blacks, some settled in one place for several generations, will need to be moved forcibly into their 'homelands'. Forced removals, a feature of black South African life since the 1960s (and, indeed, throughout three centuries of conquest and dispossession) once again intensify as the government attempts to 'consolidate' the homelands. By 1985 an estimated 3.5 million people will have experienced forced removal, while another 2 million will be facing this fate. In other words, one in five South Africans will have been turned into a refugee by government policy.

1976 Soweto uprising. Pupils take to the streets to protest against inferior education. Police open fire, killing scores of protesters. Violence escalates and, in retaliation, protesters attack official buildings. Six months later, over 600 people have been killed.

Hundreds of youths leave South Africa to join the ANC and PAC in exile. In the years leading up to 1976, the black consciousness philosophy has been widely adopted and popularized by 'Black is beautiful' and 'Black power' slogans.

1976 Transkei, one of the 10 ethnic homelands, opts for 'independence'. Three others follow during the next five years. The territories fail to obtain recognition by any country except South Africa. Six other homelands maintain their self-governing status and refuse independence.

1977 Steve Biko, the foremost proponent of the black consciousness ideology, dies in detention after torture under interrogation. Justice Minister Jimmy Kruger says his death 'leaves me cold'.

1977 Kruger bans two newspapers and 18 black anti-apartheid organizations, including Steve Biko's Black People's Convention.

Repression and Reform

1978 Vorster retires, becoming ceremonial president after the so-called 'Information Scandal'. P. W. Botha takes over as prime minister. First signs of apartheid reform emerge.

1979 Trade unions legalized and job reservation for whites relaxed. The government begins to tinker with the obviously hurtful aspects of apartheid but maintains that it will never abandon domination. For the first time, the government questions what has come to be known as 'petty apartheid' – the dogmatically imposed segregation of transport and other urban facilities and amenities, for example.

1979 Botha suggests what he terms a 'constellation of states' in Southern Africa. The idea is rejected by South Africa's genuinely independent neighbours, despite the economic inducements held out by Botha, because it would mean entering into a federation with South Africa's puppets.

1979 Botha's visit to Soweto is the first by a white government leader. Vorster resigns as President. State Security Council assumes central role in governing the country.

1979 First signs of tension between the ruling National Party *verligte* (enlightened) and *verkrampte* (hard-line) factions about apartheid reform.

1980 General election results in swing to the right. A parliament which would bring in coloureds and Indians as junior partners is mooted.

1981 ANC guerrillas attack a government petrol-manufacturing installation, which burns for days.

1981 Hard-line and pro-apartheid right-wing Afrikaners, led by Andries Treurnicht, leave the National Party to form the Conservative Party.

1982 ANC mission in London bombed. ANC accuses government agents.

1982 Botha, in one of the first African political 'safaris' undertaken by a South African leader, meets Zambian President Kenneth Kaunda.

1982 The Internal Security Act, one of the pillars of apartheid security legislation, is toughened.

1982 South Africa raids Lesotho in pursuit of ANC bases and kills 42 people.

1983 The United Democratic Front (UDF), a coalition of 600 anti-apartheid organizations, is formed to fight new legislation giving black local authorities semi-autonomy and awarding coloureds and Indians junior roles in a three-chamber parliament (while the African majority is excluded). The national launch is attended by 15,000 representatives and delegates. Archie Gumede, Oscar Mpetha and Albertina Sisulu are elected national presidents, Popo Molefe national secretary, Terror Lekota national publicity secretary. Among the patrons elected at the launch are Nelson Mandela, Helen Joseph and Revd Allan Boesak. Unprecedented and well-coordinated campaigns against apartheid begin.

1983 UDF campaigns successfully for a boycott of the coloured and Indian management committee elections in the Western Cape. In some instances, the poll is less than 2 per cent.

1983 Referendum to ask whites whether coloureds and Indians should be coopted into parliament. Botha gets a resounding 62 per cent 'yes' vote to go ahead with his Tricameral Parliament. The government regards its new emphasis on 'Own Affairs' and 'General Affairs' (the latter specifying matters on which all three houses will deliberate together) as a major apartheid reform; blacks reject it as apartheid in a new guise.

1983 Less than 10 per cent of eligible voters vote in the black authority elections following an exhaustive campaign by the UDF against the elections.

1984 UDF launches a Million Signature campaign against President Botha's reforms. Six months later about half a million signatures have been collected, despite state attempts to crush the campaign through the detention of activists, seizure of signature forms and other methods of harassment.

1984 Nkomati Accord signed between South Africa and Mozambique, ostensibly bringing peace to a devastated neighbouring country in return for undertakings on ANC bases.

South Africa becomes ungovernable

1984 (September) Coloureds and Indians brought into parliament despite massive protests. Botha becomes an executive president and is given wide-ranging powers as head of state. Massive protests against rent hikes turn into bloody confrontations between residents and the police in the Vaal Triangle, south of Johannesburg. In the ensuing conflict four councillors are killed. Violence spreads throughout the nine Vaal Triangle townships and 66 people die in the first week. Political unrest spreads to most townships across the country. South Africa becomes ungovernable. As civil unrest spreads, outdoor meetings are banned and soldiers are sent into the townships.

1984 (5–6 November) Largest stay-away in 35 years in the Transvaal. The strike is called by the Congress of South African Students (COSAS) and supported by the UDF. Demands centre on the education crisis, the presence of the police and army in the townships, increases in rent and and taxes, and detention of activists.

1984 (December) Archbishop Desmond Tutu wins Nobel Peace Prize for his anti-apartheid stance and fight for human rights.

1984 (December) The UDF backs a call by affiliates to observe a 'Black Christmas'. Anti-apartheid organizations resolve that Christmas should be regarded as a time for mourning those killed, injured or detained as a result of the township uprisings. People are urged to buy necessities only, and to do so in their own areas.

1985 (January) Senator Edward Kennedy visits South Africa as a guest of UDF patrons Allan Boesak and Archbishop Tutu. He addresses a UDF rally in Cape Town, but in Soweto a planned rally is disrupted by supporters of the UDF's rivals, the Azanian People's Organization. On his return to the US he calls for increased economic and diplomatic isolation of South Africa.

1985 (March) 20 protesters shot dead in Langa township outside Uitenhage in the Eastern Cape. It is the 25th anniversary of Sharpeville and, as on that occasion, most protesters are shot in the back. The massacre is preceded by stay-aways to protest the high cost of living.

1985 (April) UDF leaders Terror Lekota and Popo Molefe are detained and accused of attempting to make South Africa ungovernable.

1985 (July) 22 UDF, civic and church leaders, including Molefe and Lekota, are charged with high treason. The charges relate to the Vaal rent uprising of September 1984, after which upheavals spread to the country's major townships.

1985 (June) South African raid on Gaborone in Botswana is aimed at ANC bases and safe houses. (Of the four people killed, three are Batswana.)

1985 (July) Declaration of a partial State of Emergency. COSAS, one of the UDF's biggest affiliates, is banned.

1985 During this year Botha offers to release Mandela on condition he renounces violence. Mandela rejects the offer. His answer is read by his daughter, Zindziswa, to a mass rally celebrating Archbishop Tutu's Nobel Peace Prize in Soweto.

> I am suprised at the conditions that the government wants to impose on me. I am not a violent man. My colleagues and I wrote in 1952 to Malan asking for a round table conference to find a solution to the problems of our country, but that was ignored.
>
> When Strijdom was in power, we made the same offer. Again it was ignored. When Verwoerd was in power we asked for a national convention for all the people in South Africa to decide their future. This, too, was in vain.
>
> It was only then, when all other forms of resistance were no longer open to us, that we turned to armed struggle. Let Botha show that he is different to Malan, Strijdom and Verwoerd. Let him renounce violence.
>
> Let him say that he will dismantle apartheid. Let him unban the people's organization, the African National Congress. Let him free all who have been imprisoned, banished or exiled for the opposition of apartheid. Let him free political activity so that people may decide who will govern them.
>
> I cherish my own freedom dearly, but I care even more for your freedom. . . .

Reform and Repression

1985 The government's first acceptance of the principle of full and equal political rights for all South Africans can probably be dated from this year. Limited apartheid reforms, such as the repeal of the Mixed Marriages Act, now begin in earnest. But the reforms are mixed with widespread repression.

1985 (September) First delegation of whites to meet the ANC at its Lusaka headquarters is led by Anglo American chairman Gavin Relly. By 1990 more than 30 such meetings have occurred, involving clerics, students, academics, National Party members and even former SADF officers.

1985 (December) Formation of the Congress of South African Trade Unions, an anti-apartheid federation of labour unions linking FOSATU (the federation which emerged from the Natal strikes of 1973) and other unions.

1986 Apartheid reforms continue. Full property rights are extended to blacks. Central Business Districts are opened to all races. No longer are there separate courts for blacks. Hotels and restaurants are opened to all races but the government gives owners a right to refuse members of other races. Cinemas and theatres are opened to all races. Above all, the hated Pass Laws are abolished – the influx control measures which for years controlled the movements of blacks to and in urban areas. Approximately 18 million blacks were convicted between 1921 and 1986. 'My government and I have made a choice by which I have to stand or fall. It is a choice for constitutional, social and economic reform,' says President P. W. Botha. But blacks maintain that what they need is full political rights, not cosmetic reforms.

1986 A massive drive for sanctions and disinvestment begins. The United States passes a sanctions bill (the Comprehensive Anti-apartheid Act). President Ronald Reagan refuses to sign the bill. Congress vetoes his refusal. 'As far as I am concerned, the West can go to hell,' Archbishop Tutu says, referring to the reluctance of some Western countries to impose sanctions against South Africa. About 50 United States companies disinvest in the course of the year.

1986 (January) Commonwealth Eminent Persons Group (EPG) – a group of eminent politicians appointed under the Nassau Accord on Southern Africa to promote a process of dialogue for change, for ending apartheid and establishing a genuine, non-racial democracy in South Africa – visits the country for talks with people from all political spectrums, including Mandela. The EPG travels across the country to discuss peaceful negotiations to end apartheid.

1986 (February) Police and army invade Johannesburg's Alexandra township in a week later known to township residents as the 'Six Day War'. At least 18 people are killed.

1986 (March) Partial State of Emergency lifted.

1986 (May) Two million people join South Africa's largest-ever May Day stay-away. Some employers recognize the day as a paid holiday.

1986 (May) South African troops raid Botswana, Zambia and Zimbabwe. The EPG drive for peace is scuttled by government intransigence, confirmed by these raids into neighbouring states. The group leaves South Africa disappointed, blaming Botha for talking reform and at the same time embarking on repressive measures.

1986 (May) The UDF launches a 'Call to Whites' campaign in Johannesburg. Whites receive a warm welcome from Alexandra residents during a flower-laying ceremony in solidarity with the victims of police action.

1986 (June) Nationwide State of Emergency declared. Anti-apartheid activists rounded up (over 20,000 within three months). By the end of the State of Emergency four years later, over 45,000 people have been arrested at various times.

1986 (16 June) Tenth anniversary of the 1976 student uprisings. The Soweto Civic Association calls for a rent boycott to protest against high rents and to pressurize town councillors to resign. Already a number of townships have begun the boycott, despite the State of Emergency which makes it illegal for people to urge such a course of action. Soweto joins 40 other townships which are already boycotting payment of rent and service charges.

1986 (August) Plans for the independence of the homeland of KwaNdebele are cancelled by the homeland government after a nine-month anti-independence campaign in which the UDF plays an active role. Over 100 people are killed in the struggle against government-supporting vigilantes.

1986 (October) UDF launches 'Forward to the People's Power'. Street Committees, people's courts and other structures for resolving disputes are set up. Anti-apartheid organizations continue to make South Africa ungovernable despite stringent emergency measures.

1987 Opening of some beaches to all races. Job reservation for whites ended, but apartheid reforms stall. Botha blames outside interference and political violence. Government continues to maintain that reform process is irreversible, while growing numbers make the journey north to meet the ANC. Closer to home, the Revd Allan Hendrickse, leader of the predominantly coloured Labour Party, leaves the cabinet after a clash with Botha.

1987 (November) Release of Govan Mbeki, ANC leader given a life sentence in 1964. Soon after his release, Mbeki is restricted under the country's emergency regulations.

1988 (January) The ANC's headquarters in Lusaka bombed by South African agents.

1988 Botha presses on with limited apartheid reforms. Trains and stations desegregated. Educational desegregation begins. Botha appeals for Afrikaner unity, but is rebuffed by the right-wing Conservative Party. He proposes an advisory council for blacks, to be called the National Council, but no credible black leader shows any interest.

1988 (June) State of Emergency renewed.

1988 (August) The ANC publishes its Constitutional Guidelines.

1988 (November) Pan-Africanist Congress leader Zephania Mothopeng and ANC veteran Harry Gwala are released from prison.

1988 (November) Mandela is taken to hospital, suffering from tuberculosis. Botha announces that he will not be returned to jail, but to a prison warder's house. Rumours that Mandela might be released.

1989 (January) P. W. Botha suffers a stroke. F. W. de Klerk becomes National Party leader. A crisis ensues within the NP as Botha tries to cling to power. He loses the battle and seven months later resigns. After national elections, de Klerk takes over the reins as State President.

1989 (July) Botha meets Mandela. First known meeting between the ANC leader and South African head of state.

1989 (August) Newspapers release contents of a memo Mandela is supposed have submitted to Botha:

> The deepening crisis in our country has been a matter of grave concern to me for quite some time and I now consider it necessary in the national interest for the ANC and the government to meet urgently to negotiate an effective political settlement.

1989 (August) The Mass Democratic Movement (MDM), a shadowy coalition of hundreds of banned UDF affiliates, launches a defiance campaign against apartheid. Activists demand treatment at whites-only hospitals and march on white schools to demand integration. The MDM also defies laws and use facilities reserved for whites such as parks, buses, toilets, libraries and swimming pools. The campaign embarrasses the government and makes apartheid unworkable.

De Klerk, 'Man of Action'

1989 (August) ANC president Oliver Tambo suffers a stroke.

1989 (September) De Klerk launches drive for 'a new South Africa', allows demonstrations and protests against apartheid rule, and orders police and troops to adopt a 'softly softly' approach.

1989 (September) De Klerk embarks on an African safari. The government announces that communism is no longer a threat following the demolition of the Berlin Wall and the collapse of communist regimes across Eastern Europe.

1989 (September) Provision of some mixed residential areas ('Free Settlement Areas'). Blacks reject the move as another cosmetic change.

1989 (October) Eight black leaders, seven including Walter Sisulu from the ANC and one from the PAC, are released from prison. All the indications are that Mandela will soon be free.

1989 (November) The government announces that it will repeal the Separate Amenities Act, which for decades has reserved better facilities for whites.

1989 (December) Mandela meets de Klerk. Rumours that he will soon be freed intensify. Mrs Mandela says, 'This time it is the real stuff,' as she emerged from visiting him.

1990 (February) De Klerk unbans the ANC, the SACP, the PAC and 58 other organizations, and says Mandela will soon be freed. South Africa's political landscape is irrevocably changed.

1990 (11 February) Nelson Mandela is freed.

1990 (March) Political violence intensifies across the country, especially in Natal. The violence takes five forms: clashes between anti-apartheid activists and security forces; fighting between rival black organizations, with the ANC and Inkatha staging pitched battles; fighting fomented by government agents or white right-wing agent provocateurs trying to scuttle constitutional negotiations; revenge attacks; and pre-emptive attacks.

1990 (March) Police gun down 11 protesters in Sebokeng. The ANC postpones its first round-table discussion with the government in protest against the shooting. The meeting was to discuss obstacles impeding negotiations towards a non-racial constitution.

1990 (May) First meeting between the government and the ANC. Historic 'Groote Schuur Minute' signed: 'The government and the ANC agree on a common commitment towards the resolution of the existing climate of violence and intimidation from whatever quarter, as well as commitment to stability and to a peaceful process of negotiations.'

1990 (June) State of Emergency is lifted after almost four years. Many other restrictive laws lifted.

1990 (July) Inkatha cultural movement becomes a political party, the Inkatha Freedom Party. Fighting between Inkatha and ANC supporters spreads from Natal to the Johannesburg townships. At least 1,200 people are killed before the year is out.

1990 (July) The National Party opens its doors to all races.

1990 (July) Public re-launch of South African Communist Party at a rally in Soweto.

1990 (July) The PAC and AZAPO reject a government invitation to take part in preliminary negotiations towards a non-racial democracy.

1990 (August 6) Second ANC–government summit. The ANC suspends guerrilla warfare. 'Pretoria Minute' states:

> In the interest of moving as speedily as possible towards a negotiated political settlement and in the context of the agreement reached, the ANC announced that it was now suspending all armed actions with immediate effect. As a result of this, no further armed actions and related activities by the ANC and its military wing Umkhonto we Sizwe will take place.
>
> It was agreed that a Working Group will be established to resolve all outstanding questions arising out of this decision, to report by 15 September 1990.
>
> Both sides once more committed themselves to do everything in their power to bring about a peaceful solution as quickly as possible.

1990 (August) Intense fighting erupts in Johannesburg townships between members of Inkatha and township residents, most of whom are supporters of the ANC. Over 800 people are killed in the next three months.

1990 (October) Separate Amenities Act officially repealed.

1990 (December) ANC president Oliver Tambo returns to South Africa to a tumultuous welcome after 30 years in exile.

1990 (December) The ANC holds its first consultative congress inside South Africa in 30 years. Its rival, the PAC, follows suit.

1991 (January) Mandela and de Klerk remain committed to a peaceful transition to democracy. Both support a multi-party conference to work out the mechanics of transition. Deep divisions remain over the ANC's call for a Constituent Assembly and an interim government.

1991 (January) Nelson Mandela and Chief Mangosuthu Buthelezi meet for the first time to discuss how they could end, or at least curb, the fighting between their supporters. Fighting intensifies.

1991 (February) De Klerk announces that the three remaining pillars of apartheid, the Group Areas Act, the Land Acts of 1913 and 1936, and the Population Registration Act will be repealed before the first session of parliament ends at mid-year.

1991 (March) Fighting between the political factions continues in Johannesburg and Natal townships.

1991 (April) The ANC holds an emergency meeting of its policy-making National Executive Committee to discuss political violence. It resolves to send an open letter to de Klerk demanding among other things that effective steps must be taken to end political violence; that 'traditional' weapons such as spears and sticks must be banned; and that two cabinent ministers responsible for public order must be sacked by 9 May. The ANC says it will suspend all talks with the government if these demands are not met.

1991 (18 May) The ANC suspends constitutional talks with the government.

1991 (24–25 May) A government-sponsored summit on violence, shunned by the ANC and its allies, and by other groups to the left and right of the political spectrum, is held in Pretoria.

1991 (June) Parliament votes to scrap the Group Areas Act and the Land Acts of 1913 and 1936.

1991 (September) 24 organizations, including the government, the ANC and Inkatha, sign the 33-page National Peace Accord, aimed at curbing township violence.

1991 (October) 92 organizations, including the ANC and PAC, form the Patriotic Front, aimed at giving the government a 'final knock-out blow'. Inkatha is not invited, but says in any event it would not agree to 'gang up' against the government.

1991 (November) 20 organizations – the government, the National Party, the ANC, Inkatha, the PAC, the Democratic Party, the SACP, the Transvaal and Natal Indian Congresses, two Indian political parties, one coloured political party and and representatives from 10 homelands – resolve to form CODESA (Convention for a Democratic South Africa). But the PAC pulls out, accusing the government and the ANC of colluding. Chief Buthelezi later pulls out, too (though Inkatha stays at the negotiating table), saying he will not attend until his homeland and Zulu King Goodwill Zwelithini have been accorded separate delegations.

1991 (21-22 December) First plenary session of CODESA. The Declaration of Intent, a document outlining basic principles for a future constitution, is signed by 17 of the 19 parties (Inkatha and the Bophuthatswana homeland are the exceptions). Mandela and de Klerk square up in a verbal brawl.

1992 (February) Five CODESA working groups begin discussing mechanisms of transition to democracy at the World Trade Centre outside Jan Smuts Airport.

1992 (15–16 May) Second plenary session of CODESA meets at the Centre, but deliberations collapse because the ANC and the government disagree over majority rule and, in particular, the role of future regional powers.

1992 (16 June) ANC launches 'Mass Action', a pro-democracy campaign of strikes, boycotts, sit-ins and other disruptions.

1992 (17 June) Gunmen rampage through Slovo Park in Boipatong township, killing 49 people. Residents say the killers came from the nearby KwaMadala hostel, which houses Inkatha members.

1992 (21 June) Mandela announces that the ANC has suspended bilateral talks with the government in protest against the massacre.

1992 (23 June) The ANC and 10 of its allies pull out of CODESA. The ANC sends a memorandum containing 14 demands to de Klerk, saying it will not return to talks until the demands have been met. Eleven of the 14 demands dealt with violence. This is the beginning of 'the war of memorandums' as the government and the ANC exchanged memoranda at seven-day intervals.

1992 (3–4 August) Massive strike called by the ANC to press its demands. Business says it has lost R250 million because of the strike. The ANC vows to intensify mass action.

1992 (7 September) 28 ANC demonstrators marching on Bisho, capital of the nominally independent homeland of Ciskei, are shot dead by soldiers. Hopes that talks will soon resume are shattered. The killing occurs as de Klerk and his allies are attending a 'federalism' summit in Pretoria. After the killing, de Klerk calls on Mandela to meet him to discuss the violence. Mandela agrees but stresses that the meeting can only take place after thorough preparation by ANC negotiator Cyril Ramaphosa and his counterpart on the government side, Roelf Meyer.

1992 (25 September) ANC says the government has agreed to release 150 prisoners, including guerrillas convicted of killing white civilians.

1992 (26 September) ANC–government summit signs Record of Understanding which, among other things, paves the way for the ANC to return to CODESA. The understanding binds the government to fence troublesome hostels, release 500 prisoners by 15 November, and ban dangerous weapons when a permit has not been obtained. It also commits both parties to majority rule.

1992 (27 September) Angered by agreements reached at the ANC–government summit, Chief Buthelezi, his party and his homeland government withdraw from any constitutional discussions. Chief Buthelezi says most of the agreements affected him, but he was not involved. CODESA is again thrown into crisis.

Chief Buthelezi, Lucas Mangope of Bophuthatswana, Oupa Gqozo of Ciskei, Andries Treurnicht of the right-wing Conservative Party, the Afrikaner Volksunie and others form a group to oppose bilateral dealings between the ANC and the government.

1992 (November) The government and the ANC begin a series of *bosberaads* (bush summits) to pursue issues raised by the Record of Understanding. De Klerk sets dates for the transition to democracy. He says multi-party talks will begin in February 1993, an interim government will be installed by the first half of that year, and elections for a constituent assembly will be held no later than April 1994.

1992 (18 December) De Klerk admits that some white senior members of the security forces have been involved in undermining his reform initiatives, to the extent of planning to wreck the democracy negotiations. Several senior officers are retired.

Into 1993

1993 (January and February) The ANC, the government, Inkatha and their allies begin a series of multilateral talks to get negotiations back on track.

1993 (5–6 March) First fully representative multi-party forum, with 26 parties and organizations represented, holds 'talks about talks' at World Trade Centre. Committees set up to work on contentious issues.

1993 (1 April) Multi-party forum meets again to set up committees to begin full-scale negotiations after the Good Friday weekend. Committees include a Planning Committee and a Negotiation Council.

1993 (10 April) South African Communist Party general secretary Chris Hani is gunned down outside his home in the Boksburg suburb of Dawn Park. His death precipitates widespread violence, looting and the death of at least 72 people by the time he is buried on 19 April. His funeral is the biggest in the history of South Africa.

1993 (24 April) ANC stalwart and former president Oliver Tambo dies at the age of 75. Tambo was credited with building the ANC into a powerful and coherent force while in exile for more than 30 years.

1993 (30 April) Negotiation Council begins weekly meetings to discuss transition to democracy and the holding of first-ever non-racial elections by April 1994.

1993 (7 May) The 104-member Negotiation Council adopts a Declaration of Intent stating that South Africa's first multi-party elections will be held no later than April 1994.

1993 (2 July) Negotiators confirm 27 April 1994 as all-race election date. Inkatha, the KwaZulu government and the CP walk out in protest, insisting that election cannot be held until future form of state has been decoded and violence has been curbed.

1993 (18 July) Inkatha, KwaZulu and CP pull out of democracy negotiations. Inkatha and KwaZulu demand a federal state; the CP wants self-determination for Afrikaners.

1993 (26 July) Draft unveiled of post-apartheid constitution, strongly influenced by US model.

Sources

Newsfile (Reuter electronic library).
Human Sciences Research Council.
T. R. H. Davenport., *South Africa – A Modern History*, second edition, 1980.

Index